LIVING HIGH

LIVING HIGH

An Unconventional Autobiography

June Burn

June & Farrar

J & F Project
Bellingham, WA

Publisher
J & F Project LLC
PO Box 6035
Bellingham WA 98227-6035
www.juneandfarrar.com

© 1941, 1958, 1969, 1992, 1999, 2011, 2022 June Burn
First edition 1941. Second edition 1958. Third edition 1969. Fourth edition 1992. Fifth edition 1999. Sixth edition 2011. Seventh edition 2022.

Revised and expanded postscript "Eighty-one Years Later" © 2022 Skye Burn

Except as noted on page 261, all the images are from the June and Farrar Burn Papers and used with permission from Western Libraries Archives & Special Collections and the Center for Pacific Northwest Studies (CPNWS) at Western Washington University. Some of the images from the June and Farrar Burn Papers have been subject to quality enhancement and cropping by the editors prior to publication.

Summary

Living High is the compelling story of June and Farrar Burn and their unconventional lifestyle, philosophy, and experiences—homesteading a small island in the Salish Sea, living north of the Arctic Circle before Alaska became a state, touring the U.S. in the Burn Ballad Bungalow (pictured on the front cover), and how they lived in a covered wagon while June, at age fifty, earned her master's degree in soil science and nutrition. This seventh edition includes additional photographs and an epilogue by Skye Burn, June and Farrar's eldest granddaughter.

No part of this publication may be reproduced, stored in a retrieval system or on a computer disk, or transmitted in any form or by any means—mechanical, photocopying, recording, or otherwise—without written permission of the publisher. Permission is given for brief excerpts to be published with book reviews in newspapers, magazines, catalogs, and web sites.

ISBN: 979-8-218-06931-5
LCCN: 2022922004
Printed in United States of America

ACKNOWLEDGEMENTS

The June & Farrar project is made possible with support from the Burn family, Western Libraries Archives and Special Collections, and the Center for Pacific Northwest Studies at Western Washington University. We especially appreciate the assistance that Elizabeth Joffrion, Director of Special Collections, and Ruth Steele, Archivist, have given in providing access to June's writings, digital copies of historical photographs, and recordings of Farrar's songs.

Tracy Spring, the Artistic Director for the June & Farrar project, has been instrumental in bringing the project to life. Western Washington University now owns the property where June & Farrar lived in Bellingham. Tracy lived in the log cabins that Farrar built when she was a student at Fairhaven College in the 1970s. She read *Living High* and was deeply impacted by June & Farrar's story and their philosophy. Thank you, Tracy, for your devotion to this project.

We are tremendously grateful for the work of Jeff Daffron, community co-creator extraordinaire, who donated many hours of exacting labor to enhance the digital copies of photographs without impinging on their historical value.

We greatly appreciate the artistry that Janis Carper, owner of Second Chance Productions, has brought to designing this new edition of *Living High* and crafting the website—www.juneandfarrar.com.

We also greatly appreciate Village Books, Bellingham's locally owned bookstore, for facilitating the publication.

Lastly, we thank Pat Karlberg for proofreading and Richard Brummett for his generous and continous support for the project.

Best wishes,
Skye Burn
Producer, J & F Project

FOREWORD

June was living in a little log cabin in a 100-acre forest near Washington DC in 1919 when she and Farrar met. Within a month, they were married. In deciding where and how they wished to live their life together, June and Farrar chose a full and rich life untethered from convention. They pledged to keep their wants to the things that really make for happiness.

June and Farrar shared a trust in the outcome life would bring. Farrar said, "Whenever I have this hand in mine, I feel like eloping off for some adventure." June's unconventional autobiography brings the reader along on their life journey, into a story of fulfillment, curiosity, adventure, and exploration.

As newlyweds, June and Farrar crossed the country to homestead an island in the Salish Sea. The Seattle Land Office told them there were no islands available, but June and Farrar set out anyway. June wrote the Land Office every week—sharing their adventures as they worked their way toward the Pacific Northwest. When they walked into the Seattle Land Office and announced, "Our name is Burn," the staff person at the counter turned and yelled, "Here they are!!" The whole staff poured out from the inner offices to greet June and Farrar. Yes, there was an island they could homestead! Just 15 acres, no water, no beaches. It was the island of their dreams. June and Farrar called it "Gumdrop" because of the island's shape.

June and Farrar had a magical ability to create warmth and comfort in a simple camp—baking bread in a cast iron oven, sitting on beachcombed hobs around an open fire. *Living High* weaves their guiding philosophy of life with the joy found connecting with one's surroundings. In her mid-life June earned her master's in organic farming and nutrition. She created fertile soil out of beach sand and grew delicious produce.

Living High recounts June and Farrar's adventures—from homesteading to managing the reindeer herd and teaching in a Yup'ik community on St Lawrence Island in Alaska's Arctic—from touring in the "Ballad Bungalow" (Farrar performed his own songs and sold sheet music) to living in Bellingham where June wrote a daily column for the *Bellingham Daily Herald* and they published their own newspaper. For their final home in the islands, Farrar carved a sign from Alaska cedar which hung above the door. The sign read *Wishes Come True at This Place*.

Living High has remained in print through many decades since it was first published in 1941. Some of June's language is insensitive, in calling Yup'ik people Eskimos and other instances. In publishing this new edition, it was tempting to edit June's views, but we have not changed a single word of the original text except for updating some spelling. *Living High* and Farrar's songs are part of the historical record and the context of their time. The publication of this historical record should not be interpreted to mean that our family or the June & Farrar Project endorse the culturally insensitive language, and we apologize for any hurt June's words may cause.

After living in the Yup'ik community, June wrote she was even more convinced that one must find joy in work for it to be worth doing. June and Farrar believed that creativity is the pathway to joy. Through decades, June and Farrar's philosophy has shaped the lives of countless readers. We hope you find their story meaningful and delightful.

Best wishes,

Skye Burn

Owner and Producer
J & F Project LLC
www.juneandfarrar.com

JUNE'S ORIGINAL DEDICATION

    This is likely the only book I'll ever write. I'd better dedicate it while I've got the chance to: Farrar and our sons, North and Bob; Phil; Alice; the Wemies; the Heinies; kinfolks; Polly; Mary and Ray; Katy of the Mountains; the Gillies; W.E.W. and Helen; Hazel; Adelaide; the Chevs; the Cooks; the Girls; the Meigs; the Bucks; Laura; Ben; Link; Eileen; Gavin and Jim and Fred; Sally Ann and all hers; Mr. Beard; the Lenoirs; Jean; Breakie; Louesa; Art and Glad; Peg; the Eastmans; Mr. Ely; Julia; Betty and Pret; Madge; May Jetta; Wave; Edythe; Donna; Ralph; to brand new friends here in New York—to all our friends, old and new!
... to our *Puget Sounder* subscribers and contributors and advertisers; to the P.L.F. Club and the *Chickawana*;
... to S.S. who coaxed this book along and to Elinore Denniston who edited and cut and improved it;
... to thousands who have been kind to us on all our adventures including Eskimos, hitchhiker pick-uppers, freight trains, and those who have given us jobs when we needed them.

                                                                  —First Edition, 1941

PREFACE

This is a double-header autobiography, for as the ex-rib of man, surely a wife can write her husband's life along with her own and call it self-biography. Perhaps it might be called the autobiography of twenty years of happiness.

Does that sound smug? Well, of course we haven't been happy all the time. But these have been good years of what Farrar calls "first-hand living." We did set our course, from the very first, and we have followed it as closely as we could. We said we would retire first and enjoy family togetherness as nature intended, giving to our children that more than bread alone by which man lives. We said we would taste life at first hand, dig for our own food, scratch about just anyhow for what we needed, going at it the hard way, letting our children see into the primitive mechanics of living. Then when the boys were older and began to need such things as clothes, a conventional home, college tuition and spending money, why, then, we said, we would settle down and in some easier way earn what was needed. We never wanted our sons to be different from their fellows. It was a plus life we planned for them, not the other way about.

They and we have had fun, happiness, joy, splendid hardship, fine adventures. No depression can take those things away from us. No war can cheat our sons of having lived. They lived first.

This, then, is the story of how we managed to live high on so nearly nothing at all.

To our two sons, two daughters-in-law
and grandchildren, in love, June.
—Second Edition, 1958

*We are all so a part of everything in the past and future and
our little stay on this earth is so short a time in eternity
that we should tune our spirits to the more noble.*
Farrar Burn

CONTENTS

Acknowledgements	*ii*
Foreword	*iii*
June's Original Dedication	*v*
Preface	*vi*
Second Edition Dedication	*vii*

Part One. HOMESTEADING — 1

I. We Find Our Island	3
II. Breaking Rocks and Precedents	12
III. Homesteading on the Gumdrop	20
IV. The Hopeless Chest	29
V. Living on Seagull Eggs	39

Part Two. THE PALE GREEN YEAR — 51

VI. How Do You Get to Alaska?	53
VII. The Frozen Island	64
VII. We Meet Three Shipwrecked Men	74
IX. Winter of Splendid Isolation	80
X. A Few Stiff Sleeves Limber Up	90
XI. We Toss a Coin	97

Part Three. TRAVELS WITH A DONKEY — 109

XII. A Gale Blows Us a Baby	111
XIII. America by Cart and Donkey	120
XIV. In Which We Kick Over the Traces	130
XV. Burn's Ballad Bungalow	139
XVI. Winter Sunshine	148
XVII. America—Round Trip	154

CONTENTS

Part Four. PUGET SOUNDINGS   163

XVIII. We Live in Bellingham a Million Words   165
XIX. A Burn's-Eye View of Puget Sound   172
XX. I Hunt for Stories   180
XXI. Campfires in the House   187
XXII. Living on Nothing a Year   193
XXIII. We Get a Bear by the Tail   200

Part Five. THE CAMPFIRE BURNS   209

XXIV. O America!   211
XXV. Rattlesnake in the Buttercups   218
XXVI. We Ride a Freight   225
XXVII. From Now On, Everything Is Gravy!   231

POSTSCRIPT   237

Seventeen Years Later   239

EPILOGUE   249

Eighty-one Years Later   251

Photo and other credits   261

Part One

HOMESTEADING

Cabin near Washington D.C.

To live free you've got to keep your wants down to the things that really make for happiness, or you will find yourself working too hard, trying to pay for things you get no real joy from.
Farrar Burn

I. WE FIND OUR ISLAND

UP THE Potomac River in Maryland, not far north of the District line, there used to be a little log cabin on a knoll in the heart of a hundred-acre place. It had woods all about and clear cool brooks winding by on three sides. Down the trail from the house was a large tulip poplar tree that spread its huge limbs over a stone-walled spring.

In a Washington newspaper I had placed an advertisement: "WANTED, a cabin mate. Every country inconvenience. Mile walk from Cabin John trolley, through a pine cathedral. Brooks, spring, woods, wild strawberries soon. No bath, no telephone, no neighbors in sight."

Thirty girls and women answered my advertisement but I couldn't decide among them. I asked them all to come out to tea and draw straws for it.

To that party I invited Ensign Burn. It didn't occur to me that he might not like being the only man among so many women. I had never seen him. One afternoon I had returned to the cabin to find a note on the door. Ensign Burn had discovered the place in his Sunday ramblings. He had taken a few pictures of the cabin and would like to send prints.

He came to tea, ruddy face beaming, merry tongue wagging, his hair reddish in the early spring sunlight. He was the life of the party. He went to the spring for water, cut and brought in wood for the fireplace. He saw when sugar was needed and had ideas about where people should sit. He was, in short, the perfect host and from that day to this has been host at all my parties. For, in a little over a month, we were married, and the Glen Echo postmistress said, "Well, you got your cabin mate, didn't you?"

Farrar Burn, 1919.

That was a month of strange courtship. Every other evening Farrar Burn would come out to the cabin to sit before our fireplace and talk. The girl with whom I had been sharing the cabin was a practical person and she disapproved of Farrar. She thought he talked too much. But he was the first man I had known who was gay enough for me. He loved the woods in the same personal way I loved them. His father was a civil engineer in Arkansas. Much of his boyhood had been spent roaming the Ozarks on timber cruises and surveys. Before he was old enough for this rough going, his mother used to take her two little boys and spend whole days in the woods, gathering flowers and nuts and ferns. No wonder, then, when Farrar was detailed to Washington during the war, he spent his holidays exploring the surrounding hills and woods, sometimes with companions, occasionally alone, and thus had come upon my cabin.

I was the eldest, over-responsible child of a Methodist circuit rider in Alabama. I had helped bring up a family of eight. Life for me had been serious enough in one sense, but happy and carefree too, practically living in the woods, finding all my pleasures there. Hickory saplings for horses, pine needle slopes for toboggan runs. Erosion gullies to play hide-and-seek in. Wild persimmons and plums, sassafras root for tea, hickory nuts, black walnuts, chestnuts, chinquapins and muscadines for treasure trove, to say nothing of the fall gathering of tall grass for brooms—the only ones we knew for a long time.

The whole family would go fishing for days at a time. My mother was always ready to go out gathering wild flowers with us. We practically leafed out in summer and shed down to bare twigs in winter, so close to the earth we lived.

Yet along with this happy outdoor life, was the too finely drawn seriousness of Methodism—a straining after impossible perfection that left despair in its wake. Joy in the woods was the only pleasure in which I felt no guilt.

Like his father, Farrar had civil-engineered for awhile before the war. But no profession or job or adventure could permanently engage his restless spirit.

"But what do you plan to do?" my responsible cabin mate used to ask him when he would be so gaily building air castles.

"Not to keep my nose to the grindstone anyhow," he would say.

"But how do you expect to live?"

"It doesn't take much money to be happy. This cabin is my idea of what a house should be. Just a wood pile with a hollow place in the middle to crawl into at night, to get in out of the rain. The grass, trees, flowers, the sun, moon, stars are the enduring things. Why insulate yourself away from them with laboriously constructed piles of junk? A man could work with pick and shovel for three days a week, and have a place like this, with all the rest of the time to enjoy it in."

"But what if everybody did that?" she asked, making the old objection.

"What if they did? Why, men could live like kings if each one would do his share of the physical work of the world. Of course, you've got to be a king, within yourself; you've got to keep your wants down to the things that really make for happiness, or you will find yourself working too hard, trying to pay for things you get no real joy from. Then the first thing you know you'll be wondering what you're living for anyhow."

"Suppose your wife didn't like to live as simply as that—just enough for bare food and never any conveniences?" my cabin mate objected.

"But suppose she did? I'll wait until I find one who does. It seems to me the worry over payments on those so-called conveniences

June Chandler Harris, 1919.

Farrar sang songs of his own composition.

could wedge any happily married couple apart."

"What would you do when children came?"

Farrar threw another log on the fire and grinned. "Add on a lean-to," he said promptly, "work four days a week and get a cow."

"Then you wouldn't be free to go wherever you wanted, as you say," she pointed out triumphantly.

"Why not? Hitch the cow to an old cart or something and drive off."

My cabin mate was put to it to be convincing against that gay insistence on the human right to happiness provided no one else paid for it. But I loved it. His austerity appealed to my Methodism. Unwantingness was as deep in me as joy. Here was someone else who wanted nothing but the simple fruits of occasional labor.

So Farrar continued to come and continued to talk. Those word-hurricanes blew me into a new world.

"Christianity is fine as far as it goes," he said once. "But it doesn't go far enough. It isn't big enough for the soul of a free man. Heaven was invented by a defeated people. You don't need heaven if you have lived while you were here. To be yourself, to live true to your own nature, to fruit in your own way—that's heaven. Any other is just a failure's makeshift—all this struggle to fit yourself into someone else's pattern— why does a man want to get ahead, anyhow? Get ahead of whom? Pure selfishness is at the root of it. To use natural advantages, such as better education or extra cleverness or strength or good looks—just to push yourself ahead of other men—it's a lousy trick. You know who was the worst enemy America ever had? Benjamin Franklin! He's the old boy who taught us to pinch the pennies and care more about saving money than enjoying life. Be thrifty with the things that count and you won't have time to worry about whether your wallet is full or not."

March blew into April. Rooster violets came out along the trail to the car line. Snowy bells of the bloodroot began to ring in the rail fence corners. Bluets were like a dream low over the meadows. The brooks ran fat with spring rains.

On an occasional day off, Farrar would come out to the cabin for a whole day and evening of talk. We'd make fireplace toast and coffee for lunch and supper wouldn't be ready when my cabin mate came home tired from work.

I'd be cleaning up the house, leaning on my broom daydreaming, likely, when I'd hear that clear whistle from the trail beyond the spring. I'd go out on the porch and he would come running down the brown pine needle path, leaping the spring brook under the big tulip poplar, racing up the knoll to the cabin.

But all this time we never said a word about love. Not a kiss. We discussed marriage and children and life and feminism and women working. We never discussed marriage or love in relation to ourselves, though. We never seemed to get around to it.

Then one day I learned that a Red Cross job had come through for me. I must be leaving for St. Louis. That day I telephoned Farrar at his office and he joined me at a tea shop where we often went, for our last luncheon together.

Last? We didn't take that in, at first, going a mile a minute. Farrar was full of a tracer test that had just been made. He had just got back from a trip to Cape May. I told him about a pink moccasin flower I had found in the woods. We talked of the cabin. He said he wouldn't be going there any more, when I was gone.

Toward six o'clock, he said it would be lonesome without me. Perhaps he would go out to the cabin again, after all. But suppose someone else was living there?

"Why don't you rent it? You love it so."

"Why don't we get married," he said abruptly, "and both go back and live in the cabin? We've had fun from the very first day. We love the same things."

He wasn't even going to ask me whether I wanted to get married.

"Come on, let's get married right now," Farrar said. "No use putting off a thing like that."

We called the waitress who put the problem to the cook. He said we should go to the District Building. We hurried down. Having lost all afternoon, edging up to it, we mustn't waste a second now. The District Building was closed. But one man, working late, came out of his office and talked to us.

He had a friend in Rockville, Maryland, he said, not very far from Washington by trolley. An undertaker. He would see us married.

In little Rockville, we had no trouble finding the undertaker. He laughed and laughed and got the clerk to come down to the courthouse and issue a license. He got the preacher out of bed. Still laughing, he stood with us there in the little parlor while the preacher read the service in front of a big parlor lamp with flowers on the globe. The preacher had very large, thin ears. They stood out from his head and the light shone through them. Farrar gave him the last ten dollars he had till next payday.

April blossomed into May. Dogwood trees hung out their chaste medallions and mountain laurel foamed over a certain hillside along our brook. I hadn't known it was there, though I had walked that way for a year. I suppose I had been too busy watching the brook. It crossed the trail seven times on the way to the post office, every crossing different. Here it would be shallow, the sweet singing water honey-colored over fallen autumn leaves. Further on, a waterfall, noisier than it was big, was forever putting on a show. During the winter it had frozen in paper-thin layers, as though the freeze had caught each ripple and fixed it. The white flakes had piled up and up into a series of snowy ledges. It was motion caught in midair. At another crossing, the brook narrowed and was deep and still. I had to jump it here. At another, it winkled happily over flat steppingstones.

Where the valley widened, tall liriodendron trees grew. (That is the only proper name of any plant I know that is sweeter than its common name.) Now, in May, their curiously angular branches held fragrant yellow tulips up right among the leaves.

Every time I went down that brook I discovered something new. On this day I was walking down the valley when some lightness drew my eyes up the side of a hill, and there was the patch of delicate mountain laurel, queer, boxlike buds just bursting into pink-white froth. When I took Farrar to see them that evening, he called them our wedding flowers and said it meant we could always expect more than we expected.

May is a wonderful month for love. I discovered passion. An ignorant girl may have known vague, unconscious desire. She has felt urgencies and been ashamed, sure that they meant she was no nice girl, if the truth were known. (How much righter, cleaner, girls are now!) But I was an unusually stupid person. I had not dreamed that passion is the stirring of love itself toward its natural consummation.

May ripened and mellowed and it was June. We had big handfuls of wild strawberries for supper. The fields were white with daisies. Garden honeysuckle grows wild in Maryland, and the slender trumpets blew their fragrance far and wide.

In June, Farrar was given his choice of remaining in the Navy and confirming his commission, or being discharged back into civilian life. We chose civilian life.

We went to the library, then, and got down the atlas to decide where we should make our permanent home. When you begin to look at the maps with an eye for the most ideal place in the world to live in, a strange thing happens to you. You practically go blind when you look at any country but your own. You look at Scotland and think of those firm, strong people and imagine how your sons would flourish on the windy bracken moors. But you don't take yourself seriously.

But we could see islands! We practically had double vision when we came to the islands off Maine, off Florida, off Alaska. To go on an island and pull the ladder up after us and live, untroubled by anything—that would be heaven.

But which island? We chanced on an article about Puget Sound, turned to the map of Washington and saw that beautiful inland sea with what looked like a thousand islands in its pocket.

We'd go to Puget Sound, then. We would live on one of those islands. How to get one of them stumped us, until we thought of homesteading.

We hurried in to Washington to ask the Land Office about it. They said we'd have to write to Seattle—but likely there were no islands left at this late day. Nonsense. We wrote to Seattle. No, there were no islands left for homesteading. In a country that had the measles with islands! They hadn't looked hard enough.

We wrote that we hoped they would search carefully. We were coming out. We were on our way. They couldn't write to us for we'd be on the way, working as we came. We'd be there by fall. That would give them time to find us an island.

Every week I wrote them. I told them where we were, gave them the daily gossip as though they were old friends, kept them amused as well as I could. Farrar called it my direct-mail campaign for an island.

With Farrar's last check, we went to St. Louis to visit my family. They liked Farrar, though they didn't think he would be any great shakes as a wife-supporter. Then we went on to Van Buren, Arkansas, to visit Farrar's family. They liked me, too, but they didn't think I'd be any great shakes as a housewife.

Farrar's faithful uncle got him a job with the railroad, with passes for both of us to Colorado and two months' work for Farrar icing refrigerator cars.

That was in Delta, Colorado. We lived in a tent among tall hollyhocks in a motherly Mrs. White's backyard. Once some people took us up on a great flat mesa which commanded the world and I saw snow-capped mountains for the first time in my life. They reminded me of the laurels in Maryland. They might have been a row of wild plum trees in bloom, that whiteness so feathery soft, against the blue. Or calla lilies to an ant on the ground.

The job over, we sped to Seattle and straight to the Land Office.

"Our name is Burn," Farrar said to the man in the outer office. "We've come to see about homesteading one of your islands."

Without a word, the man turned and opened a door behind him.

"Here they are!" he yelled, and the whole office force came out to greet us like kinfolks. It was like getting home after a long absence. And—we held our breath—they had found our island! Someone had been buying it—the last homestead island in Puget Sound. But Farrar's two years' naval service gave him priority rights.

They would return the man's payments and we were free to move on and file. It's just a rock pile, they said. No trees? Oh, plenty of trees. But it was only fifteen acres. Fifteen acres! Why, that was a domain. They said it was so little it didn't show on the map. We looked. Sentinel Island in Speiden Channel—it had a name! And it did show—a sizeable dot. It had a topographical ring on it. It was over a hundred feet high. No water, though. Oh, we'd catch rain water. It rained a lot here, didn't it? No beaches, they said. It wasn't a beach we wanted, it was high, firm seclusion—an eagle's perch from which to survey the world.

II. BREAKING ROCKS AND PRECEDENTS

I DON'T remember where we lived in Seattle while Farrar graded a man's lawn for enough money to get us on the rest of the way. I do remember, though, that the man enjoyed Farrar's stories so much that the two of them spent half their time sitting on a low stone wall talking, and the boss's wife would come out with sandwiches and coffee, ostensibly to cheer the workmen, but in reality to set them to work again.

I got a job cooking, to do my share. But I didn't last long at it. My robust health was having a setback from too much excitement. Joy is hard work!

We got the money at last and went up to Bellingham, where we could catch the boat for Roche Harbor on San Juan Island, the port nearest Sentinel, and our future post office.

Boats for the San Juans leave the Quackenbush Dock in Bellingham at seven. On a Puget Sound morning in winter, seven is pitch dark night. In summer, it has been full day for two hours or more. In the fall and spring, it is pale dawn. That is how it was on this September day, but fresh and clear, as though the world had got up on the right side of the bed.

Little fishing boats rolled sleepily against their moorings. Another passenger-and-freight boat was loading. It left just before us. I watched its keel rip open the bright silk of the bay.

Later, I learned the names of the dark green islands we passed, but that morning they were mysterious and dreamlike. Eliza slipped behind. Lummi Island, elephant-big, reared up on its haunches in front of the boat, but we side-stepped it and went on. Eagle Cliff on Cypress, Blakely

Island, Lopez, Shaw, Orcas, Deer Harbor, Waldron, Stuart Island. From the narrow channel between Johns and Stuart, we saw a tall, long, lovely island just ahead.

"That's Speiden," the captain said. "Ed Chevalier lives there. His wife's father homesteaded part of it, and Ed has gradually got it all. Just on the other side of Speiden is the little island you are looking for."

Across another channel, seagulls screaming. Around the immense hip of Speiden—and there was Sentinel Island, like a green gumdrop, fir trees lifting their beautiful crowns into the sky, sedum-covered bluffs sheering straight down into the rich, green-blue water.

The *San Juan II* turned off its course a little, came abreast, and we saw how the sun lay close on the southern slope where there was only grass. The trees grew on the northern side. Sedum was still in bloom on the cliffs. There were delicious little plateaus where we later found grass up to our knees and wild peas, tiger lilies, camas and fritillaria in their seasons.

Captain Maxwell could have taken the boat alongside and let us off onto our own land without a gangplank, but he thought we'd better go over to Roche Harbor and work awhile for the Lime Company until we had enough money to buy winter supplies and a tent. He listed a number of things we'd need which we hadn't thought of, for neither of us had ever really camped before, except by day, with an occasional night out under blankets. He said he would introduce Farrar to the men in the office and he was sure they would give him work.

Farrar still wore his uniform, and the Lime Company proposed work in the office. But we had notions in those days about the dignity of common labor; we had a theory that only physical work left the spirit free. Farrar insisted on breaking rock in the quarry. We ate with the laborers in the village hotel where we went to live, I the only woman, for the married men had their own tenements, owned by the company, row on row, on the slope above the pretty harbor.

The men went to work at seven in the morning, worked for ten hours, at fifty cents an hour. The quarry was high up on the side of a hill, overlooking channels and islands and passing boats. Farrar would come home to our hotel room at night, bubbling over with the day's adventures. The ducks were coming in droves. The men said they were bluebills, best eating of them all. We'd go hunting! Or the seagulls would have been flying high, circling and circling, and the men had said that meant a storm. A bald headed eagle had flown overhead and perched on the very tip of the highest fir tree, on the rim of the quarry above the workmen.

Or Farrar described the rock-breaking itself.

"Huge boulders will be blasted out of the side of the hill," he would say. "When they have stopped rolling and everything is quiet, we come out from behind things, each man selects his own boulder, and the sledge hammers fall to.

"But you don't just lift your hammer and let it fall on a boulder and expect it to crack. You've got to study the rock before you hit a blow. At first, I would break off a corner and then another corner until I had a big, round, smooth lump that you couldn't crack to save your life. Then Johnson came over and showed me the principle of it. He pointed out faint lines here and there. That's where the cracks will form if you hit it just right. When you have used up all the lines, you begin on the corners. But there's a knack to hitting them, too, so they'll go on making more corners and flat surfaces and the hammer won't glance off and weaken the blow. It's great when you do it just right! There's a fine clean color to the fresh rock surface. Sometimes it is almost pink and when the sun hits it right, it is dazzling." —To get fun out of breaking rocks!

Meanwhile I'd wander along San Juan Island trails, marveling at the head-high bracken, the almost tropic undergrowth everywhere. I often used to go out to a certain point where I could see Sentinel. Salal growth was tangled and heavy on that point. Its sweet meaty berries were ripe now and very good. Oregon grapes were too sour for me, but the people here mixed the two for a delicious jam.

In the evenings I'd describe my adventures, too, but they never sounded as exciting as Farrar's. But he wanted to see the land, too. Feel its craw, he said. He begrudged ten whole hours a day to rock-breaking and began to figure how he could cut it in half.

He was making five dollars a day, but hotel bills were taking most of it. We decided to move to Sentinel where our expenses would be so low that Farrar could work half-days and we would still have enough money to lay in winter supplies, while he would have some daylight hours for wandering with me. He could row back and forth as some of the men did, though none so far.

Mr. Johnson, the foreman, made no objection to the half-day plan, and Farrar began his new schedule right away. He would go at seven, break rocks till noon, return to the hotel for a shower and dinner, and we would spend the afternoon adventuring. Fishing, walking, going over to English Camp where the British soldiers were stationed in 1872 during our border dispute with England. Gathering berries, too.

Or we'd sit on the beach, a mile or so from the village, where we could see Sentinel, and there make elaborate plans for our winter. Of building a house and digging a garden. Of exploring all the islands. We would learn the names of plants and animals, we said, and become authorities on Puget Sound. Little was known and written about it. Oh, we'd count the days and none should slip by without our knowing. Life shouldn't leak for us!

Little by little we were assembling things to take with us. A tent, rented from the company for two dollars a month. A twenty-dollar coupon book for groceries taken against future earnings. On a Saturday afternoon we borrowed the company rowboat, took aboard all our things, and started for Sentinel for the first time.

Farrar was a fine oarsman. Rock-breaking had toughened him. His boyhood on the Arkansas River had prepared him for this.

But not for tides!

When we got outside the harbor and into Speiden Channel beyond Pearl Island, that day, we saw there was a wind. Anyone else would have known it long before, from the movement in the treetops. But we didn't know it. The whitecaps were rolling. They looked formidable. We realized that it was risky to make a crossing in our high-piled shallow boat with the wind blowing against what seemed a strong, contrary current.

"Must be a tide out here," Farrar said wisely. But tides on the open ocean which he had known, are one thing; on enclosed waters, quite another.

We turned back to a little beach on the lee side of our point. And then we did something which Farrar still blushes to think of. We pulled our little boat up onto the beach, tied the painter to a branch of an old alder tree against the bank, and went back to the hotel to wait until next morning.

During the night a wind and a higher tide than usual overturned the boat and emptied its contents all over the beach. Typewriter, trunk, bags, tent were scattered, some of them open, all of them wet. That is what we found the next morning, when, in radiant sunshine, we came running to finish our trip to Sentinel. It looked so bad it tickled us. We hugged each other and laughed.

"You can always expect more than you expect," Farrar said.

The boat was unharmed, so away we went again, sodden belongings heaped around us. The sun poured apologetic warmth down over us. The sea was as calm as a lake. Butterball ducks bobbed about on the long satiny rolls. Sea pigeons had not yet gone south. Their bright scarlet legs flashed out as they skittered away from our coming.

I sat facing Sentinel and watched it leap forward to meet us with every stroke of the oars. When we were nearly there, we crossed a field of hoary grandmother kelp, thirty-foot-long streamers, like gruesome hair, spread out in the tide. The water looked dark and deep, there in the kelp bed. Nine dogfish floated out of it and followed our boat, their hideous faces leering. Small sharks they were. Farrar rowed around the shore till he found a cove where we could pull the boat far up on the rocks—farther than any tide could reach. Thus he still pulls up boats.

Farrar rowing toward Gumdrop Island.

Sentinel, the homestead island—at last we stepped onto that bit of earth that was ours. We went over to a clump of trees, trod the long dry grass, looked up at the sky through yellowing maple leaves, some of them a foot across. This was the big-leafed maple. Now we must unload the boat and spread things out to dry. But, look—a long perfect plank! We'll get that first.

Beach wood still seems to me the most wonderful thing in the Puget Sound country. It comes in as new-cut logs, broken from the rafts. It comes as shake bolts which can be split into long satiny shakes to roof your cabin. This white treasure is piled and heaped at the top of every beach on the Sound.

Grass and forest meet on the very top of Sentinel. There we made our first campsite, underneath firs three feet through, the yellowed grass sweeping up over the crest of the hill to their roots. We stood a hundred and twenty-five feet above the water. Vancouver Island, in Canada, lay to the west and smaller Canadian islands were nearer. San Juan, Henry, Pearl, and Battleship Islands spread their pattern of bays and beaches to the south; the Olympic Peninsula across Juan de Fuca, on further. Speiden rose behind us, long and tall. We could see Jones Island to the east and beyond that, the humps of Orcas. The Olympic Mountains were our southern horizon and the single white cone of Mt. Baker marked where the sun would rise.

We gathered feathery fir twigs for a campfire. In the Puget Sound country you can start a fire with one match anywhere and any time, for all its reputation for rain, for even when everything on the ground is sodden, there are always brittle dry twigs hanging on the trees.

We knew nothing of forest fires then. At home, a camp fire in the woods was seldom dangerous. Hardwood leaves and twigs are not tinder to catch fire from the suggestion of a spark. It scares me yet to think how easily we might have burned Sentinel to its bedrock that first day.

A campfire lunch of coffee, bacon and eggs, and toast. Not many of our groceries had been ruined by the drenching they had had. The sugar and salt were spoiled, of course, and there was rice running out of melted sacks. But all in all we came out better than we deserved.

After lunch we must hurry to bring up the things. Trip after trip up and down that steep slick hill. Tent, trunk, bags, boxes, our plank. Weary, back-breaking loads. We'd go down the north side, sinking half to our knees in knight's-plume moss. It was like walking in feathers—no, on an innerspring mattress, for it held together and gave some resistance. Then we'd come up the short way again, past yew trees, the kind you make longbows of, tough and red and everlasting. This wood will sink in water.

Past madrona trees, their leaves like the magnolia but sturdier, tougher, the branches hung with scarlet berries, now. The paper-thin bark was peeling off in scrolls. The madrona is Puget Sound's most beautiful and interesting tree, forever green, leaves shedding surreptitiously, the new ones already there, delicate pink blossoms in spring, bright red berries in fall, cinnamon-red outer bark peeling all the time, the under skin a jade green. It will grow on the driest, rockiest bluffs, yet it looks delicate and as though it needed protection.

All afternoon we worked until we were too tired to cook supper. We ate some cheese and soggy bread and went to our bed on the ground—a feather mattress my mother had given us, and dampish comforters.

The bed looked out over the world. The islands had pulled the dark over them and were only purple blurs in the moonlight. Not a single light shone anywhere. The forest hid all the little farms on San Juan Island. The other islands in our range of vision were uninhabited.

Our island. Our world. We had pulled the ladder up and nobody would come. Nobody knew we were here. How tall these trees, their dark crowns brushing the sky! How still it is!

A tugboat rounded Henry Island. Its lights crept up the International Boundary channel. We could hear its engines going in a soft chug-chug. It was a good sound.

The last thing I remembered was Farrar leaning on his elbow, gazing and gazing. And the first thing I saw in the morning was Farrar on his elbow, waiting to show me the morning world with only its fir tips sticking up out of the low mist which hid the water. The world had been down for a swim and was just coming up again. The sun rose over Mt. Baker. The mist sped away. And there was the new day.

"These are the 'days when,'" said Farrar. "We're happy now. This is what it's all about. This is what we were born for. We own the world."

This is what we were born for.

III. HOMESTEADING ON THE GUMDROP

ONE afternoon, shortly after Farrar had declared his half-holidays, we were on the village dock watching the flowery white sea anemones blow out and in on the piling where they clung below the lowest tide level. Some of them were as large as peonies. It was hard to believe that they were animals, though they drew in their scalloped petals when they were touched or the piling was jostled, as the rowboat jostled it now, and became vulgar-looking things, tight and wrinkled and gooey.

We looked up to see a jolly, chunky little man, short and round, with rosy cheeks and a white fuzz of hair above them, hop nimbly out of his boat, grab the painter, and pull it up onto the beach. Then he lifted out his cans of milk and cream, grunting and chuckling and mumbling to himself as people will when they know someone is watching them. Farrar went over to help and little Santa Claus began to talk a mile a minute, in a broad Lancashire dialect, about the weather and tides, about hunting and fishing, and ended by inviting us to go home with him and meet Mother. They lived on Henry Island, he said, which would be the northern end of San Juan if it weren't for a narrow channel between them, on a beach facing Roche Harbor, across the bay. They sold milk, cream, butter, and eggs to the store and the villagers.

"What ye doin' here, Lad?" he asked Farrar, on our way over, and how he laughed when we told him about our half-day plan of working.

"An' they let ye do it? . . .Well, don't ye think they will long. Lemme see, now—if we could think of a way—see here, Lad, why don't ye ask the company for all the merchandise books they'll let ye have, then ye'll be in debt to 'em and they can't fire ye?"

On and on he rattled, chuckling and bouncing his round belly as he talked. With strong, short thrusts of his oars he carried us across the harbor and channel to his own beach. While we helped carry his empty cans, he opened the gate to his backyard garden and called, "Mither! Mither! Come ye out and see what I've brought ye!"

Mother Butterworth came out. She, too, was short, though not so round as her husband, with very curly white hair and a motherly, smiling face.

"Come ye in," she said in her low voice.

We stayed for supper. "Sit ye doon," Mother said, as we went into her warm kitchen-living room. "I'll set the kettle on," which meant tea.

After that, Father Butterworth often picked us up when he came to deliver milk, and took us across to the low gray cottage on Henry Island beach. After supper, or the next morning perhaps, he would set us across on the other side of the narrow channel and we would walk around the woods trail to the village.

On Saturdays, we would sometimes go over for Sunday, giving up Sentinel for a weekend because Father and Mother Butterworth were lonely and we loved them. At that, we didn't go often enough and years later, when they were both gone forever, we thought how we might have stayed with them a lot more if we hadn't been so drunk on everything, selfishly engaged in each other and our own island.

It was a real self-sacrifice, though, to spend a night with our new parents. Mother Butterworth was the proud possessor of what she called a "flock" mattress, which seems to be much prized in England—a bed made of loose wool. It was a flock of lumps, high at the ends, low in the middle. But we wouldn't for the world have told Mother Butterworth how uncomfortable we found that bed.

It is odd about that kind of thing. You are polite, but you don't visit so often. They are lonely and wonder why you don't. All my life, I have puzzled over that. What a multitude of little comedies of errors there are in all relationships which a few words could straighten out if anybody could bear either to speak or to hear the words.

The Butterworths had a dairy farm. Father did the milking. Usually Farrar helped him, but sometimes I went instead, and Father and I would drink all we could hold of the fresh warm milk before taking it down to be strained. Farrar would turn the separator and we would have fresh cream on canned fruit for supper.

After supper, Father would tell stories, with Mother correcting every date, every fact, every event in her gently persistent way. Father would give a curiously musical chuckle and go on. They had been in South America on a sugar plantation, Mother acting as housekeeper of the owner's establishment and Father as manager of the plantation, I think. That made them upper servants in the English tradition, which, for all their loyalty to England, they didn't like. In our tradition, they were business people, plain and simple, and they came to live in America for that cleaner standard.

As Father Butterworth had warned us, it wasn't long before the other laborers began to complain about Farrar's half-day arrangement. "He gets paid only for what he does," the foreman explained; but it wasn't done in the best laboring circles and the men didn't like it.

Meanwhile, Farrar had wangled two or three twenty dollar books out of the company. He is a plausible devil, and now the company couldn't fire him, as Father had said, until he had worked out the books. Anyhow, we had moved to Sentinel by now and Farrar was rowing the two and a half miles to work every day. He had the necessity of working on his own place as an excuse for the short day's labor.

But at last the foreman said he couldn't have Burn in the quarry any more. It made the men discontented. The company bookkeeper called Farrar in and told him that his accounts were even, and they thought they had better let him go.

Even! We must have owed them at least forty dollars. Father Butterworth nearly bust his galluses laughing at that. It was the first time in the history of that company that a laboring man ever got ahead of them. That night Farrar came back to Sentinel with his boat loaded with the last supplies we'd ever get from the company merchandise books. He was jubilant. He had been fired, but we still had Sentinel. Time enclosed us in a world of our own.

A check for thirty-six dollars came from Washington, some kind of back flight-pay, and with that we bought a rowboat for twenty-five dollars, laid in more supplies, and bought a fishing outfit: line, lead, spoon.

With our own rowboat, our world stretched out. We often rowed over to the Butterworths, and almost every day we went fishing. We ate so much codfish, you'd think we would have tired of it, but the more we had the better we liked it. Even when the days came when there was nothing but cod, we still liked it.

"What did you do on Sentinel all day long, week long, month long?" people have asked. "How could you stand to be so idle?"

Idle? Our days were so full we had to write down a schedule to get anywhere. We got up at the first crack of dawn, had breakfast, tidied the camp, and set to work.

The work was writing. We worked until noon, and I wonder where all those written words can be. Somewhere, we dropped the fruit of a whole year, like an apple tree, and forgot it ever was.

After lunch we fished for our food, dug in the little pockets of soil to get it ready for spring planting, explored the islands, rowed across the channel to Speiden for ten gallon cans of water, gathered beach wood, and, later on, built our cabin—after we had stolen the materials to build it from.

During the afternoons, when our occupations were physical, we would talk. And many a writing morning we've wasted at it, too. Evenings were particularly dedicated to talk, of course, and there were the early mornings, before dawn, with islands sneaking up out of the dark, when Farrar nudged me to wake up so I could feel myself and see whether I was still happy. We talked then, too. And once in awhile we talked all night, the stars slowly wheeling into new positions as we watched them.

Farrar could make such convincing plans that it seemed they would surely come to fruition if I'd strain a little, as you push against the floor of a car when it is going uphill. But before anything could be done about one plan, another would get me just as excited.

Whenever high slack tide came in the afternoons, we went fishing. We learned how to rig the troll, polish the spoon, where to fish, and what to do under every condition. We trolled on the end of the flood and at the beginning of the ebb.

While Farrar rowed, I gave the spoon its final polishing with a bit of old flannel blanket we kept for the purpose. We used a Number 5 McMahon with its huge cruel hook, heavy top cord for the line, and a half-pound lead sinker. We crossed the narrow channel between Sentinel and Speiden before I let out the line. About twenty feet off shore, I would unroll the hundred and fifty feet of line, let out fifty or sixty feet of it, make a loop around a spring stick, and sit there hoping the stick would begin to bob madly up and down.

Farrar's job was to row just fast enough to keep the lead and spoon from catching on the bottom, but not so fast the cod couldn't overtake him! Sometimes the hook would catch on kelp or a rock and then the stick would bob and I'd leap to my job of pulling in the line, hand over frozen hand, only to find a bit of kelp on my hook.

After awhile we could tell when it was a fish and when kelp. "When it's kelp, you think you've got a fish, but when it's a fish, you know you've got one!" There is no mistaking the feel of a fish, even a very eggy mother cod, sodden and limp at the end of your line. I hauled it in until the prize was at the gunwale of the boat, when Farrar took over.

The cod is the ugliest fish in the world, I expect. Great gasping mouth, bulging, slimy eyes, wide gills going in and out, gray spotted body. I didn't like to haul them in and kill them. Farrar did that. One day I caught a forty pounder. It was so big and ugly that I burst into tears—a silly thing to do—when Farrar lifted it up to bring it into the boat. It had so much good eating on it that we could live a week without going fishing again. Not that we minded fishing, except for the cold. Puget Sound water is icy any time of year, but in late fall it is iciest. You get used to it after awhile, but for those first few weeks I thought my fingers would break off.

One day, when we were fishing the kelp bed on the southeastern end of Sentinel, I got the spoon caught on a great grandfather kelp that wouldn't give it up. Farrar tugged and tugged; the kelp would yield a little, but never quite break off or the spoon quite pull through. The kelp was stronger than our line and we lost the only spoon we had. It had cost a dollar and we didn't have another dollar either. Yet we had to have fish—there wasn't anything else to eat just then.

Then Farrar had an idea—we would sell the fish we had already caught at Roche Harbor and buy another spoon. The idea of selling fish to the company store hadn't occurred to us. Sometimes we had taken a fish to the Butterworths and come home with homemade bread, butter, winter carrots, but I suppose our own guilty consciences where the lime company was concerned had kept us from thinking of selling fish to them.

We counted our catch. There were seven, some of them twenty pounders.

Farrar rowed back to the landing on Sentinel and dressed the fish on his favorite tide-washed flat rocks there. Then, while I took a couple of them up the hill to hang on the empty spikes on the shady sides of the trees around our camp, he went to the Harbor with the rest. About two hours later, he came back with another Number 5 McMahon spoon, some coffee, beans, rice, and whatever else the sixty pounds of fish at ten cents a pound had bought. "We've got the world by the tail, now, sure enough!" he said.

He was a little premature. On the next good fishing tide we caught over ninety pounds. With over nine dollars we would be rich, and that night we celebrated in advance the money which we would send to the mainland for supplies, which were cheaper than at the company store.

But it happened that the company also ran the post office. They knew what we had done and they didn't like it. The third time Farrar went over with fish, the store keeper handed him a merchandise order.

"What's this?"

"It's an order for seven dollars and forty cents of supplies."

"But I don't want supplies; I want cash."

"You'll have to take this. You can't sell your fish anywhere else and you'd be spending your money here, anyhow."

Farrar took his beautifully dressed fish outside on the dock and threw them into the bay. "It's cash or nothing," he said and rowed home, wondering why he hadn't thought of peddling the fish direct to the villagers.

That is what he did from then on. One day he came home gleeful. "I have a fish hanging out on the back porch of every house in the village," he boasted. And he had enough money for some boots for me and long underwear for himself, for the cold weather had come by then.

But one afternoon he discovered that everybody in the village already had fish. Old Ole, hearing that people were buying fish for cash, decided to cut in on the market, and he sold for five cents a pound. After that, Farrar couldn't get the price back to ten cents and he stopped taking them fish.

"It just shows what cutting prices can do to a big business," he said.

By then it was summer time and the cod were going out to deep water, anyhow. It was difficult to catch enough for our own use. But we had had several batches of supplies, during the year, which had given us reprieves from our codfish diet, at least.

One crisp, sunny fall day, we heard a motorboat coming toward Sentinel. Lots of them came near our island, of course, but this one sounded as if it meant to stop. We ran down the hill to see who it was.

The blunt-nosed boat eased up to the sheer bank below our clump of maples. A bareheaded man with a long nose and a shock of curly black hair threw us a line.

"We're your neighbors from Speiden Island," he said. "We've come by to take you home with us for supper." Just like that.

I had on breeches. Would I do? Sure! Jump in!

Farrar held the boat close in. I stepped aboard and he followed. The man pushed off with his long boathook and started up the engine again. He backed up to clear our rocks, then headed across the narrow channel between the two islands to the boat landing on Speiden.

Above the noise of the motor, we met the Chevaliers and found our second set of Island parents. Dad Chevalier, half-French, wild and rough and good, had come to Puget Sound when he was fifteen, worked in the Roche Harbor lime quarries, and married a lovely half-Indian girl whose father had homesteaded part of Speiden Island. Gradually he had bought the rest of the island and now owned nearly everything in sight, on islands all around. He was, and is, the best storyteller this side of heaven and on that first day began telling us tales of the old days, and we haven't heard them all yet.

Ma Chevalier was shy, gentle, and pretty. She is the kind of woman who can seat a dirty old fisherman at her table beside a spick-and-span banker from Seattle and make both of them feel perfectly at home. That day she said something reassuring about my breeches and I forgot all about them.

There were five children: Bill, about twenty-five, kind and dark like his mother, but with his father's quick temper; Ellen, twenty-three, blond and daring like her father; Alfred, twenty, a dark, brooding boy of few words and unruly temper; Elmer, sixteen, with his father's looks and his mother's disposition, lies now in the little burial plot on top of Speiden; Caroline, twelve, called Tootsie, the baby, so quiet you might have dreamed her there, but growing up into a dark beauty which rivaled Ellen's.

These were the boys and girls whom we came to love like sisters and brothers. That day the glamour of the big island and a boat to travel in hung about them all. They were like people from Mars to us. We discovered later that to them we were the "educated fools."

It was a long, steep walk up the narrow switch-back trail from the boat landing to the top of Speiden. But what a view up there! White Olympics to the south, white Cascades to the north and east, green islands everywhere. How small Sentinel looked, down there in the blue channel! Across on the Canadian side a ship moved along so smoothly it might have been towed by the International Boundary Line.

The Chevaliers lived right on top of Speiden. Here was the blue cottage with chrysanthemums still in bloom in the garden. There were horses, cows, chickens, turkeys, pigs, sheep, and pheasants running about their secret ways.

We went around to the back gate to enter. We always did; I don't know why. The dog, Ring, came to meet us. Two great sheep came waddling up. "Ma's pet lambs," Dad said, laughing. It seems that every spring there are two or three orphan lambs that Ma brings up by hand. Then, by butchering time, she has grown so fond of them she refuses to sell them and they are pests to everybody. But when they are a year old—that is, when the next lambs come along, and Ma has one or two or three more to bring up—she loses interest in them and they are allowed to join the herd.

We stayed all night in the blue cottage. After supper, Dad took off his shoes, propped his feet on the rung of a chair, filled his pipe, and began on the story of his days in the islands which, like Scheherazade's, never ends. Ma washed dishes out in the pantry. We could hear her laughing, now and then, at his exaggerations, but she never interrupted or corrected him. Elmer had gone out to his own little cottage in the yard, to play his accordion, and we could hear it faintly from the kitchen.

After awhile, Farrar wandered in to the piano and began to play. A music-loving family, they gathered around; even the shy Elmer crept in to listen. Then Dad wanted some old songs. Farrar plays only his own music. I took over, and we sang "Old Black Joe" and "My Old Kentucky Home" till long past midnight. Many a night on Speiden we sang every book in the house straight through. Early next morning Bill rowed us home. Dad couldn't understand why we had to go so early. Farm work was light at that time of year and he had leisure. What nonsense to go off just to write!

After that, our second—no, our third home was on Speiden.

It was Dad Chevalier who taught us what we knew about fishing. We were crazy to catch a salmon. He told us a salmon had pink flesh. He meant inside, but we thought it would be pink outside. One day we caught a beautiful red fish off the San Juan shore. We were so excited we rowed for dear life to Speiden, ran up that steep, long hill to the house at the top and showed our prize.

"Red snapper," said Dad, "just a common red snapper," and he laughed fit to kill. We laughed, too. The mistakes we were forever making seemed funny to us, which was a blessing—there were so many of them.

June and Farrar on Chevalier's front porch.

IV. THE HOPELESS CHEST

WE STOLE our first house. One night Bill asked when we were going to build one. We were still living in the rented tent, doing our cooking and having our meals among some gray boulders on the first plateau below it. When Bill came over to see how we lived, he looked very dubious. There had probably been a family conference about it on Speiden, the upshot being that we must build a house, and at once, before winter set in.

"There is a cabin over on Johns Island that you can get," Bill suggested.

"How?"

"Just go over and tear it down and row home with it. You can build it again on your own place," he said. "Some fishermen built it several years ago. They will never come back. Nobody owns it. It is often done in the islands."

And that is how we got our first house. Just rowed over to Johns Island and stole it. For though it belonged to no one in particular, it certainly didn't belong to us. That is, not at first. But after those nights when we tore it down and rowed home with it in the moonlight—then it belonged to us.

You would think that building our first little home on Sentinel would be the outstanding adventure of the year. It was nothing of the sort. Sentinel itself was our home.

We loved the camp among boulders up on top. We loved the tent with one whole side open to the south, where we could lie at night and watch the stars, and in the early morning see the day slowly break. We didn't feel the need of any more home than we had. But we were beguiled by the notion of getting a house as easily as birds get theirs.

And now that we had it, there was nothing to do but build those four dark, in-shutting walls. So we built them. Two-by-fours for studding and rafters. Two-by-tens for floor joists. Beach boards for walls and floors, shakes for the roof, two tiny windows. We had everything we needed. It lay in a heap on the level plateau on the western side of Sentinel where we meant to build, in the lee of the hill, sheltered from the prevailing southeast winds.

Farrar decided on a shed roof because it was both useful and easy to build. I decided that the shack should be as near the ground as we could squeeze it—I like a floor on a level with the ground so one can feel he isn't really going into a house at all.

It took us two weeks to build the little eight-by-ten house, working in between other tasks. We set up the stove at the front end of the shack, a little railed galley stove which Dad Chevalier gave us. We built a table under the window in the front wall and another under the window diagonally opposite in the side wall. With boxes for seats, we were equipped with desks which could be transformed into dining tables or shelves for cooking at the proper times.

Across the back end, we built a narrow double bunk, with closet space between the end of it and the wall. Farrar made the bunk springy by using slender poles for lengthwise slats, which gave easily under our weight. Thin shakes over the poles kept the bedding from going through. It was comfortable, and fragrant of cedar and fir. We gathered fir

June in their outdoor living room.

boughs to put under the bed so that it would seem like out of doors. But we couldn't see the sleeping world from our bunk.

There was ample shelf room for papers, books, supplies, fishing tackle, jars of pebbles, and everything we had, over the tables and bunk. And if there was no room left to walk in, we had plenty just outside on the mossy ledge.

After a morning's work inside, we stepped out through that little door into living room. The tide would be making whirlpools down below the big madrona tree. Ducks would fly up, their wings whistling as they sped away. Bald eagles, out on Sentinel Rocks, would heave themselves up and go flopping off over Speiden. The *San Juan II* would pass on its way to Bellingham, pushing its little white wall of water ahead of it. Ever since we had moved down on the ledge, it gave a gay toot as it went by.

Early in December, Bill Chevalier came over to our new little cabin. "Dad says for you kids to come over to Speiden. It's too cold for you to stay here during the winter, he says, and you can live in the log cabin over there just across from Sentinel. He says I am to move you over today."

I can't remember that we hesitated. Dad's word was law and if he said we must come, we must, and we began packing.

The little cabin had a fireplace. Farrar built a double chair of poles and we would sit in it by the hour, talking and philosophizing before that fire. We discovered that island willow makes a fragrant fire, and so had incense with our philosophy. I wish I had those nights again. I thought I had them

Farrar leaning against Chevalier's house.

tucked away where nothing could nibble away the bright recollection of them, but they are fading.

Sometimes we lost track of time. Once we lost, or gained, a week. It wouldn't have mattered, except that we had to keep track of the tides for our fishing. This time we went out on what we thought was a slack tide. We rowed around Speiden to the north side, up to the bay where the codfish were hanging out those days. When we got there, we found ourselves in the maddest tide rip, and the swiftest ebb we had ever seen. Before we knew what had happened, the thing had grabbed our boat and flung us far out into the channel. We rowed for dear life, barely gaining an inch, zigzagging back toward shore. At last we made it and I got out on shore to pull the boat around the bad spot while Farrar kept it off the rocks with his oar.

My hair had grown long. It came down over my eyes. My stockings came down over my shoes. The bank was slippery with seaweed and steep, and I had on rubber soles. Hair-blinded, stocking-lamed, nothing but fear kept me from falling into that tide rip. Meanwhile, Farrar was pushing with his oar—he had to stand up in the boat to use force enough to keep it from being dashed onto the shore. Even so, the water boiled over into the boat and the rip jerked it about. It was all he could do to stand up.

It must have taken us an hour to inch our way up that shore and around the dangerous point. At last we gained the comparatively calm water of a little cove at the upper, narrow end of Speiden. And there, on shore, standing in the middle of a potato field, was Dad Chevalier, doubling over with laughter. I was furious, but Farrar laughed, too, and I saw I would be in that hateful woman position of seeming a spoilsport if I lashed out, so I bottled up my anger and sat down in the sun until I could stop trembling. We had come as near to drowning as people can come and live. If I hadn't been born with a caul, we would probably be in Davy Jones's locker right now.

Once when we had sold ten dollars' worth of codfish at Roche Harbor, we bought coffee and a hand grinder and a sack of island wheat. After that, we had ground wheat hoecake with our fish, and once in awhile mush with milk from Speiden's cow.

But the fish-selling episodes were rare. We decided that before we should run out of supplies again, we would put away what we called our hopeless chest. Rice, beans, coffee, a can of butter, salt, sugar, some ground wheat—enough, we thought, to last a week with fish to eke it out. If it should ever be necessary, we could row to the mainland and get jobs, living till we got them on the hopeless chest's supplies. Now, whatever came, we were safe. On the leanest days, we used to haul out the neat box and think of the good things in it. It helped to keep up our courage.

For by Christmas, what with the storms that prevented our catching a surplus, we hadn't a single thing left to eat but codfish. We hadn't even salt—except salt water. We had run through a considerable batch of supplies, like the prodigals we were, and now we lived on boiled codfish for breakfast, dinner, and supper.

That was the sweetest winter! Only one snow. It didn't even rain much. I remember that we took a dish of fish with us down to a secluded slope on Speiden and spent the day after New Year's lying naked in the warm sunshine, talking about all we were going to do and be and write and see.

Of course, we tried everything that grew in the Puget Sound country to add to our diet of boiled codfish. Ma Chevalier told us about Indian potatoes, which are also called camas. She dug up some for us one time—striking down into the grass and hoping to find them, for the tops were long since gone and there were no signs of them. She brought up a few tiny little slick onion-like bulbs which, when boiled, tasted precisely like solid air. Not a particle of taste, and a slimy texture. I couldn't eat them then, but now I could, and with relish, because I have grown used to the earth and its tricks and I'll eat anything that is edible. My body is decently submissive and civilized; I am not such a slave to it. But then, with our supply of codfish, we were still choosy. We never tried Indian potatoes again, although whole tribes of Indians had practically lived on them in the old days.

We had the same experience with sea urchins, which the Indians call sea eggs. Crack that beautiful cluster of spines, pour out the slime and there, tight against the shell, in little yellow strips, is an egg-like, rich marrowy stuff which the Indian children eat raw but which we didn't like, even when cooked. It was too rich.

Sea cucumbers were good. Bother one of these flabby creatures enough and he will obligingly dump all his insides outside and you won't have to clean him. Peel off the warty-looking, slimy outer skin to expose a broad, flat, sweet muscle which, fried in butter, is delicious.

It was fun digging clams on a low winter tide by the full moon. Once we went with all the Chevaliers over to the clam beach on Johns Island and dug three or four gunnysackfuls in an hour. We gathered gallons more than we ever used—there were so many of them, who could have helped it? Minus tides didn't always come on full moon nights. Better take a lot and be sure you have enough. Now the bed is so depleted it would take a week to dig as many as we got that night.

When we had all we wanted, we stumbled back across the rocky beach to the dry upper beach where we built a fire, dried ourselves, and had a clam bake—the first one for me. Ma Chevalier chose the clams and the flat rocks, placed the clams with their backs to the fire and we all sat and watched them fling open their shells from the heat. Then she turned the faces of the clams to the fire and let them brown a little. They were sweet-flavored, though you had to watch out for sand and gravel. Ma had brought along homemade bread and butter and coffee, and Farrar and I ate that with more relish than we ate the clams.

Once we got into serious trouble, experimenting with all kinds of food. We were fishing one day when we saw a mass of pearls under a rock. They were tiny, perfectly round, iridescent, tough but not hard—so beautiful we knew they must be ambergris or something even more valuable. We stopped fishing at once, carefully gathered up the mass, and ran up Speiden with it.

"Fish eggs," said Dad, perfectly unconcerned. He laughed at our delight in their beauty. "Just fish eggs."

"Good to eat?"

He saw a chance for a joke. The Indians sometimes ate them, he said. We must boil them gently, otherwise they would get tough.

I simmered them just a few minutes. Then we ate them. Or Farrar did. He always believed in going through with eating anything we found, whether we liked it or not. He admitted that his teeth bounced on the eggs but he swallowed quantities of them. And that night nearly died of acute indigestion. He was sick for two weeks, and unashamedly I took milk from the Chevaliers for him and we got through it. Dad still laughs about that. If Farrar had died, none would have mourned more deeply, but since he didn't die, it was a grand joke.

When spring came, there were tender shoots of thimbleberry to eat, boiled like asparagus or eaten raw. There was miner's lettuce, flavorless raw, but delicious as cooked greens. Nettles grew in the marshy places. We gathered them with gloves on, I sloshed them up and down in a pan of water with a wire potato masher and cooked them without being stung. They were a bit medicinal in flavor, but good, too. Later in the summer, there were quarts of blackcaps—a wild sweet raspberry that is delicious.

Over at the Butterworths, carrots and potatoes and everything good began to grow in the garden, and whenever we visited there, we would bring home baskets of vegetables in exchange for the fish we took them. How good they were to us, always! Understanding and kind and tactful. It is curious that the more you need a thing, the more sensitive you are about taking it. Something false in our lives has made us that way. But the Butterworths understood and contrived all manner of things for our undoing, and we always had plenty to eat for a day or so after visiting them. Which made us visit them less often, and was another silly comedy.

Once Farrar took one of Dad's guns out and shot a seal. A hair seal. We had heard that it was grand eating. You shot it at the end of its breathing period so it would be so full it would float until you got to it. Farrar had gone to Roche Harbor for the mail. He often carried that borrowed rifle on the chance that he might get a seal. On this day he got one and he came running up the hill to our cabin, so full of the news he was fit to burst. Now we could eat for a week!

Then, true to the Arkansas in him, he left the seal down at the foot of the hill overnight. He was too comfortable to go down and get it. And it was a hot day. The fat, which is the strongest and the worst flavored part, melted into the flesh. By the time Farrar brought it up and dressed it, the flavor of the meat was utterly ruined. It tasted the way Eskimos smell. Like carrion. Like nothing fit to eat. But, having committed his sin, Farrar ate that seal. He cut it in hunks and hung them to dry on the shady side of the cabin. We would boil it and it would smell up the whole island, and he would eat it. I couldn't get down a single morsel.

Once, after all the codfish had taken to deeper water, and we had not yet learned how to catch salmon, Dad Chevalier told us that there was a halibut bank off our island.

Halibut! Not only would one of them last us a long time, but if we caught a big one, we could sell it at the Harbor for twenty cents a pound, or fifteen cents anyhow. Halibut was in great demand. Here was our chance to get back our lost fish market.

Dad said you had to have live bait for halibut. They wanted herring. And you had to catch the herring first. You could do that if you had a herring rake and a very thick school of fish. The thing to do was to rush the rake through the school, impaling dozens per scoop.

The first thing, then, was to get a rake. Dad said we could make one with a strip of cigar box on a pole and a lot of straight pins stuck through the thin strip of wood. It sounded plausible and Farrar used up my paper of pins making a rake.

We had lately had some supplies, from our last sale of codfish, and now had one mess of ground wheat, one mess of navy beans, and one bit of codfish left. We cooked them all together in a kind of pemmican hoecake. Taking the pemmican and our new rake, we set out for Friday Harbor, where Dad said the herring could be found. It was twelve or fifteen miles, and with a fair tide we could get down there in three hours.

It was a lovely day, no wind, a good strong tide going our way. We never felt happier, plenty of food for today, two pairs of oars so that I needn't sit idle in the stern of the boat, boats passing and people waving to us.

We made Friday Harbor by noon, took out a hunk each of the thick, brown pemmican and ate it slowly, swinging our legs off the dock. After lunch, Farrar got out his rake and we rowed around and around, under the docks, hunting a herring school. We found only one little cluster of fish, candlefish, or about that size. Not more than a few score. But it was the best we could do.

I held the boat against a piling, while Farrar poised, like a big brown Indian, and prepared, with one sweep of the rake, to gather in what he could. He misjudged the depth, struck the soft bottom of the bay, broke his rake, and came up with one little broken fish hanging on one pin. He looked a bit rueful. But he said, "Anyhow we got one. One herring, one halibut."

We filled our bait bucket with sea water and put the little broken fish in. Before we got home he was in two and we knew that no self-respecting halibut would look at him and that we had lost our chance.

But we still had plenty of the pemmican for supper. It was a big thick cake and dry going; a little of it went a long way. We made the end of Speiden along about four o'clock—still hours of daylight to go. We were living on Sentinel Island again, but we planned to spend the night on the neck of the reclining lady that is Speiden and row home early the next morning.

Farrar gave a loud cry. "A devilfish!"

He had beached the boat and was down by a pile of rocks at the end of the beach. I ran down to see, taking an oar along, for you have to have something for a devilfish to cling to or you can't bring it up.

Farrar took the oar, teased the octopus with it, got a few legs wound around the handle, and dragged the evil looking beast up on shore. I ran to get the boat and we managed to maneuver that eight-legged, big-bellied, red, slick, hideous thing over the gunwale onto the floor of the boat. Then we got in after it, and started for home, two miles away. With all this food, we had new strength for the rest of the trip.

That devilfish is properly named. We were rowing, hell bent for leather, when the thing began to reach out with one leg, then with another, toward our legs. Farrar told me to get on the back seat where I could tuck up my legs, so we could manage to keep the thing in the space between us. But that wasn't its idea at all. It kept edging toward me. Farrar couldn't stand it any longer. He stood up in the boat. "I'll fix him," he said. He lifted his oar, handle end down, and brought it down on the back of the octopus with all his might. The oar slid right off the tough back and through the bottom of the boat. A geyser of water shot up. We were two hundred feet from shore in deep water. With an octopus laughing fit to kill at us.

Farrar grabbed one of my oars, left his plugging the hole as best it could, and with the unmatched pair, rowed for dear life. I grabbed the herring bucket and bailed as hard as I ever did anything. And we made shore just as the boat quietly went under. We waded out. I grabbed the boat while Farrar set about tangling the octopus on his oar. We weren't going to lose him after all this.

The anticlimax of that devilfishing experience, was that we cooked one of its legs just as Ma told us to do, but it was as tough as the fish eggs, and we couldn't chew it into fine enough hunks to swallow, to save our lives. She had forgotten to tell us that it must be softened in vinegar first, and anyhow, we had no vinegar.

The way to kill a devilfish, by the way, is not to hit it, but to turn the thing over and there, big as life, is a head with a beak—somewhat like a parrot's beak, which you cut out and the creature is dead. Farrar cut out that hard beak, and then threw away the unsavory-looking stomach. We found out later that the stomach is the choice part, and the only part that is tender enough to cook as it is.

V. LIVING ON SEAGULL EGGS

WHEN spring came to the islands, she brought more than dandelion greens and thimbleberry shoots for hungry homesteaders. Wherever she went, her quick light footfalls left beauty prints.

In March, flowering currant came out on Sentinel and Speiden, in sheltered sunny crevices of the bluffs. In shady spots those spicy scarlet tassels hung on through June. Ma Chevalier said it would rain if we picked it, and she always looked a little troubled when we came in with a spray of it for our cabin.

The wild Easter lily is one of the earliest bloomers in the Sound country. Those six-petaled toy lilies were like white butterflies over the tender new green of open, grassy headlands. They grew in among the sharp-spined Oregon grape, too. Sometimes there would be sheets of them on a bluff—a flock of butterflies basking in bland new sunshine.

Tall Oregon grape bloomed in March, too—fragrant sunbursts of flowers in the crotch of the spiny leaves. The low Oregon grape blooms later, deeper in the woods. Salal hung out its sweet waxy pink upside-down chimneys for doll-sized lamps. Madrona trees wore clusters of the same delicate pink, bell-like blossoms.

In April the ground of the deep loamy woods was purple with lady slippers, deliciously fragrant. In the open grassy places there were blue camas, and dark-brown, mottled fritillaria drooped on thin stems. Wild peas and vetch and everlasting sweet peas bloomed in the level pockets of soil.

Puget Sound dogwood is different from the eastern variety. It is not quite so radiant a white. Each medallion has five petals instead of four, and the great spread of them is not "pure as the driven snow" against the dark green of the forest. They are—hateful admission!—just a little messy. But the flash of dogwood among the maples high on a bluff is a quickening sight for all that.

In June the ocean spray burst into feathery white foam on the bluffs. We'd be rowing along and look up to see creamy Holodiscus and scarlet flowering currant hanging together on a cliff, with a humming bird dipping its flying siphon into the currant cups.

We found a few bluebells, and along damp ravines, bright orange monkey flowers, or mimulus. On Speiden, the meadow larks sang all day long from the fence posts.

Farrar said, "All this is what makes a country. After a fellow gets a bellyful, he looks for something else. And here's something to go with your bread!"

In the spring the Indians went sluckus gathering. One of them, whose given name was Major General Scott—he was called "General," for short—had a forty-foot-long dugout canoe with high curved figureheads at each end. He would pile all his family into that dugout and strike out for Sucia Island and Waldron, to gather sluckus.

Sluckus is the Indian name for a glutinous seaweed that grows on the rocks below high tide level. On long low tides, this weed dries on the rocks and can easily be picked. That is, the first few handfuls are easy. After that your fingers hurt. You can't help rubbing them against the rock surface, scraping tiny barnacles, sometimes cutting them. There are loose grains of sand and small gravel everywhere. By the second day it takes sheer grit to pick sluckus, your fingers bleeding, the weed slick with blood. One day we saw an old Indian woman doggedly picking the black bits off rough rocks, her hands so torn and cold that she didn't feel them any more.

The Indians sell their sluckus to the Chinese who put it in soups and eat it raw, too. There are thousands of Chinese in Victoria. The Indians on our side of the border thought nothing of rowing their sacks of sluckus the fifteen or twenty miles to Victoria, where immigrant Chinese bought it, shipping some to China. The fine, narrow weed brought as much as thirty cents a pound, and the coarser, fifteen cents.

One day General came over to Speiden. He always walked with his head down, as though he were charging, shoulders slouched forward. Now, that stoop has become a fixture and General looks like an old man, though he can't be over forty.

But that day, when he came into Ma's spotless kitchen, he was very much excited, puffing from his run up the hill.

"What's the matter, General?" asked Dad, who was a friend to all the Indians and always ready to help them.

Farrar and I were there and General seemed ashamed to speak. Dad went outside with him. Then, in the curious, invisible way men have, Farrar melted through the door, too. I heard the tale that night.

"Sarah is gone," General said.

Sarah was General's new wife. But she hadn't wanted to be. Now, the young, shy girl had run away and General had come up to get Dad to bring her back to him.

"Gone?" Dad said. "Gone where?"

"Across the border," said General, the tears running down his face.

"Oh, she'll come back," Dad said.

"She has only gone over to Victoria to visit her folks," Farrar told him.

But General was inconsolable. Sarah was gone and all was lost.

"I wouldn't mind so much," General said at last, almost sobbing, "but she took my new soo-ootcase!" dragging out the word into a wail. Farrar and Dad roared. They haven't stopped laughing about that yet, though Sarah came back years ago.

Every now and then, the Indians came to Sentinel to spear cod with a "dolly." They had a wooden block that might have been cut off a broom handle. One end was sharpened, and near that end, and all around the block, they had fastened bright feathers to make a whorl. The block was weighted at the bottom to make it stand upright in the water, but not enough to make it sink.

When the fishermen reached the rock cod hangouts, they pushed the dolly down among the rocks with their long spears. Then they jerked the spears up quickly and the dolly came whirling up to the top, the feathers making a beautiful and colorful pattern as it rose. Codfish have more curiosity than monkeys. They swarmed up in the wake of the dolly, and there were the long cruel tines of the Indians' spears ready to impale them. Curiosity killed the codfish, too.

Farrar never tried to fish with a dolly—indeed, I believe it is illegal for anyone but the Indians to spear fish—but he did learn to jig for cod. A jig is a fish made of babbitt with a sharp, strong hook on the end. You tie the fish to the end of a hand line, stand on the stern of your boat, and give short, quick, strong jerks on the string, hour after tiresome hour. The theory is that the curious codfish will swarm around the babbitt figure and

Farrar jigging for cod at slack tide.

while they are then, one of the jerks will impale a live fish. Farrar never caught one by jigging, though he would try for half a day at a time—as long as I would stay on the bank and watch. When my arm got tired from watching him and I would call for him to come in, he would say, "The jig is up."

One day in May, Dad Chevalier said, "Why don't you kids go over to Flattop and get some seagull eggs? They're just starting to lay."

We thought he was up to some of his tricks, but eggs were eggs and meaty food scarcer and scarcer. It might be worth trying.

The gulls laid their huge, mottled eggs right down on the ground in open nests, which were hardly more than a billful of grass. They laid three eggs. If you found only one or two in a nest, it meant the gull had just started to lay, and the eggs would be fresh. You could take an egg and the gull would lay more until she had three to sit on. If you found three in a nest, you didn't take them, of course, for there was no telling how long they had been sat upon.

"The Indians used to think seagull eggs a great delicacy," Dad said, but then he had said that about the pearly codfish eggs under the rocks. If it hadn't been that we had eaten wild bird eggs many times down South, as children, we would not have believed him. But this did sound reasonable.

One day we rowed over to Flattop Island. A blind man could have told we were nearing the place, from the smell. As we rowed up onto the beach, thousands of gulls rose screaming into the air. We didn't have to look far; the nests were everywhere. Eggs lying on a ledge within an inch of rolling off. Eggs in a cozy nest of fully three straws on a rock. Eggs in grass on top of the bluff. Bluish, with brown spots, somewhat like oversized turkey eggs.

As we gathered their eggs, the gulls screamed overhead and beat their wings. We gathered fifteen dozen and rowed away. As our white boat left the island behind, the gulls began to settle down again, their wild screams tapering off into little querulous murmurs.

Back on our own island, we dug a deep hole in the ground and buried thirteen dozen of our eggs, keeping out the other two dozen for immediate use. We boiled them, for cold lunches. They were so large that I could barely eat one at a meal. They were tough, too, if cooked quickly or too long. It was best to coddle them. But how good they were! The whites were pinkish, the yolks very orange. We liked them best as fluffy baked omelet. Yolks beaten to a creamy orange color, whites to a stiff pink froth, folded together, poured into a greased deep pan and baked like a souffle. Like snow-capped mountains rosy with sunset.

A few days after the post-Easter egg hunt, Farrar and I rowed over to the Harbor for the mail. On the way home, I read the letters aloud as Farrar rowed.

Here was one from his mother. They had had a late frost in Van Buren that had blackened the peach blossoms and may have killed the crop. She worried about us, she said, up in that far northern state. Did we nearly freeze? Did the wind almost blow us off the island? Did the waves ever threaten to roll over us as they did down in Galveston? Was there danger of floods as on the Arkansas? She said she never could make up her mind whether to worry about us or to envy us.

There was a thin envelope from *The Country Gentleman*. That would be Farrar's little poem coming back.

We had run out of postage for mailing manuscripts. and could send letters home only when we caught and sold a fish. This was the last thing we had sent out, and here it was, back again. I slipped the envelope to the bottom of the pile.

We were about halfway home across the wide channel when Farrar said, "Have you read all the mail?"

"It's just a rejection slip," I said. "You don't want to see it, do you?"

"No, I guess not," he said, trying to sound indifferent. Then, "Oh, why not? Maybe it's a good rejection slip, anyhow."

Good rejection slips were personal notes from warm-hearted editors. Bad ones were printed slips worded by sadistic genius to sound indifferent down to the last comma. I took out a sheet of letter paper—"It's a good one, all right"—unfolded the letter, and out fell a long green slip of paper!

"It's a check! You sold the poem!" I jumped up, holding the papers out to Farrar. He dropped the oars and came to meet me, and what with laughing and crying and hugging each other, we almost upset the boat.

"How much is it?" Farrar asked, and I looked to see. "Three dollars and a half," I said.

Farrar let out a yell that could have been heard to Jericho. "We'll frame it! I'll make a frame out of madrona bark. I'll carve one from yew wood. We'll save it for our grandchildren. Why, we're authors ... maybe, though, it would be better to cash it and buy some postage. Shall we cash it or frame it?"

He was weakening. He was beginning to see cups of steaming coffee beside campfires with hoecakes made from new Island wheat. I waited, determined that he should be the one to say, "Coffee and wheat and lard." After all, it was his check; it had been his poem.

"Let's buy food," he said. What joy to have a husband as hungry as oneself! He turned the boat around, heading back towards the Harbor. "Might as well buy it now," he said. "Three dollars and a half will buy a hundred pounds of wheat, pounds of lard, coffee, butter, some sugar for you, and enough stamps for a few manuscripts besides." And that is what we did.

The poem was called

THE WAIL OF A SHEEP HERDER

All about me are the sheep,
  Baa, baa, baa, baa.
O'er the greening plains we creep,
  Baa, baa, baa, baa.
Up along the mountain steep,
Down into the valley deep,
Gosh, the critturs never sleep!
  Baa, baa.

Every sheep now has a lamb,
  Baa, baa, baa, baa.
Every sheep that's not a ram,
  Baa, baa, baa, baa.
Wool into my ears I cram,
Still, no matter where I am,
I can hear that constant damn
  Baa, baa.

When we went over to Speiden that night, with our great news, Dad said he ought to have half the money; the poem was about his sheep. He said he had beat the man who sold everything about his pig but the squeal; the very bleats of his lambs had gone to market.

In June the sheep had to be driven up, lambs corraled and sold to the butcher. Farrar helped, and so did I. Yelling like Apaches, we ran all over that big island driving the sheep out of the brush, up into the corral on top. There an Indian man separated lambs from ewes, lifting each fat young thing for the butcher to see, then shoving it into its own pen. When the lambs were all separated, a gate was opened into the lane that ran between rail fences down the shank of Speiden to another corral at the water's edge. In the flying dust we followed the bleating lambs down the hill, to drive them onto the waiting barge. All the way down, the meadow larks sang from fences. They flew up as we passed, and dropped right down again, without missing a note.

Sweating, cursing, yelling, prodding, pulling, the men got the bewildered lambs out of the waterside corral onto the barge. Now the butcher's boat started up. The barge moved out into the channel, the round gray woolly animals huddled solid against the rail of the red deck. They were not bleating now. They had given up. All of us straggled back up the hill to sit in the shade and rest. We could see the barge out on the sunny water. It got smaller and smaller until it might have been one lamb on a log, drifting off towards Friday Harbor.

The butcher wrote a check for five hundred dollars, which came back from the bank marked "No funds." Dad never got his money. "Too bad," he said, "he was a nice old man, that butcher. I guess he ran out of money."

In summer, the tides are low in the daytime, the high ones often coming along towards night. High slack tide at sunset—that was the very choice time and tide of all our days. Puget Sound is bank full. The green water laps your very doorstep. It joggles the beach wood that some higher tide has deposited there. The sun comes walking across the full-bosomed sea, its eye on a level with yours, and you see the birds flying across its path on their way home toward their nests in trees and bluffs. If the salmon are running, you see one jump now and then, and a school of herring boiling up in a wide circle out there, somewhere.

Farrar and I loved to row to the Harbor in late afternoon, just to get home in the high slack tide at sunset. For one thing, the high water helped us up the skids with our boat. But mostly because all Puget Sound seemed to be dreaming then, breathing deep—replete.

One summer day—in August it was—we were rowing lazily along over the full-breasted water when we saw an immaculate, cool-looking lighthouse tender sweep in through the pass and come to anchor in Roche Harbor. Officers in cool white stood about on the deck.

Now, Farrar and I were as contented as porpoises. But that day we were hot and tired and hungry. We were wearing shorts and sleeveless shirts. We were thin from lean meals, brown from exposure. Our hands were rough and hard. What was there about this clean, cool, big ship that made us homesick for something else?

A phonograph was playing, and Alma Gluck was singing, "In the Land of the Sky Blue Water."

Farrar looked at me—a queer lonesome look. "What does that make you feel like?" he said.

"Like going to some far place."

"Me, too—where shall we go?"

All spring we had watched the purse seine boats going up to Alaska in pairs. People around here talked of Alaska as familiarly as they spoke of Seattle. "Seymour Narrows," they would say, as we said, "Speiden Channel." The Inside Passage, Queen Charlotte Sound, The Aleutians—names of romance. Calling names.

"Let's go to Alaska," I said, and Farrar said, "Alright," and turned the boat around. "We'll go back to the Harbor and advertise this boat for sale so we'll have some money to get to Seattle on," he said.

We rowed back. Farrar went up onto the dock and wrote his advertisement on the bulletin board outside the store. FOR SALE ONE ROWBOAT AND TROLLING OUTFIT...$30.00. FARRAR AND JUNE BURN, SENTINEL ISLAND.

After work next day, the blacksmith from Roche Harbor came over to Sentinel. He talked us down to twenty five dollars and bought a fine sixteen-foot clinker-built rowboat with one copper patch on its side, and one fishing line with a Number 5 McMahon spoon on it. He got a bargain and so did we. "It never is a bargain for anybody, unless it's one for everybody," Farrar always said. We stored all our things on Speiden—papers, books, household odds and ends. We took our bedding, cooking things, typewriter, and every scrap of clothing—two trunks, altogether, and left for Alaska.

Good-by, Father and Mother Butterworth, in your little gray cottage on Henry Island. Good-by, gentle Ma Chevalier. Huge, hospitable Speiden, good-by!

As the *San Juan II* went off down San Juan Channel and we looked at

Sentinel for what might be the last time, we sat on deck, feeling mighty quiet.

But when we got round Limestone Point and beautiful, round-topped Sentinel was out of sight, we turned toward our next adventure with all sails set. We were off to Alaska. We hadn't begun to worry yet about how we would get there. "The longest journey begins with one step," and we were already expecting more than we expected.

"We'll retire now," Farrar said. "We'll have to settle down when our children get ready for college, you know. They will have to have some money, then. But now we'll see the world while we can!"

I wonder why everybody doesn't do their retiring first, while they have the zest for everything, and settle down later on when they don't feel like doing anything but work, anyhow.

San Juan II *at Patos Light Station, Washington, 1915.*

Part Two

THE PALE GREEN YEAR

Bear *being towed by* Algonquin *in Bering Sea.*

Always expect more than you expect.
Farrar Burn

VI. HOW DO YOU GET TO ALASKA?

WHEN we went ashore in Seattle, we knew the time had come to start thinking about how we were going to Alaska.

We went to a clean hotel down near the waterfront and started on a simple program of asking everyone we saw how we could get there.

"I beg your pardon—do you know how a couple could find jobs that would take them to Alaska?"

"Hello, Sonny, if you wanted to get to Alaska, what would you do?"

"Good morning, Ma'am, can you think of any way to find a job that would take a couple to Alaska?"

Down on the waterfront we asked, "Where is your captain? Any chance of getting on your crew as stewards or cooks or deck hands?" Into the offices of the steamship companies we went. "Do you need cooks, stewards, typists, deck hands on your boats going to Alaska?"

Every person we asked made some courteous reply. Nobody was gruff or abrupt. They would scratch their heads, figuratively, anyhow, and consider the matter at more length, sometimes, than was convenient. Boys, men, women, executives, captains, sailors—they all gave the best advice they could.

One day we were walking down First Avenue when we ran into a gray-haired Negro. "Good morning, Uncle, can you tell us any way to get to Alaska—get jobs that would take us there?"

The old man stood a little while in thought, then he said, "Yassir, I uz down heppin to load de ship Saturn, jist yistiddy, and I heerd de capn say dat he wuz a-lookin fur a man an his wife to teach school up on de

Pribilofs. You-all schoolteachers?"

We said we could be and we hurried down to where the Saturn was tied up at the dock. The captain, a Scandinavian, was cordial and kind, but thirty minutes ago, he had hired a man and his wife for the Pribilofs. He suggested, though, that we go to see Mr. Lopp of the Bureau of Education. It was late for this year, but there might still be a vacancy somewhere in Alaska.

Mr. Lopp interviewed us within an inch of our lives. He wanted to know all about our pasts, our beliefs, education, experience, personalities. But the upshot was that we both got jobs in his service, Farrar at $135 a month, I at $120, lasting for twelve months, with the possibility of holding them for three years, if we were good and didn't go having babies right away—for we were going into the Far North where there were few other white people.

Years later, we learned that Mr. Lopp had been in a tight spot that week. The *Victoria* was due to sail for Nome on its last trip and he hadn't yet found teachers for St. Lawrence Island. He admitted that he would have grabbed much worse prospects than we seemed to be. But the stage lost a good man when Mr. Lopp went into government service, for nobody would have guessed from his severe manner that we were his last hope for the year.

Tom Lopp was one of the greatest friends the Eskimos ever had. That is why, no doubt, he lost his job in the Bureau of Education during those boom years. For in our country, as in England, the procedure seems to be to take care of our primitive subjects with half an eye to them and an eye and a half to the few members of our own race who live by exploiting them. Mr. Lopp worked the other way, and though he came to be regarded as the outstanding authority on Eskimo economy and was often called into consultation in later years when things got in a mess, he lost his position, and died recently, a strong, young, gusty man, still mourning his lost charges.

Farrar was to be manager of the island, the native cooperative store, the reindeer herd—a sort of governor and father combined. I was to have charge of the school, with one native assistant. Store and medical supplies had been ordered and were ready to go, Mr. Lopp said, but we would have to buy our own year's food supplies and winter clothing. He advanced $300 against our salaries for that purpose.

We could hardly suppress our glee until we left the office. How much better the reality than anything we had expected! What was it that brought us such fabulous luck every step of the way? Three hundred dollars in our pockets and a first-class ticket to Nome, Alaska! We were going to St. Lawrence Island, in sight of Siberia, out in Bering Sea. It was within the Arctic Circle. Nobody but Eskimos there, and we were to govern and teach a primitive people. We were filled with determination to do some really worthy work, and with exhilaration at our sheer luck. I have never been sure whether we were almost ribald honeymooners on a lark sponsored by the government, or pure missionaries burning with zeal for the work ahead. A little of both, I guess.

I don't remember what we bought in the way of clothes. Mr. Lopp said that the Eskimos would make us some skin garments when we got to St. Lawrence Island, but that we might need some woolens of our own. But I do remember how we splurged buying food. After a year of semi-famine, all we could think of was food. Nine sacks of clean seed wheat and a new grist mill. Five sacks of seed corn for real hand-ground cornmeal mush and spoon bread. Two sacks of steel-cut oats. Two dozen two-pound cans of butter. Powdered milk and eggs. Cans of spinach, beans, milk. Cans and cans of coffee. Sugar, candy for the children's Christmas, huge chocolate bars for use on the trail, which the sailors on the Bear nibbled clean out of existence before we got to St. Lawrence. One day we overheard them talking about our supplies—the oddest selection any of the teachers had carried up, I expect. "What can the Reverend Burn want with these sacks of corn?" one of them said, with insinuations in his voice. Formerly it had been missionaries who had gone to Alaska to teach the Eskimos, and though they were now government-employed teachers, most of the sailors still spoke of them as "the reverend and his wife."

In a week we were ready to sail, and so was the old *Victoria*. With supplies for the native store, medical supplies, school books, thirty-five tons of coal in sacks, and our own food supplies and baggage, "the teachers" for St. Lawrence must have filled a pretty big hole in the hold of the ship.

Here we go, then! Cast off the lines! The old boat backs slowly out into the Sound and heads north. We are taking the outside passage, out Juan de Fuca, around Vancouver Island, straight across the Gulf of Alaska to the Aleutian Islands. Our first stop will be Akutan, Aleutian whaling station.

We found a sunny place on deck where we could sit and write letters home. Planning out loud for a year of such happiness and learning and progress for the Eskimos as they had never known before. Farrar started inventing ways to mark the reindeer, for among the many things Mr. Lopp had told us, Farrar remembered that the ear markings which were then in use were not satisfactory. By the time the marks were all on, the reindeer had practically no ears left.

I began to plan reading lessons that would use Eskimo facts and situations, remembering the joke about the Eskimo who had come outside and been most surprised to find that horses had long legs and hoofs. He had seen pictures of horses in mail-order catalogues, advertising harness, and their legs had all been cut off at the knee, for lack of space. Oh, we were going to do wonderful things!

Now we sight the Aleutians off the starboard bow. We are steaming up to the whaling station. Suddenly an off shore breeze makes passengers grab their noses. We'll be here only a minute, surely; we can hold our breath that long. No, we shall be here two hours or more. It seems the *Victoria* borrowed some oil on the last trip down and she must return it now.

Two hours in a Chicago stockyard, multiplied by the difference between the size of a cow and that of a whale. The captain says we may go ashore to gather flowers if we like. Long-stemmed wild flowers from the knee-deep grass of the rolling, treeless tundra. Many do go ashore. Farrar and I choose to stay and watch them whale.

On the long plank docks, men were stripping foot thick fat off the carcass of a ninety foot blue-back whale. One man walked down that mountain of flesh, drawing a huge knife like a long brush hook through the fat, to separate a strip from the whole. Then he fastened a big hook into the end of the strip, up at the head. The donkey engine whirred, the immense ribbon of fat peeled off the prone giant, curled back over itself, fell to the floor at the tail of the whale. Man, hook, and donkey engine returned for another strip, baring the red-black muscle flesh of the animal.

When the fat was all off, the men swarmed over the carcass to cut up the rest of it for various uses: fertilizer, dog food, and perhaps even steaks for human consumption, though it may be a smaller species from which our whale steaks come.

In the old days, the whalers saved only the fat to be rendered into oil, and the whalebone from the mouth. The rest was wasted—tons and tons. Imagine the stench then! There is still a good deal of waste, they say, of blood and viscera, but far less than formerly.

When this blue whale opened his mouth to take in a whole school of herring, there wasn't much of him left shut, for his head measured a third of his length and was the widest part besides. The great lower jaw was heavily furred with what they call whalebone—wide, thin, black, gristle-like slats, edged, along the upper side, with long black coarse hair. This odd timber work inside the mouth is a huge sieve; the herring lie on top of the fur mass while the water strains through. Then the whale reaches out with a hungry tongue and draws the fish in.

The donkey engine was going. Men were running about on the dock and on the carcass. There were noises on the *Victoria* of winches and cables and voices. We could faintly hear the cries of the flower-gatherers up on the tundra. It was not surprising, then, that a tugboat slipped up on the other side of the *Victoria* without our knowing it. It brought another blue whale, towed alongside, belly up. The queer, washboard-like hills and valleys of the whale's belly were all stuccoed with barnacles. This, they said, was a hundred-footer—a whale of a whale. It would be drawn up onto the dock by the donkey engine and men would set to work stripping off its blubber, cutting out its whalebone, hacking up its flesh.

A collective handkerchief still at its nose, the *Victoria* called its children in from play and slipped out of Akutan, heading north again. The next time we stop, we shall be at Nome.

It was early morning when we began to be put off the *Victoria* and taken aboard the lighters at Nome, where the sea was too shallow to admit the big ship to the dock. It was jolly going ashore in such an informal huddle. People love that secure togetherness of shared adventure, whether of disaster or good fortune. Farrar says this human hunger to be all in the same boat together is not only an amelioration of war; it is actually a cause of war.

Nome was the whispering village. Plank houses, wooden sidewalks, muddy streets, two or three brick buildings, a few hopeful window boxes, a row of the false-front stores peculiar to frontier towns, thunder of surf at its front door step, dead silence of frozen wastes behind. Nome might have been built for a moving-picture set. Nothing about it seemed real. Plank hotels with typical Bret Harte land ladies, and restaurants with reindeer steaks and buxom waitresses were bits on the cutting-room floor. The people, all talking in whispers or guarded low tones, were actors. Farrar and I, apparently, were the only audience. Everybody else seemed to belong to the cast. It was the spookiest town I have ever seen.

On the *Victoria* we had struck up an acquaintance with one of those plain-spoken, likeable, frank girls, who was going up to the hills beyond Nome to cook for her miner father and his partner that winter, and have the time of her life in the wild, rough wilderness. A hearty girl, full of laughter and noise. We saw her a week later on her way out from the visit. She had begun to whisper. We asked about her father and she was furtive and secretive. She whispered that she could not tell us anything. Everybody was like that.

But when we walked out of the village onto the endless frozen tundra toward the hills, we saw that the earth was fair up here, too. The sunsets on that strange, pale land were eerily beautiful. Bering Sea lashed the beach day and night and loped off in green rolls toward the west. The sea on the west, wide and lonely; tundra to the east, wide and lonely, and an unhappy little lonely village in between.

Down the beach the King Island Eskimos lived under their upturned skin boats, and in tents, carving ivory for the traders. Along the waterfront, a few hard-bitten miners still panned the sand for gold dust.

From Nome we were to go on to St. Lawrence Island on the old Coast Guard cutter, *Bear*—which Admiral Byrd now uses for his supply ship in the Antarctic. In two weeks it would return from Point Barrow and pick us up.

We were not the only ones from Nome to board the *Bear*. Every summer the King Islanders leave their cliff dwellings, and paddle their immense skin canoes across the wild waters of Bering Sea to Nome. On the mainland, they spend the summer fishing for their coming winter supplies of dog food, carving their precious winter's catch of ivory, and selling it to tourists. In the fall they return on the Coast Guard boat because by then it is too rough to paddle home in open boats. The *Bear* set them down at the foot of the black bluff which they called home, and the sailors hated the job. For the Eskimos smelled worse than the whaling station.

June and Farrar on the deck of the Bear.

When we took them aboard, we found we had not only all the inhabitants of the island, but also their dogs, food, boats, unsold furs and ivory, dog food, reindeer sleeping skins, white leather pokes full of this and that, and a thousand other things which only a museum curator could count.

But how quiet and orderly and merry they were! Eskimo mothers gathered their possessions and their children close about them. Eskimo fathers improvised deck shelters from their skin boats and tied up the dogs. They prepared their smelly meals on primus stoves. Babies hung onto breasts most of the time. Old men sat and carved, old women worked on leather, young women did the work of the temporary camp. The young men sat and gazed out to sea.

Except for the fact that the air on deck grew heavier and heavier, we should hardly have known the Eskimos were there. They were the most perfectly behaved crowd of people we ever saw.

On the third day we sighted the perpendicular cliffs of King Island. The high plateau upthrust from the sea was covered with fog. But we could see

The cliff dwellers of the north, King Island, Bering Sea, Alaska, c.1913.

the houses set on stilts against the side of the bluff. They looked frail, as though they might hobble off down into the sea almost any day.

The Eskimos scrambled and chattered, gathered up children and skins and dogs, and gleefully lowered themselves into their huge, open walrus skin boats and paddled for the bleak black bluff. How was it possible, we wondered, for them to have for this flat mountain top in the sea the affection we knew for our soft earth? How precarious the little houses on stilts against the wall of the bluff!

Now the Eskimos were gone, but for all the great scrubbing and washing down the *Bear* received, their smell followed us, like the albatross, up and down the mighty waves of the storm-tossed sea.

We turned south again, to St. Lawrence Island, where the *Bear* would leave us and go outside for its own long winter of rest in Seattle. But not yet.

The captain said that all the storms in the world are hatched in Anadir

Bay, off Siberia. It was the season of the Equinox; time for the fiercest storms of the year. As though the sea weren't rough enough already.

The storms came down. The *Bear* sailed round and round St. Lawrence Island, but the surf was so high we couldn't land. For one solid month we searched a lee. Twice we returned to the mainland for coal, but still no let-up in the storm.

Then one day the crown sheets of the boiler fell. The fires had to be pulled. The *Bear* wired to the Aleutians for the cutter, *Algonquin*, to come to our rescue. Meanwhile we wallowed in the waves of Bering Sea.

At last the slim-hipped *Algonquin* came rearing and plunging up from the south. They shot a thin little rope across our bow. Our sailors grabbed it, began hauling in, first the small rope, then a larger one and a larger until at last they pulled with might and main on the heavy three-inch hauser itself, inching it aboard . . . and we traveled again.

Thus ignominiously we were towed back five hundred miles to the Aleutian Islands. On the way down, we passed the Pribilof Islands, where the fur seals come at mating time and are killed for their hides. We saw St. Matthews Island in the distance. Men have died on that narrow curve of land, trying to weather a winter there, hunting fox and ivory. It looked so desolate and the officers on the *Bear* told such tales of its danger that Farrar and I longed to tackle it. That would be pulling the ladder up after you! But later on, when the Smithsonian Institution suggested that we go back there to collect for them, we were already knee-deep in the great adventure of starting our family and thus never knew that winter of splendid isolation. Perhaps it wouldn't have been splendid, anyhow.

We were taken to Dutch Harbor, the Coast Guard's base, where, after long conferences, during which we were afraid they were going to refuse to take us back to St. Lawrence, and wires to and from Washington, we were transferred, with all our goods, to the cutter *Unalga*.

North to St. Lawrence Island again. The storm had not abated. For two weeks we cruised around the hundred mile-long narrow island, hoping for a lee and a lull at the same time.

At last one morning the Captain came in and bade us get ready to land. We were off Southwest Cape, some forty odd miles from our base on the Island. But it couldn't be helped. Already one heavy snow had fallen. Soon the ice would come. If we were going ashore at all, it would have to be here and now, where there was some lee. We were to be rowed to that blizzardy bluff we saw out there—that lost land that was already covered with a foot of blue whiteness.

Boats were lowered. Sailors began unloading our stuff. And as though at a signal, Eskimo skin boats began to swarm out. The people climbed aboard the *Bear* with happy welcoming cries. Teacher had come! "Hello, Teacher. We glad you here! More better you come ashore now."

One of the old men wore a parka made of the breasts of beautiful black and white birds. I thought it was the loveliest thing I had ever seen and later in the year I traded him out of it. It can be seen now in the collection we later sold to the Museum of the American Indian in New York City. [St. Lawrence natives always said parki with a short i sound; never parka.]

Back and forth the boats hurried, dumping our supplies helter-skelter onto the beach of St. Lawrence. The storm might come up at any second and when it did, off the *Unalga* would go, leaving us with what stores we had, to our winter's fate. Fortunately, nearly everything had been unloaded by the time the wind came howling down out of the Arctic again and the *Unalga* steamed off down the lonely gray sea. We watched her over the hill of the horizon.

Farrar in parka made of bird breast feathers.

VII. THE FROZEN ISLAND

THE *Unalga* went out of sight over the horizon and we turned back to our supplies piled at the foot of a high, steep, snow-covered bluff—tons of coal in sacks, boxes of guns, sacks of sugar, stores of prunes, pilot bread, tea, apricots, dried apples, to say nothing of our own personal stores.

"How shall we ever get it up on the plateau?" I asked Farrar. "How shall we get it to Gambel? And where in the world will we live, meanwhile?"

"Oh, plenty good white-man house here," said a beaming Eskimo. He was Oktokiyok, and during those first helpless weeks he took charge of us and, gracefully seeming to take orders, gave them. "Me and my family move out that house now. You live there."

We moved into that "plenty good white-man house" on the bluff of Southwest Cape, forty miles from our destination on the island. But first, Oktokiyok and his family moved out.

What a moving it was! Out of the little twelve by fifteen frame house, built of lumber brought from Nome by a trader, came six people, hundreds of reindeer skins, seal skins, fox skins; bundles of white leather, dog harness, ivory, parkas, pants, boots; tubs of seal skins soaking in urine to tan: seal-oil lamps, wooden platters, precious scraps of old papers and magazines; little bundles of dried willow-root bark, dozens of five-gallon tins of gasoline for their outboard motors the next spring. Eskimos in an endless line went into the little house and came out again, laden with bundles. It was like moving a five-and-ten.

At last it was empty and Oktokiyok said, "Come see you nice home."

I went up the steep, slushy bluff with him, across the windy point of the plateau, to the forlorn little shack that was so proudly Oktokiyok's "summer house like white man." I had had abundant pre-sampling of the smell that awaited me inside those four walls, but even so I was not prepared. We entered through the storm shed. Inside the empty room shy women and children stood together. The coal range was red hot. The unfamiliar odor that rose up bodily and rushed out to meet me was like a foul-breathed gale to blow a man down.

I smiled and spoke, shaking hands with them all—sticky damp little hands. I took short breaths and exerted all my charm just as fast as I could so as to get outside before disgracing myself, which I did by the skin of my teeth. It would be weeks, I thought, before the house would be clean enough to endure it.

I was wrong. For, while two Eskimo women and I were scrubbing out the house, I was getting used to the odor, which was not one of filth but simply of foods and ways and garments I had not met before. In a few days I could tell by sight alone whether my house was clean. And in a month or two, Farrar and I were smelling like Eskimos ourselves in our own beautiful urine-tanned skins.

It was great fun cleaning house with the Eskimo women. They were jolly companions, but inept workers. I hadn't the skill to make them do things over and over; there was nothing inept about the way they could get out of work! When I showed them that more elbow grease would make the floor look white, instead of gray, they teased me by stroking their portion and saying, "Oh, very nice!" and of my clean spot, "This place very sick," meaning pale. Then they laughed and laughed. I fell for them hard.

And so did Farrar, working with them down on the beach. For days, that first week, he and the Eskimo men toiled up the steep bluff with loads on their backs, making jokes with every puff of their breath. Fortunately, news travels fast up there, and on the day after we landed, dozens of sleds, dog teams and drivers poured over the white hills beyond Southwest Cape and everybody began to buy supplies. Everyone carried his own purchases up on to the bluff, which was a great help.

At that "store" on the beach, Farrar sat on a keg and kept records while Iwurrigan, who spoke excellent English, waited on the natives and reported their purchases to him. They sold sacks of sugar, guns, tea, pilot bread, prunes, tea, candy, tea, calico, boxes of cube sugar, tea; everything the store had brought up including tea and more tea.

Short, fat little Boosha bought a hundred-pound sack of sugar, piled it on his little sled and went back to Gambel. On the way, he had to cross a big lake which had frozen over for the winter—else the Gambel people could not have come. Boosha's sled broke through the new ice and he lost his sack of sugar. The next day he came back for another, and couldn't understand why he had to pay for it. But he accepted Farrar's dictum philosophically. "Me rich man," he said. "I'm buy sugar for feeding fish."

Storekeeping went on for many days after our arrival. Gradually the supplies were brought up to the little warehouse which Iwurrigan owned. All except the coal. Long before the last of it was carried up, snow began to fall. It snowed so hard and fast that many sacks were deeply buried on the beach and may be there yet, for no teachers may, since then, have been landed at Southwest Cape.

It was a busy little community, those first weeks. Farrar and Iwurrigan kept store all day, while the other Eskimos stood around watching them and joking. Atonga, Oktokiyok's wife, and I kept house, she faithfully standing by until windows, shelves, bunk, attic, storm shed were as clean as we could make them, the water freezing under our hands as we scrubbed.

Nearly every evening the dogs at the Cape set up a wild, yodeling howl, and presently the dark forms of sleds and teams would skim over the white slope back of us and seem to flow down into the little settlement. We thought people would never stop coming.

When the natives had bought their fill of white-man things, Farrar engaged them to haul sacks of coal to Gambel. There must be a supply for the schoolhouse and teacher's quarters before we could move.

One hungry, lean, dog team could haul one sack of coal at a time. A good team could haul two. It took three days for the trip: a day to go, a day to rest the dogs, and a day to return for another sack. Farrar paid them a dollar a sack, and we employed as many teams as we could get. The Eskimos were delighted to make the money, in the form of merchandise orders to be cashed at the store.

At last, losing all patience with the slowness of the dog teams, Farrar ordered reindeer harnessed and brought from the reindeer camps to Southwest Cape. It was a revolutionary order, but the Eskimos did it cheerfully. Sled deer could carry four sacks of coal at a time, but they were not so fast and they had to stop and eat. It was a clumsy arrangement. The only food the deer eat is reindeer-moss and the Eskimos have not yet found a method for storing it as we do hay and grain for horses. On each trip, it took so long to graze the deer that we gave it up after a few trips and returned to the dog teams. The Eskimos were delighted at the joke on Farrar.

Meanwhile, the four Eskimo women of Southwest Cape—a mother and a grandmother-in-law in each igloo—were making skin garments for Farrar and me. Immense seal skin breeches and a very tent of a reindeer skin parka for Farrar. How they laughed at the size of his garments! And they laughed because, when they made my parka hood like theirs, it stood out from my face several inches, instead of fitting snug around it. Their faces are broad, and parka hoods, made to fit over their smaller heads, are snug around their large faces and keep the cold wind from their ears. They never figured out how to make a hood large enough to slip over my head and small enough to fit around my face. They thought it a splendid joke, and used to run their hands around the space between head and hood and say, "Patsarok plenty fresh air." Eskimos love a joke more even than Negroes. They are the laughingest people I ever knew. And the most loveable.

In our new skin garments we felt like conquerors, whatever we smelled like. It was good to be able to brave the elements like natives, and so win freedom to move about over the arctic land.

At last we had enough coal at Gambel to risk moving there, and school could begin. It was late October, or early November, nearly a month since we had landed. I was to take my first dog-sled ride over the vast undulating land that was hardly more than a huge, permanent iceberg. Farrar had been to Gambel several times and he was keen for me to experience that day-long journey by skimming dog-sled.

On the morning of a trip, the Eskimos get up at dreadful times. It wasn't long after midnight when Oktokiyok called us on that great day.

But when we had breakfasted, cocooned ourselves into layers of warm garments, and gone out to join the party, not a soul was about.

It was fully two hours before we got under way. What was time in the Eskimo's timeless eternity? Who minded getting up at midnight when there were days on end to sleep when storms raged? Oktokiyok was probably inside his igloo with his family, drinking hard-boiled tea, and laughing with his brothers and friends. The dogs were not harnessed, for they might eat the walrus-skin rope in their eternally unappeased hunger. They were alert, though, sensing that they were to go somewhere.

Losing patience, Farrar called out the men and bade them get under way. The Eskimos laughed at his hurry. "Plenty time," they said. "Patsarok see Gambel bymby."

Just before dawn, we were ready to go. The dogs were harnessed in a fan-shaped arrangement, with the leader out in front, like the fingers of a hand with a very long middle finger. That was the St. Lawrence Island style. On the mainland, dogs were harnessed tandem or in pairs.

Before the start, the three of us sat down on our sleds, Farrar alone on his, Oktokiyok and I on the other. Farrar was a veteran by now and could drive his own. He was, in any case, too big to ride double. Oktokiyok sat in front on his six-foot-long, eighteen-inch-wide sled, his legs going off sidewise, up forward, mine going off the other side behind him. Nothing to hold up my legs. Try it, sometime, for a day.

The dogs were not straining at their leashes, raring to go. They sat down, as we did, and snarled unhappily at each other, or chewed at their harness and had to be cuffed.

Now we are ready. Oktokiyok strikes the ground with his whip. "Huh! Huh! Huh!" he shouts. "Hooh! Hooh! Hooh!" shouts Farrar, never quite getting the exact sound of the Eskimo "Get up!" The lean beasts strike out up the rise behind Southwest Cape and we are off.

Behind us the villagers stand outside the two igloos to watch us leave. But they are not saying unfriendly things behind our backs. Just little chuckly things, laughing together.

Behind us, the sea was pale green under the new ice edging out from shore. Eskimos call it green ice, meaning that it is not solid yet. When the sun came up, the cliffs of Siberia would rise beyond the forty-mile stretch of sea. Before us rolled hill after white hill, so much alike that I had no sense of direction or of progress. Under the cold dawn the land was palely gray.

Then, after a while, the sun came up. By a chance turning of our way, it was behind us as it rolled up over the horizon, making the snow blush like a rose, and all the white hills were vivid pink.

When the sun was higher and the rose color had faded, the snow began to take on blue lights. Under the eaves of immense drifts, the shadows were a rich sapphire.

We put on our dark glasses, but still the glint of snow was painful, coming in from the sides. We hadn't gone many miles before I began to fidget. A little more and I could no longer maintain my position.

"Aren't your legs getting tired, Oktokiyok?" I knew a hint would be enough for him.

He laughed. It would have been a joke on him if they were. "Oh, no," he said, "my legs got bone in him all same stick. You legs no got bone?"

"Yes, but my feet seem to be getting heavy, all same rock. What shall I do about that?"

"More better you get off and run little bit," and without stopping the dogs, Oktokiyok hopped nimbly off the eight-inch-high sled and began to run alongside. I rolled off into the snow, pushed and pulled at the bundle of skins which was myself, and sure enough, I could run, too. For though it looks clumsy and heavy, the skin clothing of the Eskimo is surprisingly light. But without our weight, the dogs could run much faster, and in no time I was left far behind.

I don't remember any way of stopping those dogs. The driver has no lines, only a whip to make them go, and once they are off, he depends on himself to keep up with them. But there must have been a way to stop them, for when I was tired of running, I dropped down on the sled again and rode the rest of the way to Gambel.

We skimmed those frozen hills in four or five hours. When we topped the last high bluff above Gambel, we had passed no sign of human habitation.

Below the bluff, only three or four miles from our destination, we must cross the frozen lake where Boosha had lost his sugar. The wind had blown it free of snow. The ice was strong and thick, now, and as slick as glass. The dogs' feet skidded as they flew across it, the sleds swinging from side to side, faster and faster, making at last considerably more than a semi-circle. The dogs smelled the end of the trip and nobody could have stopped them now; we clung on for dear life.

Beyond the lake, at the very edge of the ocean, on a low, out-jutting sand spit, the igloos of Gambel huddled together. We could hear the dogs of the village, and ours gathered still more speed for the last mile or so, whimpering hungrily as they flew along. Now we saw that all the people stood outside their houses in solemn rows, like penguins, waiting to welcome "the teachers."

How the Eskimos welcomed us that bitter cold day! Not that their welcome took any such practical form as having cleaned the schoolhouse, or even having built a fire for us in our living quarters. They were as passive as children. But we felt welcome, for all that. And when the whole village followed us into the house and stood around while we shook off snow and set about building a fire, we felt flattered.

Silook, a meek young man, was the assistant teacher at Gambel. He assumed gentle authority over the crowd of visitors, pushed them back when they threatened to swarm over us, advised us to serve them tea and at last dismissed them for us, so that we could unpack a few things for the night and be ready to open school next day.

After our supper that first night in Gambel, Farrar and I went outside to look around. We knew, from the weeks at Southwest Cape, that the Eskimos would already be inside for the night. We would not ourselves be objects of attention. Snow was falling again—earnestly, steadily falling. It snowed with all its heart.

I wish I could find the quiet words that would be a picture of evening, night, and dawn in the Arctic. Eskimo children are quiet, even at play. But their soft noises abate at early twilight when they go indoors. The men have all returned from hunting or setting fox traps. They are indoors, too. Women have gathered in whatever they had hanging out on the whale-rib and walrus rope fences. Some of them have been to the deep cave in which they store their "rotten meat," and brought up what they needed for the night. Outside, nobody moves about.

Even the dogs are as still as the snowbanks they resemble, for they are curled up in the snow and it drifts over them.

The village of rounded walrus skin igloos is utterly silent. The gray sky darkens. The line of sea, far out on the point, is black silence. Snow falls on snow, quiet as thought. Night comes down. There are no stars. Now the falling flakes are no longer visible against the white darkness. Nothing can be seen except the dark forms of houses which might be sounds, so much do sight and hearing seem one, up here.

Inside the igloos, one imagines the family group sitting, naked or almost, on the walrus-skin floor of their hot inner-skin living room. They are drinking tea. Or they may be gathered around a huge wooden platter, eating hunks of meat—seal, fish, walrus from last year which has become exceedingly "high," duck, or even seagull if the family is poor. They may be eating half-boiled prunes and pilot bread in celebration of teacher-come; white-man food is doled out sparingly and only on rare occasions. If it is a wealthy family, they may be playing the phonograph with an unchanged needle, on a dusty, scratched record.

When the food is eaten and everything cleared away; when the children have all used the little wooden chamber pots in which urine is carefully saved to be dumped into the tanning tub; when the little fund of jokes from the day's happenings is exhausted, the family and visitors are ready to sleep.

The Eskimo woman brings out the roll of skins, spreads them over the floor up to a log which lies across the entrance of the living room, and which is the common pillow. Eskimos lie side by side in a row, heads on the log, naked bodies on the long-haired, soft skins of reindeer, killed in mid-winter. They lie sardine fashion, fathers and brothers outside their own women, visitors beyond them. The old grandmother, or some dependent, watches the seal-oil lamp so that it will not go out all night and the sleepers grow cold. There are skins for cover, too, but they are not always needed, unless the lamp goes out, or the inner skin house is so old and thin and worn that it is not complete protection against the air in the outer igloo.

There is no ventilation except for one small hole in the skin flap which is the door of this inner house. Steam continually pours out of this hole, as though from the spout of a kettle. It is the steam from breathing, from the lamp, and from cooking.

Morning breaks slowly, even in the fall. If you are up before dawn, you look out into the smother of white darkness that is falling snow, and see nothing. Then, after breakfast, the snowflakes are separate things, coming down onto visible drifts. Day has wedged in through a crack somewhere.

Outside, the dogs budge their little hills, erupt from them, shake themselves, stand at their chains looking forlorn and hungry. After awhile, each dog will curl down again in a tight roll, like a caterpillar when you touch it with a stick. Then the day snow covers them again with its light warmth and they sleep in lieu of eating. Once a day, except in lean times, they get food—generally one salmon each from the whale-rib racks high out of their reach where the dried fish are kept.

After awhile, you will see a man crawl through the little square door of his outer igloo and stand there. His arms are folded inside his parka, against his bare, warm belly, his sleeves hanging limp. If he is a lazy man who does not work hard enough to soften the skin sleeves, they will stand out stiff from his parka when his arms are folded inside. The Eskimo expression for a lazy man is "He got stiff sleeves."

A man or a woman or a child will come out with a vessel in his hands. He is going out to chop some frozen snow to be melted for tea. Early in the morning, they must have tea.

Tea-drinking is the great indoor sport of the St. Lawrence Island Eskimo. Boiled over and over, tea is their water, beer, confection. They drink it continually. And though they ruin it in the making, they buy the very best to start with.

When Eskimos come to call, one serves them tea, or else. (Or else they will ask for it.) When you visit them, they serve it as a matter of course. Eskimos drink tea scalding hot, sweetening it by letting it slip down past a lump of sugar held in the jaw. They learned this, no doubt, from Russian or Scandinavian sailors. It accounts for their demand for cube sugar.

Old Agoolki used to come to our house, grinning toothlessly, his feather-filled pipe going full blast. He would sit flat on the floor, his short legs stretched out in front of him, arms and body so completely relaxed and motionless that he might have been molded from putty. He spoke little English, but he could ask for tea. And he would drink it hour after hour. He was the oldest man on the island and the only one who remembered clearly the first white man's ship stopping there.

"My little boy when big ship come here," he would say. "I'm think bird coming. Bymby, go out that big white bird. Lalurumkit (white man). Bump arm, not hit."

What had impressed him most, he meant, was that these strange white men did not fight like dogs at the slightest provocation. If they bumped against each other, they did not turn and rend one another, savagely.

I think it is the most interesting thing I have ever heard about the Eskimos. It meant that, within the memory of one man, the Eskimos themselves had come up from snarling dogmen, fighting each other, to being the peaceable, happy natured children we knew.

Yet how strange that they could so completely have changed. It is true that the wildest and fiercest animals can be tamed by removing the conditions under which they fought, namely, trouble in getting enough to eat. Perhaps it means that human beings can be tamed when they make the sweet discovery that food and safety can be had without dog fights. Eskimos never lift their hands against one another now, whatever must be said of their brutal treatment of dogs.

VII. WE MEET THREE SHIPWRECKED MEN

ONE day, before we moved from the Cape up to Gambel, a sled arrived with two passengers, one of them a white man—an immensely big, very bald, ominous-looking white man—who plunged at once into an account of his troubles. He and two companions had been shipwrecked upon the Island during the storm which had kept us circling round it for so many weeks. It was his companions who were the source of all his trouble. They were in Gambel, awaiting our arrival; he said, without enough spirit to run with the Eskimo dogs, as he had done, to meet us. Anyhow, he wanted to get to us first with his version of the quarrel, for the leader of the expedition, he warned us, was a slick proposition and would tell everything his way.

We were destined to hear versions of that shipwreck and that quarrel all year. But the first consideration now, was where the man could sleep. We had no extra bedding, and he none at all. When he saw that it was impossible for us to put him up, he decided to bunk in with the Eskimos—he said he often had, in Nome, and didn't mind. He would have his meals with us, though, he said blandly, for he didn't relish Eskimo food except as a last resort, and he knew from the look of her that the little missus was a good cook, whereupon he gave me a great toothy leer. If there ever was a forbidding-looking man, he was. But before the year was out we knew that his looks did not tell a fair story of him; he had many good faults.

We never really grasped the story of those three men except in the vaguest outline. So far as we could gather, a doctor, a very tall, thin man, something of a mystic, had decided that he was called by God to go to Russia to stay the Revolution—or help it on—we were never sure which.

The Bible had prophesied that the second coming of Christ would be out of the north, and he would come in a time of world trouble. This was the north. This was such a time. Was this, then, Christ again? He never came right out and said so.

The Doctor had a round disc of elephant hide about the size of a dollar which, he said, would admit him to the forbidden land of Tibet. He was financed by some religious zealot in Los Angeles. He had with him several thousand dollar bills, one of which Farrar was able to change from the Eskimos' co-operative store cash. From Los Angeles, the Doctor had come to Nome, early in the summer, where he bought a small boat and persuaded the big old prospector and a young Russian to join him. The Prospector was to navigate him to Siberia in exchange for free passage there to prospect for gold. That was what the Doctor said. The Prospector said it was to be in exchange for the boat, which he would navigate back to Nome. The Russian was to go on with the Doctor, acting as interpreter and guide through Siberia, up the Amur River and so to Moscow—America was not then recognizing Russia, and it was illegal for Americans to go there. Hence this back-door entry.

When the three men got out into Bering Sea, it became apparent that the old Prospector knew nothing at all about boats. He had fourflushed his way into the party. The storm which sent the big ship *Bear* marching around and around St. Lawrence for a month had driven this small boat all over the sea before it came to rest. With the Prospector prostrate with seasickness, the Doctor and the Russian had made a storm anchor of oars and a piece of canvas, and so loped the waves in comparative safety. The wind blew them north to King Island. Then it shifted and blew them south to St. Lawrence and piled them onto a beach where they had been rescued by the Eskimos seasick, frightened, and hungry.

Here they were, our major problem for the year. Farrar assigned them the only other white-man house in Gambel, but the old Prospector stiffly refused to live with the Doctor and the Russian, and spent most of his time going from one Eskimo igloo to another, finally coming to rest in a little frame shack belonging to one of them. We let him alone and he went about his lonely way, unbefriended by us all. The Doctor bought his food. I wish we had been kinder to him in spite of his surliness.

That winter the Doctor spent endless, sometimes tiresome evenings at our house, talking politics, religion, mysticism, biblical prophesies, the right and wrong of the quarrel. All year he gave generously what help we needed in the treatment of illness. He was a good man.

Our house at Gambel was an unnecessarily large, roomy, porous board structure, thrown together as though for use in the tropics instead of the Arctic. It was not triple-sealed against the elements. Weather made itself right at home with us. In no time we were on intimate terms with snowdrifts. With our short supply of coal, we had to confine ourselves to a single room—the kitchen. Here, with coal for the range, we cooked, ate, slept, and entertained the Doctor and the Eskimos.

The other rooms of the house were ghost chambers, bitter-cold, bleak, empty. After our year of homesteading on Puget Sound, we didn't mind the cracks and crannies. In fact, we thought it great fun, huddling together in the very innermost room of the big old empty house. Nowadays, the teachers have better quarters.

The schoolroom was part of our house. It too was un-arctic in construction. But the Eskimo children came to school in their furs and needed no airtight house. Those nearest the big-bellied stove nearly cooked, and we had to rotate them there.

On the first day of school, children tumbled in like puppies. Silook introduced them to me and gave them their seats. He knew each child's grade and place. We passed out the books, some of them bright and new, some old and tattered.

The most advanced children had reached the sixth grade. I gave Silook the three upper grades, on the theory that he could do the least harm there. I took the young ones, and all the reading classes, and sometimes I had to take over Sixth Grade Arithmetic. But, on the whole, Silook was capable. He was earnest, quiet, and, if a little lazy, he did his work as long as I was there. When our coal would give out and we had to return to Southwest Cape until another surplus could accumulate (for we used it faster than the men hauled it), Silook shirked a bit, but there was no help for it.

Lessons went smoothly on. If you had come into our warm old barn of a room full of skin-clad children and teachers, the stench would probably have sent you outside again to catch your breath. But in school as at home we couldn't smell ourselves. We were as happy as snowbirds—all of us. I never loved teaching so much, never loved any children more. Yet there was one little boy who kicked the dogs whenever he got a chance. Just as the dogs themselves would tear to pieces one of their number who was sick or weak, so these boys seemed to despise hungry or whining dogs and delighted in tormenting them.

One day I saw this child kick a dying dog. It was lucky for him that the schoolroom was very long. By the time I reached him, I had reminded myself what his upbringing had been, how little he could feel for helpless creatures. But I lectured him and all the rest of the children. I gave Silook a tongue-lashing for not having taught them better. And I made Farrar call a council about it a few nights later, and there I stormed again, and so did Farrar in his milder, merrier way. But except for their treatment of dogs, I found no fault with my children.

Meanwhile, Farrar and Oningayu, the storekeeper at Gambel, were arranging goods in the little frame building that was the co-operative store. And before long, Farrar went over the snowy hills and far away to see the reindeer herders who lived some fifty miles down island and were his special charges. I was left alone in the great, loose-joined, empty, roomy house. The Doctor spent the evenings with me, generally getting there in time for supper. I got awfully tired of him, poor fellow. And by night, the snow came sneaking in through all the cracks and had to be swept and shoveled out next morning.

When Farrar returned from Reindeer Camp that first time, he was a chastened man. I ran out to meet him. "Keep away from me," he said. "Bring me some clean things and a can of gasoline and heat some water on the stove—I will wait here in the shed."

It seems he had caught lice from a blanket which one of the Eskimos had lent him to sleep in. The shed was nearly full of snow, icicles hung down through its cracks. But there he stayed until I had heated water and fixed him up. Then he washed his garments in gasoline and I took them outside to hang on whatever whale ribs I could find sticking up near our house. The wind froze them at once and we later beat them until everything living or dead must have fallen to the ground. It was surely the most thorough de-lousing anybody ever had.

Farrar had had another adventure. He had eaten seagull. He said it was far from palatable and very tough. The dirty old woman at whose igloo he had stopped on his way, eager to serve him, grabbed a cup at her feet, a filthy rag from a corner to wipe it, and poured him some tea. Then she pushed the family platter towards him and bade him help himself to the bird. He took a piece and chewed and chewed, his stomach protesting at the taste. But he downed it.

One evening after school, Farrar and I took a walk out to the beach, about a mile away. The sea hadn't begun to freeze over at this outthrust, wind-swept point. The surf still beat there, night and day. We wondered whether there would be any agates here, and there were. We were walking along bent nearly double, peering into the gravel, not talking for a wonder because the noise of the surf was too great, when a big wave rolled in from Siberia and knocked us both down. We had been twenty feet above the highest wave and now we were sitting down in a froth of water, a determined undertow tugging at us.

Farrar struggled to his feet, grabbed my hand, and we lit out from there as fast as our high, water-filled boots would carry us. By the time we got home, our garments were frozen stiff. That was the last time we ever hunted agates on St. Lawrence beaches.

In time we settled down to the steady routine of our work: school five days a week, sewing classes for the women on Saturdays—which turned into storytelling festivals and ended as scrubbing bees, all of us on our hands and knees trying to get the week's dirt out of the place. Each woman was paid, of course. Catch an Eskimo doing work for nothing! On Sundays we held a sort of community sing and council meeting at which we discussed our problems of living.

Once a week, Farrar held another meeting, in the evening. The people loved meeting to sing and to talk. If there was nothing to settle, they made up something, I expect. They were capable of it.

Christmas found us at Southwest Cape. We celebrated there with candies and gifts for everybody, found, somehow, among our things.

There was a gale blowing. Risking going off the bluff in a sudden gust, Farrar crept out with the gifts and returned with the many thank-yous from people who lived in the two houses. They would all come to tea with us that evening, they said.

When the gale blew away to Japan, we returned to Gambel and had another Christmas there. With our buckets of candy and whatever there was in the store we could buy—prunes, cube sugar, and so on—we managed something for each person in Gambel, but it was a tight squeeze. Nobody had prepared us for this Eskimo greed for gifts.

Still, we reflected, we could not alternately exploit them and bestow beneficent largesse without creating this cunning rapacity in them. One minute we found ourselves hotly championing them against what had been done to them, and the next ruefully defending ourselves against what they were doing to us.

Wherever you find primitive people looked after like children by some benevolent and alien white government, you also find this servile demandingness—a hateful paradox. How long would it take some wise administrator to set them firmly on their own spiritual and physical legs, make proud adults of them on all levels of their being? Perhaps one generation? If we have brought them so quickly from an almost barbarous existence, we could take them on the rest of the way.

IX. WINTER OF SPLENDID ISOLATION

ST. LAWRENCE ISLAND is a hundred miles long by about thirty wide. It is within the Arctic Circle but almost the length of California from the North Pole. It is a hundred and fifty miles west of Nome, but only forty miles east of Siberia.

In winter, when the sun is given to making only polite little party calls, life on St. Lawrence goes on just as usual. The Eskimos do not huddle in their igloos and say, "Now long night come. More better we sleep now." They pay no more attention to the grayness that passes for daylight than we, outside, to the shorter days of our winter. They go out hunting every day except when there is a gale blowing. For St. Lawrence Island is whipped by stinging winds so violent that they will literally blow you off the island if you don't look out. When children go out in those gales, their mothers tie them to the igloos by walrus-skin ropes. In the big blows, grown men sometimes go on hands and knees.

We kept our lamps going all day and felt curiously separated from the world, but it was not really dark—not with all that snow-whiteness with its stored light.

On the shortest day of the year, the sun came above the horizon about a foot, rode across a little arc of sky for perhaps two hours, and went down again. On the longest day of summer, the blazing wheel ran around the full circle, slowly edged down toward the horizon at midnight, took a dip for about an hour, emerged again, and rolled up and on to light the blinding white world for another twenty-three hours. But we could read small print all night, long before that longest day arrived.

The lowest temperature which our minimum thermometer registered before it froze and burst was minus 55°—no colder than it gets in Minnesota. In summer—in mid-August—the temperature may go up to sixty or seventy or more on still, sunny days, mosquitoes hovering in clouds over the thawed-out swamps.

The loose gravel that passes for land on St. Lawrence is frozen clear to China, I expect. In summer it thaws about two feet down. But that is enough to turn the land between mountains into lakes which can be crossed only by birds. Travel is by boat, around the island, and Eskimos who have none are water-bound in their own villages.

Before I saw it, I imagined the frozen sea to be smooth, and I thought what fun it would be to cross to Asia by dog sled. That would be about as easy to do as crossing the roofs of a city in a horse and buggy. For the ice is like a hodge-podge of wrecked buildings. Wind and current push it together, jumble it, open sudden channels down into the cold watery depths, heap up blocks nearly as high as the pyramids. Even on short hunting trips, it is hard for the Eskimo dogs to find any passage through the rectangular ice hills to the dead animals which they must haul home.

Then there are the icebergs which come sailing down from the Arctic to settle on the St. Lawrence shore for the winter. They are pale green, beautiful, almost translucent. They are the last things to melt in summer, and they are hardly gone when the first snow falls and it is time for them to come again.

If some epidemic should destroy the people of St. Lawrence Island, I would like to write their epitaph. I would say that life was fun for them. The Eskimos don't need our manufactured pleasures; everything they do is recreation. It is rare fun to gather beach wood to build the base of their skin houses—to watch for the chunks or logs or planks drifting in out of the sea from Japan and Alaska and Russia—to run and pull them from the surf. The hard jobs are hunting, fishing, trapping, making white leather, building houses and boats and sleds—but they are fun, too, and it is evident that the Eskimos enjoy them.

They are a small-bodied people, seldom fat, though their broad faces and the swaddle of skins they wear make them look so. But they are strong. The men think nothing of running beside their dog sleds all day long. I've known them to do it for forty-five miles at a stretch. A man will take gun and harpoon, and sit all day on a hummock beside a hole in the ocean's ice, waiting for a seal, and pity himself no more than a man who sits at his desk all day. If there is any meat or food left in his igloo before he sets out to hunt, he will take some with him. But if there is none, he will sit and watch that deep blue lake rimmed with pale green ice, thinking—who knows what?

They think nothing of physical hardship. But then, most improvident people regard mere physical hardship a good deal as the provident ones regard monotonous routine—as an inescapable part of the way they live. Nobody works monotonously hard on St. Lawrence Island. They take time out for what we call laziness. Perhaps we were too long misled by pioneer necessity into calling laziness a fault; we have undervalued this gentle virtue. In a good life, a right life, all people would have as much sheer joy of living as the Eskimos have.

Perhaps it is more fun for the men to hunt seals than it is for the women to skin, dress, cook, tan, and sew them. But the women laugh at their work too and seem contented—if a shade too quiet about it.

For the children life is a continual festival. They run about, helping or not, as they choose, quickly learning the skills, playing quietly, laughing easily.

Seal hunting lasts all winter. Wherever the wind has blown the ice away from some tiny hole of water, you will see from one or two to a dozen hunters sitting with their guns, watching for a seal to poke its head up. If food is scarce in the village and water-holes as well, all the men may huddle around one hole all day without catching a single seal. That is a great joke. No food. All mans hunt one hole. Not one man got one seal. Very funny.

Seals are found in the open water-holes because they must come up to breathe. When one of the slick, dark, doglike heads slips up through the blue water, the Eskimo waits until the seal has breathed his fill. Then, pop! goes one of the surest guns in the world. Whiz! goes the ivory harpoon into the flesh of the seal. Whish! goes the long walrus-skin rope, if the seal was not shot in a vital spot. Flrrp! go the sealskin floats as they strike the water and are jerked partly under.

The blue water is stained with red, now. The floats ride it like big toy balloons as the seal thrashes about. They are so buoyant no seal can long outplay them. After awhile they are still as dreaming seagulls on the water. The seal is dead.

The hunter begins to coil his line. The floats come to shore and are taken in. The line is coiled onto the end of the ivory harpoon, and there is a helpless floppy seal secure on the hook. He is drawn out onto the ice and the Eskimo laughs.

While the fight was going on between seal and white floats, somebody was sent to the village for dogs and sled. If hunting has been good and food is not at the famine stage, only the one team and sled sent for will come, and the hunter will put his seal aboard and haul it home with some dignity.

But if it has been a hungry time, many sleds will come lolloping over the rough ice. Women and children come, too, laughing and chattering. They are given pieces of the seal and their sleds will go racing back to the village with a pound or so of meat aboard. When the hungry ones reach home, they cut the meat into hunks about the size of a fist, boil it a little, and fall to. Three meals a day do not mean as much to an Eskimo as they do to us. But a meal any day means something to him. And how much gusto they put into eating it—all sitting on the floor around the big wooden platter or the pot in which the meat was cooked over the never-dying flame of their seal-oil lamps.

If several seals are caught at once, there may be a waste of meat. Even the dogs may be given a scrap each. Farrar and I occasionally bought a piece of red-black tenderloin of seal which we broiled in butter and liked.

The common hair seal, weighing a hundred pounds and more for the larger kinds, is probably the most valuable product the Eskimos have. From its strong, smooth-haired hide they make waterproof pants, mittens, and—from the hide of the very large varieties—boots. By rotting off the hair, first, and freezing the skins, they also turn them into harpoon floats, using them whole; or into white leather which they cut up for trimming for their garments. The flesh, liver, and heart of the seal are standard food, and the fat is rendered into oil for their lamps.

Next in importance to the seal is the walrus. It is hunted in spring when the ice is breaking up. Herds will be sighted, miles away, on drifting ice floes. Eskimos go out in boats to hunt them, invariably killing more than they can possibly bring home. They leave whole mountains of flesh behind them for the polar bears. Someday there will be a shortage of walrus there. But perhaps, by that time, it will matter no more than our wanton waste of buffalo mattered by the time we had exterminated them. Walrus skins are used to make the roofs of the outer igloos, the floors of the inner living rooms, and, when they are cut into strips, ropes for dog harness and other uses. But their most valuable use is for the long, deep, canoe-like boats, up to forty and fifty feet long, with a carrying capacity of forty people.

Walrus intestines are cleaned, flattened, and sewn together for raincoats. The tusks are carved into trade articles. And the stomachs are treasured most of all for the undigested fresh clams sometimes found in them.

All the flesh is eaten, but we did not like it, though we found the liver very good. It is this meat which they store away in their underground caves literally to rot. But the modern Eskimo does not like this high meat as much as his ancestors did.

Reindeer herding has grown to be an important business on the Island. Since the days of Mr. Lopp, many of the Eskimos have owned reindeer. There is a little community of herders on St. Lawrence who see that the herd of some five thousand deer is driven to good feeding places, who corral and mark them once a year, and watch out for the does at fawning time.

From the reindeer the Eskimos get their beds and the walls of their inner living rooms, which are made from the winter skin with hair four to six inches long, and very strong. The summer skins are used for inside trousers, inside boots, mittens, and outer parkas. Fawn skins make inside parkas and all the children's garments. The tendons of the legs are used for thread.

Every year the herders sell a few hundred carcasses for cash. They seldom eat the deer themselves; just as farmers outside sell cream and use skim milk for their own families.

Farrar and I ate nine reindeer while we were there. The carcass would freeze solid and we would use a hack saw to cut off thick steaks which, broiled quickly, were tender as butter. Reindeer stew is good, too.

Nearly all the men trap white and blue fox, getting two or three hundred beautiful pelts a year. But they do not wear them. The only fur they use as decoration is wolverine, with its harsh, snow-rejecting hairs. They sew bands of wolverine around parka hoods to keep out the snow, and around the bottoms of the parkas for decorations. As there is no wolverine on St. Lawrence, the natives traded with the Siberian Eskimos for it once a year. Now, however, the Soviets keep the Siberians at home.

No whales were caught the year we were there, but polar bear is sometimes killed. The flesh is eaten, but it was too strong for us. The strong, heavily furred skin is much prized for sled seats.

When the wind blows too hard for hunting or trapping, the men help the women with the tanning or carve ivory. They make napkin rings, salt cellars, paper knives, cribbage boards, and all manner of trade articles which have been taught them. Sometimes they can be induced to turn out a long necklace of ivory lace, each link a fragile medallion fastened to the next by ivory rings, with slits in them which can be sprung.

Sled building, house building, boat building, tanning; making intestine raincoats and parkas of bird breasts and white leather of whole seal skins; carving, skinning fox, and drying the skins; gathering driftwood for houses and sleds and knees for the boats; herding, hunting, fishing in summer, gathering willow roots and dry wild grass for boots—there is not a dull job in the lot.

But while the daily activities were enjoyable in themselves, the Eskimos have storytelling to beguile long winter evenings. They will gather into a little cluster anywhere, any time, and start telling stories, their voices rambling along in a sing-song fashion, without any colorful inflections to mark the periods. To indicate the end of the tale, the storyteller puts his little finger in his mouth and blows hard. It is the only way you can tell the story is finished. From our standpoint, the stories are not interesting; they have no crisis, no theme, not a resolved ending among them.

A raven, wanting to show off, bragged that he would jump into the fire. His neighbors built a fire for him, he jumped in and was burned up.

A blind man, mistreated at home, ran away to the moon. There, too, he was mistreated. An old woman reached the age when it was customary to be killed by the younger people. She did not want to die just yet. She ran away and got into so much trouble you'd think the moral must be that she would return home and say, "Yes, my people have wisdom. It is, after all, time for me to die." But no such thing—she just went on having trouble. Thus their stories are the closest approximation to realism we have found in literature.

Eskimo dancing is like strenuous setting-up exercises. Drums and sticks beat the complicated, broken rhythm, voices sing, and one or more individuals stand in a cleared space and dance. They do not move about the space but keep their feet in the same position all the time. In the heat of their contortions, shrieks, and yowls, they may leap into the air, but they always come down in the same place.

The women dance more quietly. They neither leap nor yell. Theirs is more a dance of the torso and arms, their feet together on the floor, never leaving their position. But they too get more and more excited as the drummers increase their tempo and the singers whoop it up, and they are exhausted at the end.

The St. Lawrence Island drum is a reindeer stomach stretched over a hoop. It is roughly the shape of a palm-leaf fan, with a handle about as long as the fan's handle. It is beaten on the rim with a stick, the skin head giving out a shallow, booming sound. The rhythm is impossible to reproduce. It is not syncopation; it has its own plan or continuity, each dancer or singer making up his own tune and tempo. The air pulsates with the living tide-rip of sound. It is tremendously exciting.

Running foot races seems to be the chief outdoor sport. Of course, they used to have many others, but as this was the one white teachers could best understand, it has persisted. They practice with weights on their feet, increasing the weights as the time of the contest approaches. "Suppose run fast, load on feet. Run fa-a-st, suppose take load off."

There were fewer women than men on St. Lawrence, but this seemed to give them no particular advantage. As in biblical times, the young man works for his wife, joining the family, helping with hunting, building, trapping. He is a prized addition to the family. He works a year—

sometimes two, for his wife. When his time is up and the bridal night comes, the ceremony of taking a wife is very simple; the father moves over one place, leaving his daughter outside the family line and she sleeps next to the young man who, with her, now constitutes a new family.

If the young man is well-to-do, the couple may move to a skin house which he has built. Or they may live with either family, for an extra man means more food for everybody, particularly if he is a good hunter; and an extra woman means less work for the women in the mother-in-law's house.

Occasionally there is a shrewd old Eskimo who will overdo this business of exploiting a son-in-law. Old Shulook, one of the wealthiest men on the Island, had a beautiful daughter. She was Amamunga who worked for us. She was about twenty-five and quite lovely, with hair that reached the ground. And she was sweet.

One day she told me shyly that she wished Nanook (Farrar) would speak to Shulook about marrying her off. "More better I'm marry now," she said. "All time womans laugh me, for not marry." Farrar did speak to old Shulook, and Amamunga was being worked for once more when we left. I hope she married, at last, and lived happily ever after.

The Eskimo morals are different from ours, but they stick to their code as well or better than we do. They easily lie. They tell you whatever you want to hear. They will cheat you in trading if they can. Their hands are always out for gifts. But all that is conditioning from their exposure to some of the less moral individuals and groups among the whites—ignorant or unscrupulous traders—and others.

Polygamy used to flourish on St. Lawrence Island. While we were there, one man still had two wives. But changing conditions, and the fact that it is now illegal to say nothing of the shortage of women—have gradually let the custom die out. It is not for moral reasons, however, that the Eskimos are not polygamous. It is a matter of economy. They are children of nature and could as easily reason that polygamy is right because the seals have more than one mate, as that it is wrong because their favorite duck has only one. They have a legend about the faithful, monogamous duck. Once we were driven past a lake where a lone drake swam round and round. "That duck never marry again," our guide said.

"Him love wife ve-ery much all same Eskimo."

Before our government took charge of them, the Eskimos of St. Lawrence Island buried their dead on a ledge of the high bluff behind Gambel. They could not dig graves in solid ice. Even in summer, they can dig only two feet down. So bodies were laid out in the open—and there were times when things happened to the bodies and other arrangements had to be made. It seems to us that water burial is the only solution. They are a sea-living people. They should be given the seaman's funeral. Even in winter, there are water holes. But, fortunately, we did not have to face that problem.

In the old days, the St. Lawrence natives killed their old who had outlived usefulness—when their teeth were worn through the gums from chewing leather, when they could not see to sew or carve ivory, or even to tend the lamp. That custom, too, has been outlawed. It would have gone anyhow, when greater security for all came to the Island.

We found no indication that the Eskimos ever lived communally. Their stories, which go back to their earliest traditions, tell of the rich and the poor, the kind and the cruel, the haves and the have-nots.

When, as occasionally happens, an Eskimo woman is coerced into relations with some white sailor, the tribe is bitterly ashamed and angered, and the half-breed child is hated. But in the spring some of the Eskimos trade wives among themselves. This is not a breach of their own moral code; it grew out of their love for and need of children. When one brother's wife was found to be barren, another brother would lend his wife so that there might be small folk in that igloo, too. So many of the women are barren, indeed, that it seems inevitable that if the natives are to survive, new blood from the mainland will be necessary.

There seemed to be no sexual delinquency between young people. People lived together so intimately; there was so little mystery about bodies, everybody going naked inside the hot skin living rooms; getting married was such a simple affair that there was neither opportunity, necessity, nor desire for pre-marital relations between the young folk.

We never knew whether or not the Eskimos were clean, according to our standards. Amamunga declared that they bathed in melted snow water just as we did; that the women often washed their hair. They washed it with urine sometimes, as it kept down lice, was a good tonic, and made the hair shine. She also said they rubbed their bodies in oil. But while I believed the part about the urine and the oil, I never knew whether or not to believe in the water baths. The women, Amamunga said, use moss for their personal needs.

Sanitary cleanliness was rare among them. They drank melted snow from any source, casually fishing out the undrinkables. When our water boy, Iyu, brought us blocks of snow-ice chopped closer to the village than the bank we had chosen as apt to be free of foreign matter, we would find hair, a lost mitten, and nameless other things in it when it was melted. Iyu could not understand why we didn't simply fish them out and use the water. We had to watch him on every trip to the ice bank.

The disposal of human refuse offers no problem. The dogs eat it. Then the ravens eat the dog refuse. There is an Eskimo song, wondering what becomes of the raven droppings.

The Eskimos are subject to skin disease, venereal disease, tuberculosis, sore eyes, and—since sugar and prunes—tooth decay. They are not outstandingly healthy or long-lived. But while they do live, they make a wonderful job of it.

X. A FEW STIFF SLEEVES LIMBER UP

MORE than anything else, Farrar and I wanted to leave St. Lawrence Island better off than we had found it. We wanted to manage so well that every human being on the Island would have enough to eat, would improve his status, and make some progress toward adult living without sacrificing the values and good customs already obtaining.

Part of our job was to raise the price level of Eskimo goods and lower that of the trader's goods, so as to make it more worthwhile for the Eskimos to work. All Eskimos are easy-going, but some of them are so lazy that their families are reduced to extreme poverty, hunger and disease. These live off the bounty of others—for there is little margin in a primitive society, even among the wealthy.

Our task, then, was to find some way to persuade the laziest ones to work. We tried preaching, scolding, shaming, cajoling them off to the hunting and trapping grounds, the white-leather making—all with little success. They agreed to everything we suggested graciously, admitted their laziness humbly, resolved to improve themselves earnestly—and went right on behaving as before.

Then one day we saw the laziest man on the Island running a race with his dogs, apparently just for fun. He won the race.

"We'll try turning the work into play," we said, and knew we had the answer.

So, early in the year we decided to hold an Eskimo fair. It seemed the made-to-order answer to all our problems. It would encourage productivity, even among the laziest, and provide them with goods which they could exchange for the supplies they would need for the coming year. And they would have fun doing it.

Before Christmas, I typed twenty copies of a "Proclamation" telling about the fair, which we sent by messengers to every group on the island, explaining what fun it would be and what a lot everybody would have to eat.

It took time to work up any enthusiasm. At first everyone thought how much work it would be to make boots fancy enough to compete for prizes, to carve ivory lace, trap fox until the choicest pelt on the island was caught. We had to emphasize the fun, the prizes, and the "plenty grub."

At last we began to get a flicker of interest here and there. The idlest old man on the Island, as it happened, was also the best carver. By a campaign of flattery we finally got him stirred up, and after that things ran along with more spirit.

The Siberian Eskimos, who came in the spring, were always entertained with races, dances, and "big time." That, then, would be just the time for the fair. No one knew, of course, exactly when they would come, but we set the date for the fair for sometime in March or April—I cannot remember exact dates from our year in this timeless land. That would be before the land ice had begun to thaw, but after the days had begun to get long and bright. By then there would be good hunting, too; the Eskimos at Gambel would have food for their guests from Siberia as well as for those from all the other parts of St. Lawrence Island.

Early in the fair month, Farrar went to the reindeer village to select a couple of fine government bucks, which were to be our contribution as hosts-in-chief. By that time the co-operative store, and we too, were running short of food. We still had a hundred-pound sack of steel-cut oats left. It would make washtubs and boilers full of oat-reindeer stew for our three hundred guests. And thereby hangs a tale.

The great day came. Eskimos began arriving in their dog sleds. There was dog-pandemonium on the little sand spit on which our cluster of igloos and frame shacks sprawled. The great tea-drinking began. Everyone came to pay respects to us. Fortunately we had plenty of tea, plenty of snow to melt for water, plenty of sugar and hardtack. But not plenty of pots in which to boil the water; everything was filled with reindeer stew.

However, we managed to serve tea just the same. To fail in that would doom the festivities at the outset.

Silook and I had decorated the schoolroom with maps and drawings which the children had made. Now we added the fair exhibits: soft, strong-haired, great snowy fox pelts; ivory chains intricately carved; beautiful hair-seal boots, decorated with finely cut white leather; gloves, parkas, pants, ivory toys, rare old ivory in many colors, harpoons, miniature walrus-skin boats, miniature houses, perfect facsimiles of the big ones. Everything Eskimos use was represented at that fair—proof that they could do sustained work over a long period of time if there was incentive enough. I doubt if any of them thought that by working now they would have food next winter. They worked for the fun of competing—"I'm get prize. I'm plenty laugh for big time in March."

In spite of all our cajoling it was the wealthiest, least needy Eskimos who made the greatest number of fine articles for trade after all. But every man and woman had done something, and we saw that there would be a money surplus for all of them. They could buy what the store had left now, and still have money left for fall when they would be more in need of it. I felt like asking them all to stand up, hands inside parkas, to see whether there was a stiff sleeve left among them.

First we elected the judges. The Doctor was chosen by acclamation, for he was popular on the island; Silook, who, at our request, had entered nothing in the fair; Sepilu, the wealthiest and most intelligent man on the island; and me, to make sure that everyone got some sort of prize, if only a stick of candy for the little boots fashioned so clumsily by Maskin's sickly girl-wife. We kept Farrar off the judge's bench to act as supreme court in case we couldn't agree.

The display exceeded all our hopes for it. With what patience old men had sat and carved all winter that these blackened tables should hold delicate ivory chains! Farrar and I bought every prize-winning object, at top prices, partly because we wanted them, partly to show them—as nothing else could—that there were prunes and sugar and calico and tea to be had by all, if they would work for them.

In one of our private financial depressions—so frequent that Farrar calls them our status quo—we sold this collection, and they can now be seen at the Museum of the American Indian in New York City.

On that first day of the fair, the Siberian Eskimos did not arrive. But the weather was calm and sunny and the ice floes well-broken as far as we could see; they were sure to come the next day. Meanwhile those merry people were immensely enjoying their first fair.

At noon we served our tubs and boilers of reindeer stew. The Eskimos brought their own plates, cups, buckets, pie pans, lids, wooden platters, on which to receive their helpings. One little boy had an old rusty tin can. I lent him one of our plates, and after that had much trouble not to lend all the rest of them to people with shallow bucket lids or too-deep buckets. There was plenty for everybody.

With singular bad judgment, we gave second and third helpings of that rich food to those who wanted it—the hungriest or the greediest. That day the Doctor dined with us, and the stew was so good that the three of us ate too much of it, too.

Then, to cap our foolishness after that heavy meal, we held the preliminary races. Without the weights which they had worn in practicing, the men ran, losers eliminating themselves for the big races with the Siberians later. Between stakes or ice blocks or natural hummocks, they ran, nimble and fleet. They wore only their soft light skin boots and one pair of skin pants, and nothing on their upper bodies. Their feet seemed barely to touch the snow as they flew, their coarse hair lifting and falling on their heads. The middle-aged men were the best runners, easily outdistancing lads and old men. The women, too, were surprisingly fleet runners. Before that day was over, everybody had run. No one was winded. No one needed a rubdown. They ran as simply as they laughed, and thought no more of it.

But that night nearly three hundred persons—including ourselves—paid for eating too rich food after abstemiousness, and too much exercise after eating. Every single one of us had diarrhea.

Next morning, Silook came in, looking limp and wan. He wanted some medicine.

"Oh, everybody plenty sick," he said. "My father, he go outside, inside, outside, inside. Bymby he just stay outside."

Farrar and I nearly finished ourselves off laughing, though we were frightened, too. Presently the Doctor arrived to prescribe for us all. He had been sick, too.

On the second day of the fair we went right on with the contests and games. The Eskimos are a hardy lot. They aren't particularly Spartan; it simply wouldn't occur to them to miss anything interesting by being sick.

We had a rifle match, using powerful thirty-thirties, and I won second place. It must have been an accident for I wasn't used to such a heavy gun, but the generous Eskimos crowded around, patting me on the back. "Patsarok fine shoot," they said.

The dog races were next. Scrubby, dirty, scrawny, hungry, sullen dogs in teams of three or eight or nine were hitched to sleds, leaders out in front. The sleds were lined up, drivers sat ready to shout the first "Huh!" when Farrar should give the signal.

"One—two—three—go!" said Farrar.

"Huh! Huh! Huh!" screamed the drivers, slashing their whips on the ground, now on one side, now on the other side of their teams to direct them along the course.

The dogs ran belly-low, straining out. The sleds flew over the hard trail. We watched them sail over the last snowbank onto the lake ice, swing around the far edge of the lake and start on the homeward stretch. By that time, Farrar and I had shouted so much we had begun to get up some excitement among the imitative Eskimos, but it all turned into shouts of laughter when young orphan Iyu's three mangy dogs came in trailing the pack. Iyu was carrying one of the dogs in his lap, the other two pulling them. "Him not keep up," Iyu said, perfectly cheerful. The fun was the thing.

It was late in the afternoon. The scheduled games were over. Callers from other parts of the Island had come in to have tea with us and had gone again. Farrar and I were thankful for a little quiet beside our kitchen range.

Suddenly Silook ran down the hall, poked his head in and shouted that the Siberians were in sight. We grabbed up our parkas and ran with him down to the beach—or to the massed shore-ice that served as a beach at this time of year; it was about a quarter of a mile beyond the summer beach.

A huge walrus-skin boat had slipped into the open channel to our shore, and presently some forty smelly, cheery, casual individuals tumbled out of the deep, open craft onto the pale green ice. They pulled their boat up onto the shore-ice to make room for the one behind. And then they turned to greet us. Silook stood nearby to act as interpreter for the visitors. By this time the second boat load had come ashore, and we were proudly presented by our Eskimo names—Nanook and Patsarok. The Siberians laughed at our names, gazing appreciatively up at Nanook, the polar bear, as though they thought he had been well named, and at me, the little weed, and thought that funnier still. Everybody beamed.

Now we streamed back along the ice trails, over the dirty snow, homeward. The seventy-odd Siberians were so much like our own Eskimos that I couldn't tell them apart at a little distance.

That night we had a dance in the outer chamber of Shulook's big igloo. It lasted nearly all night. The Siberians were much dirtier than our Eskimos. They didn't laugh as much or as happily. But how they could turn themselves loose in the dance!

Lanterns stood about on boxes or hung from the roof. The air was close and strong. Small children lay on reindeer furs in the corners. The larger ones were given places of vantage around the dancing ring. The drummers sat in a row on boxes, close about the dancing space. Everyone was silent, waiting. Waiting for some dancer's spirit to urge him out into the ring.

Presently one of our men came, then one of the Siberians, another, another, until there were six or eight naked men in the ring. They wore loincloths, beads, fringed bands around their calves, white reindeer skin mittens to accentuate the rhythm, for it was a hand, not a foot dance. They danced their wild, shrieking, leaping, writhing, contortion dances, each according to his own impulses, but, to our untrained eyes, all looking the same.

Amamunga danced, her long dark hair loose, sweeping the floor. She wore her daytime clothes, dropping everything down around her hips to leave arms and shoulders naked and free. Another girl came into the ring with her. There seemed to be rivalry between them. Without moving their feet from their place, the two girls bent at knee, hip, shoulders. They turned and twisted from the ankles up. Their hair flew about. The drums went faster and faster. They danced so violently and with such swift movements that I began to fear they would kill themselves. And when I could bear no more, they stopped in the middle of a drum tap, walked calmly out of the ring, out of sight behind the crowd.

On and on into the night the drummers beat, the howls and shrieks burst open the skies. Then—out of a dark corner, a white woman came to dance! We had not seen her before. Where had she been hiding? I asked Silook.

She was a half-breed, he said. "Him not like to be seen. Sailors come ashore at Siberia, too," he said.

The woman's eyes were blue, her hair and skin fair, her expression one of infinite pathos, as though she felt completely outside life. But when she danced, she flung herself into it as though it were the only way she had ever found to say, "I live, too—I am."

Next day, there was trading between the natives from across Bering Sea and our own. They had brought soft fawn skins, for they had more reindeer than we and no government regulations to say how many should be killed each season. They had brought wolverine, beautiful brass samovars in which they made their own tea en route, and which they didn't want to trade. Silook got one, however, which he later traded to me for my best boots. He no doubt had that in mind when he wangled the samovar.

From us the Siberians wanted sugar, tea, calico, and white-man things in general, including fine guns. Our men were the sharpest traders, having had more dealings with white men, and the poor Siberians came out at the short end of the horn, but everybody was happy.

In the afternoon of the third day, we held the long-awaited foot races. Our Maskin won first place—and the fair was over. Soon the Siberians would go back and life would fall into a new pattern for the Eskimo spring.

XI. WE TOSS A COIN

SPRING comes with a rush and a roar on St. Lawrence Island. Ocean ice begins to crack like cannon. Winds blow the floes about, opening up long blue channels to tempt the natives out in their whaling and walrus-hunting boats. The sun glares down on the eye-blistering snow. The pale green icebergs, like a city of skyscrapers along the shore, begin to look uneasy, as though they knew their time had come. Sapphire shadows underneath the curling eaves of snowdrifts darken to a rich purple in contrast to the dazzling whiteness around them.

Immense flocks of birds ride the winds from the south, settle on the rocks and bluffs of their summer home. They fill the air with happy, homecoming cries. The days have lengthened rapidly and amazingly. Even in March, night has receded so far beyond our bedtime we never know when it comes down anymore.

But spring really comes when the Eskimos take off their heavy winter reindeer parkas and don white-man clothes. One night we went to bed in a land of people we knew. Next morning we looked out to find a flock of scarecrows over the landscape. It was the Island's Easter parade. The women seemed to have lost twenty or thirty pounds overnight. Their calico parkas hung limp without the padding of heavy fur underneath.

But the men! They were unbelievable in coats and trousers bought in Nome or traded from former teachers. Silook walked solemnly up and down in a khaki officer's uniform which Farrar had traded him for something or other, and the pair of boots for which I had got the samovar.

Farrar is on the biggish side and Silook was small, even for an Eskimo. The trousers were tight below the knee, puttee style. The bloused portion came nearly to Silook's ankles, and the tight leggings were rolled up. The coat hung far below his hips and the sleeves were doubled back to the elbows. The cap came down over his ears and eyes. But Silook was the envy of the Island. And when Farrar complimented him on his appearance, he nearly burst with pride.

The reindeer fawn in the spring. Farrar and I went to the reindeer camp for a month, I to give the dozen children of the herders some schooling, Farrar to superintend the counting of the herd and its new additions.

It was a crazy beach-wood, whale-rib, walrus-rope corral into which the milling deer were gathered. The Eskimo lariat is a walrus-skin rope, pliable and easily thrown. But they weren't cut out to be cowboys. Farrar lost all patience with them and would come in at night fuming at their ineptness. They ran a deer down instead of lassoing it. That seemed a good way to me, if they could catch it, but he said it ran off too much fat, was bad for the mother deer, and anyhow wasn't good cowboy.

At reindeer camp we lived in a tent. Sepillu, chief herder, and the only man on the island of whom we made a real friend, had fixed it up for us. He had put up a tiny ship's stove in one corner, railed off a space at the back for our bed in which he had spread down all his own cherished supply of boot grass—a strong grass which they gather in summer and save to pad their boots with, for it is springy and breaks the hardness of ice underfoot.

June and Farrar in sled.

There was a box for a table and two whale vertebrae for seats. The floor was frozen ground, of course, and the unbearable glare of the sun on snow outside was scarcely dimmed by those thin canvas walls, but we loved it. After a winter of living in a house it felt like adventure and freedom.

There is something exciting about a tent. A sense of impermanence, as though one weren't committed to this forever. The closeness of air and sky and ground—all the outer world. In a tent one has the delight of camping in the open beside a fire, plus the thrill of being hidden in a cave.

The reindeer-camp children hung around so hungrily, in their eagerness to learn to read and do sums, that I rang the schoolbell—or rather beat on the frying pan with a stick—as soon as we had had breakfast and Farrar had gone out to the herding. The children sat flat on the snow outside the little tent, and I on a sack of coal. I wore sunglasses but they didn't seem to mind the snow. We had few books—only those that could be spared from Gambel but it seemed riches to them.

June teaching children.

We read and wrote and sang, and I told them stories, made up on the spot, about the things they knew. Once upon a time there was a young seal that decided it would rather be a little Eskimo boy than a seal and so it went off to school to learn how it could be done . . . on and on, not knowing where the next word would lead, the children motionless as long as I kept going. Never was there a jollier school, or pupils so eager to learn—or a teacher gladder when the term ended. For they nearly exhausted me that month.

In the spring the women have their inning. With the children they go to the "woods" to gather bitter tonic willow bark from the roots of the six-inch-high shrubs that grow wherever there is soil. Later in the summer they gather the boot grass, too. And with their families they go to the lakes and streams to scoop up hordes of spawning salmon to be dried for their dogs the next winter.

Spring is walrus-hunting time. All winter long, occasional herds of walrus are watched as they move slowly up or down on the currents, dark masses on the white ice floes. But even during semi-starvation, the Eskimos dare not go out to hunt them so far from shore. A sudden wind might come up, break off the floor of ice on which the hunter travels, and sweep him to Japan. That happened to Athelingok's father once. Before he got there he had eaten everything he had along with him, even the dog harness. And he is not sure it was Japan he reached. All he knows is that it was a long way south, and that, three years later, when he was again out hunting off the shore of his new home, he was blown away once more—northwards this time—and actually landed on St. Lawrence Island. He lived many years to tell that unbelievable tale.

But when the boat channels are safely open and the calm weather has come, how quickly the hunters get under way! All over the Island, men get out their outboard motors and prime them for the start with ether.

"Suppose see walrus this day, we hunt," Sepillu said one morning while we were at breakfast in the tent.

Out over the sea, long ribbons of blue wound about among the ice floes. No wind threatened. It was ideal walrus-hunting weather. Men stood on their roofs and searched the ice fields with their long spyglasses.

"Ievuk, Ievuk!" they said after awhile. "Walrus, walrus!"

They had sighted a big herd. Everyone hurried into winter clothes again, for it would be cold out in the boats with ice all around.

Eight or ten of us equipped with big thirty-thirties piled into Sepillu's whaleboat. The outboard was attached and off we sputtered, the noise shattering the winter-long silence.

The herd was miles away. In and out of cul-de-sac channels we wound, finally approaching so close to the herd that engines must be shut off and paddles broken out. Silently, then, we crept up on it, approaching on the lea.

At first the brown beasts had been a thin dark line on the ice floe. Then they were black hummocks. Now they began to stir, to lift their two-tined, clam-digging heads. They were very mountains of flesh.

"You shoot first walrus, Nanook," the Eskimos urged Farrar.

He protested he might miss and cause them to lose all the walrus. But our polite hosts insisted. Farrar stood up in the boat and aimed a gun that all but had buck fever. The gun roared. A half-dozen Eskimo guns echoed it.

A dozen walrus slipped off the ice into the blue water and we saw them no more. Two great wounded fellows thrashed about, making a red sea around them, roaring out defiance. They were dangerous. Shots rang out to silence them.

We turned, then, to the kill. Nine dark forms, some as big as draft horses, one a baby walrus, lay on the bloody ice. Sepillu pointed out the biggest one as Farrar's kill and laughed in delight at Nanook's prowess.

Now to the butchering. It is impossible to take back all this meat. The heads are saved for the tusks, the pair of baby tusks given to us. The guts are piled out in a huge mass, stripped of their contents and loaded in the boats to be further cleaned in the village and made into raincoats. The stomachs are carefully felt for clams, and those that have them put into the boats. The skins are hacked and ripped off for houses, boats, ropes, harness. Livers and hearts are saved and as much of the tons and tons of flesh as we can pile into the boats.

We had a tea-party there on the iceberg. The butchering took hours. We had all brought lunches. At noon, Sepillu got out the ubiquitous primus stove, boiled some snow cut from the top of the ice floe and made tea. We ate and drank sitting on carcasses and ice hummocks.

When we left the floe, the sun was swinging down over Siberia. We traveled in its glittering path all the way back and I saw setting suns in my eyes for days afterwards.

The whole village met us at the shore. That is one of the things I like best about the Eskimos—they make a celebration of everything.

In those days, the great event of the spring was the coming of the trader, usually in early June. One day, shortly after the close of school, we saw a flock of children running toward our house. Something had happened. We ran out to meet them.

"Pederson come! Pederson come!" they said, pointing out to sea where, tangled up with icebergs, the masts of a ship could be seen. Already dog-sleds had been harnessed and were skimming down the worn trail toward the beach. People were streaming out of the houses, some of them plopping down on the sleds as they shot off, some running in their clumsy boots. We joined the crowd flowing toward the big ship.

Over the ice blocks, through puddles of slush, around icebergs, along fairly good trails over level ice, Farrar and I hurried. The ship was jammed up against the shore-ice so that we could walk to the foot of the ladder against her side and climb aboard.

Pederson had been coming here for years from a house in San Francisco. He was on his way to Point Barrow where the year before he had married the station's nurse. She was with him now. Farrar and I stayed for lunch on shipboard—a lunch of canned foods, prepared by one of those inevitable oriental cooks favored by ships' captains but not by us. After a winter of fresh reindeer and our own hand-ground wheat bread, we were spoiled. But the captain was so solicitous of what he believed to be our semi-starved condition that we had to pretend we thought it a feast.

After lunch we watched the trading. The natives swarmed all over the boat, fingering things, delaying trading for very joy of the business. They loved Pederson, for though he was canny he dealt more fairly with them than other traders had done. And he was genial and friendly. He brought them the best of trade goods, too, not trying to palm off cheap tea or guns on them. He respected their desire for oh-plenty-fine-thing.

Then, too, since Mr. Lopp had set up the government co-operative stores the natives had discovered what standard prices were, so if they were willing to sacrifice something in every deal for the fun of trading on shipboard, Farrar thought they were justified in the name of romance and adventure. Nowadays, the natives have both the romance of trading aboard and the security of not being cheated, for the government Bureau of Education ship takes things up to them.

Pederson stayed three days. By that time the dog sleds had worn a sloppy brown path over the ice to the ship. The Doctor offered the captain five thousand dollars to set him and the Russian across on the Asiatic shore and was refused. And one morning early, the ship slipped away from its ice-moorings and glided off through the dark green channels to the North. Nearly three hundred persons stood on the pale green ice banks and watched it go.

That very day the Doctor and the Russian began to load their whaleboat which they had hired for their trip on to Siberia. Cans of gasoline, boxes of food, bundles of garments, trade goods which they had got from Pederson who had changed another of the thousand-dollar bills—everything was easily stowed away in the big open boat. The Doctor covered everything with canvas. His Eskimos were ready. They left next morning.

Earlier in the spring the Doctor had offered to pay our way to Russia and clean on around the world, back through New York and on to Puget Sound, if we would only go with him across that fearful Bering Sea, with Farrar navigating the boat. The Doctor wasn't afraid. But he was in earnest about his mission and wanted to make sure that he got there. He felt that Farrar, just out of the Navy, would take care of that, and that if he and the Russian undertook it alone they might come to grief again.

We were tempted by his offer. But it was an illegal venture and we were taking government pay. Moreover, we wanted to start our family, because it seemed a shame not to wait for the children so they could enjoy our adventures, too.

On the one side lay danger and uncertainty and, perhaps, loss of standing with the government, but it was tempting. On the other lay safety, legality, security, our first c:hild. Farrar tossed a coin. Heads, we'd stay safely in America and start the family; tails, we'd go to Russia and maybe never see America again. Luckily, the coin came up heads. If it hadn't, though, I expect Farrar would have kept pitching until it did.

On St. Lawrence Island, people announce a new addition to their family as soon as they are sure of pregnancy. By the time we had come back from Reindeer Camp, we were sure that our first-born was on its way and had proudly made the announcement. Everybody was greatly excited, and I felt like some kind of sacred cow. Women would come up and say, "Patsarok got baby inside. Fi-i-ne!"

I like that custom. Somehow your child seems more real to you, acknowledged and talked about like that. To the poor Doctor, the baby spelled the doom of his hopes. He took it gracefully enough. But from that time his restlessness increased. He was all for starting right away. Farrar had difficulty in persuading him to wait for a time when the ice was more nearly gone and there was less danger of getting cracked between floes in a sudden wind. Now, that time had come.

It was a calm sunburst of a day, the light from the ice splintering off in our eyes, when he finally left. How near the bluffs of Siberia—surely not more than an hour's paddle away!

At last everything was ready. The Eskimos pushed the boat into the water. They primed the outboard motor. It would start at the first turn. The immensely tall, lean Doctor shook hands with all of us and stepped in. The stocky, short Russian followed. We pushed them out into the channel. The sputtering roar of the outboard was their final word as they moved swiftly out along the winding blue passage toward Russia. When the Eskimos returned, they brought us a pitiful little note that said, "When you see the face of the world change, you will know that I have accomplished my mission."

Poor Doctor—kind and humorous, strange and a little befuddled. A year later we heard that the young Russian, who had been so eager to return to the land where everything was now for men like him, had been killed by the Bolsheviki; that the Doctor had been robbed of his money and sent back home, broken and defeated.

Now, our good Doctor and the silent Russian were gone. School was out. Our reports were all written. Farrar and I had compiled a sort of census taker's survey of the Island, listing every inhabitant and describing him fully with all relevant matter concerning him. He had written down the Eskimo names for things, the stories we had heard. We had set down all the legends and superstitions and rites we could persuade them to tell us. We had given the schoolhouse a final cleaning, made out the order for books, medicines, store supplies for the following year, and were waiting for the *Bear* to come and get us, to take us back to Nome.

Then good old Sepillu arrived from Reindeer Camp to tell us that the men from there were going to Nome in Sepillu's whaleboat and we could go with them if we liked. Go a hundred and fifty miles between ice floes in a thirty-foot boat, with a wind as likely as not to come up and crush us like an egg shell? We didn't hesitate. It might be a month before the *Bear* arrived, and we had had enough of that ship. The old Prospector was going back on the *Bear* and we had had enough of him, too.

We had set our hearts on the baby being born on Sentinel; we didn't want to stay on St. Lawrence Island another year. We hurried our packing. Willing Eskimos—their hands out for parting gifts—took our bundles and ran with them out to Sepillu's tiny boat, invisible from shore behind the ice blocks. Trunks, boxes, bedding, suitcases went off on sleds or backs, and we followed.

No wind blew. The ice lay in great, still, broken fields over the sea, leaving winding channels between the floes. Sepillu steered his boat back to Reindeer Camp to pick up the rest of the party and then straight east to Nome, on a gamble that for two days the wind would not come up.

As we rounded a point below the highest mountain on St. Lawrence, Sepillu told us that the Eskimos used to worship up there. He said there was a perfect, three-tusk walrus head there—one of their old objects of worship. Farrar offered him twenty-five dollars to get it for us. Sepillu ordered the anchor overboard and set off with one companion up the mountain. After what seemed hours, they returned bearing the huge head with three, long, perfect tusks. It can now be seen in Dr. Hornaday's famous collection of heads at the Bronx Zoo. It is, he told us, the most perfect three-tusker he ever saw, perhaps the most perfect one in existence.

We were off again—thirteen of us. There were no sleeping accommodations, no conveniences of any kind. We sat or half-lay on bales of reindeer skins. The men took turns atop the dinky little mast looking out for open channels, but even so we had to back up and try again, time after time. We stopped for lunch on an ice floe, got out to stretch our legs, made tea on the primus stove, and thoroughly enjoyed ourselves.

The Punuk Islands lie not far off the eastern end of St. Lawrence. They are famous for the enormous flocks of waterfowl that nest there. Sepillu wanted to stop and gather bird eggs for dinner. We went ashore on the long beach of the largest island and Eskimos began running up and down the beach like wild things, stooping down every now and then to pick up something.

Sepillu alone behaved with his usual dignity and restraint. He said the men were gathering old ivory. "Sea wash him up all winter. You look, too," he bade us, and we did. And there on that beach we found a gunnysack full of rare treasure which the Smithsonian Institution later pronounced to be prehistoric ivory. There was a half tusk of solid black — the rarest piece we ever saw. One fine whole tusk of a rich deep rusty rose. We found blunt, broken tusks of beautiful amber, one tiny point of a baby walrus tusk, yellow as gold all through.

When we had picked up all the ivory that showed itself above the water line, the men turned their attention to egg gathering, and soon they were scattered all over the perpendicular bluff, holding on to inch-wide ledges.

It was supper time before we left Punuk. We broke out the primus stove again and scrambled two or three dozen of the white shag eggs, as good as hens' eggs ever were, and ate them with hardtack and tea.

Now to sea again, the sun still riding high. At midnight it took its brief dip, rose again a foot or so away, the sky a radiant yellow all around it. We were going east. But the sun had gone down straight in front of us and was still in front of us when it came up again.

It was early morning, and the sun was straight overhead, when we left the ice and went galloping out into open choppy water off the mainland. Fifty miles of this. And now for seasickness. I kept my head low against the hides and was completely miserable all day until the man on the mast called out, "Land ho!"

We had made it. Cramped, weary, and nauseated, we went ashore on the bleak beach of Nome and not long afterwards took passage for the Outside.

Reindeer Camp.

We learned from the Eskimos that if you don't live as you go, you don't live at all. Since occupations fill most of our time, they must be made interesting, lively, delightful. They've got to be, or at least to seem, important.
June Burn

Part Three

TRAVELS WITH A DONKEY

June and Farrar and North visiting family in Van Buren, Arkansas.

We wanted to teach our children to be rich without money, how to live like millionaires without a cent, how to compel life to yield them what they wanted without selling their beliefs for it.
June Burn

XII. A GALE BLOWS US A BABY

WHEN Farrar and I had settled our affairs with Mr. Lopp in Seattle, we found that we had almost two thousand dollars of our salaries left. That was more than either of us had ever had before. And we didn't know what to do with it.

Of course, the baby would take some—a couple of hundred, we thought—for we didn't know then that we would have that baby for ten dollars, all told.

Then we decided to go over to Victoria on Vancouver Island and have an English tailor make us some clothes. After all, you could wear clothes, but there was nothing we could do with money but sit and wonder what to do with it.

But first, we outfitted ourselves with all sorts of household things which we had gone without in the past, such as a washboard and tubs and wringer, and even clothespins. We bought a big army tent for Sentinel; the baby couldn't be born in our tiny shack. We laid in a lot of supplies, and even bought a Toggenburg milk goat from an Italian family in the outskirts of Seattle.

In Victoria we splurged on clothes, handsome suits and dresses and handmade shoes. The money slipped through our fingers. The prices were high: we practically wore that two thosand dollars on our sleeves.

Then we went back to our island. Dad Chevalier met us at Roche Harbor in the Norine and landed us on Sentinel with all our supplies. There she was, the gumdrop, as lush and green as ever, lapped in swirling tides. Dad helped us up the hill and around to our shack with load after load of supplies, and he and the boys built a platform and put up the tent for us, Dad talking to himself all the time about these kids who hadn't learned a thing. A tent for a baby to be born in. A goat to be a pest around the place.

His murmurings lasted all day, scolding us under his breath as though we had deliberately planned to make it hard for the baby. Yet it was Dad Chevalier who was always complaining that modern women were soft—look at the way the Indians had their babies—out in the bracken, on the beaches, in a canoe, anywhere. But it was different with his family—or practically his own family.

The pattern had changed a little during our absence. People had married and moved away. Even Father and Mother Butterworth were talking of selling out and going to Seattle to live with their son. But they hadn't gone yet. And on Speiden there were still Dad and Ma, and Tootsie, Elmer and Alfred. But a different generation of pet lambs ran around in the backyard.

For the second year on Sentinel we each had a rifle and we could shoot ducks for our dinner. We shot something like a hundred and fifty of them that winter. Big-breasted bluebills, occasionally a canvasback, mallards, and once a beautiful wood duck. The Butterworths gave us some milk-fattened pork. We baked the unskinned ducks with strips of the sweet fat across the breasts and spices over the whole. With hot hoecake made of our hand-ground wheat, sweet butter which we could now afford to buy, greens, and goat's milk, we dined like kings, those days.

We had chickens that year, too. The old woods were so full of grubs that the hens either had to lay or get too fat to walk. They roosted in trees and made their nests everywhere except in the boxes we had put up for them. Hunting for eggs in the deep moss over the island was more fun than in the hayloft down in Alabama.

For water, we caught the rains in huge barrels which we had bought in Seattle. During August, Farrar hauled water—for we had bought another rowboat, of course—but after the fall rains began we were never without it again, except in the quantities needed for washing clothes. But we solved that by taking the washings to the water on top of Speiden Island. Farrar did the heaviest work, and I did the hanging out and helped with the rinsing.

Washdays were fun. We had learned from the Eskimos that if you don't live as you go, you don't live at all. Since occupations fill most of our time, they must be made interesting, lively, delightful. They have got to be, or at least to seem, important. Farrar and I had determined that we would never again do anything that wasn't rewarding in the doing. We had a theory that a good life, right and true and independent, could be lived on that principle. The Eskimos loved all the everyday activities of their lives. What could be more fun than hunting seals? What more fun than gathering boot grass in summer? Yet their economy was as complicated as ours.

Surely, it was possible for us, too, to strip our wants down to the minimum and live as heartily as the Eskimos lived. We had already learned that life could be beautiful if we could find a way of keeping clear of cluttering possessions beyond what actually contributed to well-being.

Farrar had the instinct for economy of effort which we so patly call laziness. He loved large leisure for trying out new tunes, new word combinations, new ideas. His more gracious attack on everyday living was hard work to me at first, for I cared about white clothes and immaculate houses, clean corners and tidiness.

"Don't you see," he kept at me, "that energy-margin, time-margin left over from doing a washing is more important than getting the clothes to a certain degree of whiteness? If I'd wanted a housekeeping wife I'd have married a servant and gone out for friendship and companionship."

In November we rowed over to Deer Harbor, on Orcas Island, to visit a cantankerous, lame, lovable old man who lived alone in the dustiest cabin in America. He had written one of his precise, witty, scolding, charming letters, inviting us over, goat and all, for Nanny had to go wherever we went, so we could milk her twice a day.

It was the season of rough weather, rainy and cold. No time to go visiting. But when our friend's lonely letter came, we piled into our rowboat and set off across wide, blowy channels. We meant to remain overnight and return next day. A longer visit in that house offered no charms for me; it was full of books, trash, dirt, old rags—the unaired accumulation of years and years. Our friend didn't care. He sat all day beside his fireplace, facing the motto he had tacked above it—OH, WHAT FOOLS THESE MORTALS BE—and paid no attention to the rest of his house.

He was well-read, canny, and gentle. His quick, acid wit and rare understanding marked him a personage even when he was neck-deep in rags and dirt. We treasured his friendship and were ashamed not to accept his discomforts as casually and large-mindedly as he did.

The wind came up that night, and we stayed a week with the philosopher, living on crackers and cocoa, sleeping on the floor with books piled all around us. At last I said, "I'm rowing home today," and Farrar knew that I had reached my limit.

The wind had abated a little, we thought. We piled our things in the boat, led Nanny down the long steps to the beach, and our host limped down to watch us off, grumbling that it was foolhardy, and that women were stubborn creatures.

We rowed across the Harbor and there were struck by the full force of what was almost a gale. Had the wind come up again, or had we been sheltered and unaware of its force? Every once in awhile a "willy" would flatten out the water under its sudden swoop, but a second afterwards the sea would unflatten itself with a vengeance. It looked dangerous.

The next two or three hours wouldn't have been so hazardous for us, though, if it hadn't been for the worms we had eaten for breakfast. That morning our friend had insisted that we have oatmeal instead of the usual cocoa. He had hobbled about, making it himself, while we packed. We ate it with goat's milk. Just as I was finishing my bowl, I saw a worm—the unmistakable brown head and sick white body of a weevil's larva. Looking closer I saw that we had practically breakfasted off larvae. I went outside and was sick, but I thought I wouldn't tell Farrar. What he didn't know wouldn't hurt him.

But now we were facing that gale on a wide channel. The *San Juan II* would be along soon, and if we could get into the middle of the channel, she would stop and take us in tow. But the wind was from the southeast. In order to keep our boat directly across the waves, we had to head northwest. That would take us to mid-channel all right, but if the *San Juan II* should miss us, it might take us bang into the high bluff of Mt.

Disney on Waldron Island. There was no beach at the foot of the bluff and the waves would dash us against the rocks in spite of all we could do to keep off.

We stopped around a point to tie Nanny's four legs to four equidistant points, so that she would keep in the middle of the boat. Then we dove into the breakers, Farrar maneuvering the boat directly across the waves. I held my yellow slicker outside the stern of the boat, trying to keep out as much water as I could. Farrar looked frightened. He began to look pale. After awhile he said, "I'm going to be sick." But he couldn't be sick now. If he let go of the oars one of those waves would turn us endwise in the trough and that would be the last of us.

"You're just scared," I told him. "Don't you dare be sick!"

Farrar bent his shoulders and rowed.

It seemed hours before we heard the *San Juan's* whistle and hours more before she came leaping the waves across the channel. Now we were safe! But when we saw her head into the channel we realized we were still a long way out of her course. What if she didn't see us!

"You'll have to stand up in the boat and flag them down," Farrar said. I took off my coat and flung it around my head, yelling and crying, Farrar shouting as loud as he could.

The *San Juan II* went galloping across the channel utterly unaware of us. Every time we went on top of a wave I'd fling my coat and shout. Every time we went down, we couldn't see the boat at all. At last we realized it was no use. I sat down again on the wet seat and began to bail out the water we had taken in. Farrar kept rowing, his lips pressed tightly together. Nanny gave a half-uneasy, half-consoling baa every now and then and I spoke to her reassuringly in return.

Farrar rowed and rowed. I bailed and bailed. The bluff of Mt. Disney was getting nearer. Farrar was whiter and whiter. "I can't stand it much longer," he said. The impulse to vomit had turned into diarrhea.

"You can stand what you decide to stand," I said, and he kept on rowing.

Then, when we were near the mountain and almost certain destruction, we saw a boat. Someone else was caught in this storm—someone in a motor boat. Why—why—it was Bill Chevalier!

"Hi, Bill," I yelled. "Grab our line quick. Farrar is sick!"

Bill grabbed the line I threw him, Farrar leaped out of the boat and into Bill's and was sick for a long time. When I told him what we had had for breakfast he laughed and laughed, and Bill said we were fools.

Bill had come around to get some logs he was told were in a sort of pocket of the tide and storm, beating themselves to kindling against the bluff. He had been foolish, too, but before the days of the log patrol, islanders could turn a tidy penny in a year by salvaging logs, and Bill needed the money. His propeller had got fouled in his tow-rope and he was in about as bad a fix as we were when we found him.

When he and Farrar had cleared his propeller, Bill took our boat in tow, leaving the logs where he had found them. Nanny was still tied in the rowboat and she bleated pitifully all the way around the island to the Graignic beach on Waldron where Bill and Lizzie lived.

When we got back home and Dad Chevalier found out what we had done, he shook his head. A rowboat couldn't cross the channel in a blow like that, he said. But he wasn't impressed that ours had. "Beginner's luck," he muttered.

Drawing by Skye Burn.

Farrar made the baby's crib out of a chicken crate. He took it down to the salt water to wash it, dried it in the sun, lined it with clean sheets and a pillow, and made it cozy and sweet. It stood, now, on a high box behind the stove in the warmest corner of our tent. I hadn't bought or made anything beyond the baby's elementary needs. We had his name ready.

> *My name was North*
> *Before my birth*

Farrar wrote in a day ledger which was to be filled with "Rhymes for North." And:

> *Our big black rooster has long spurs*
> *And struts about the place*
> *As though he owns the whole shebang*
> *Of chicken populace.*
>
> *Our small white rooster*
> *Has no spurs*
> *But watches every chance*
> *To drag a wing around a hen*
> *With flirtive arrogance.*

I had been writing letters to North—a handy way to keep a diary. We sat in front of our semi-Franklin stove in the tent and talked and talked about how we would bring up our children. They should be let alone to do things for themselves. They should be taught not to care for position or fame, for possessions or ease or comfort, so that they might be free to choose how they would live. We would bring them up, we said, to love the earth, simple pleasures, independence of action. We thought if we brought up our children in austere poverty that they never knew was poverty because we had so much fun all the time, we could make them really free of the hateful wantingness which is the destroyer of men.

We talked more about how happy our children should be than anything else. We meant to show them America before they started to school. We meant to give them a taste for adventure and romance—the exquisite adventure of camping in a hickory grove when the leaves are turning yellow and you feel a very shower of gold all around you when the sun pours down through them. Adventure of hunger in the desert, and thirst.

For physical hardship is adventure. We wanted to teach them how to be rich without money, how to live like millionaires without a cent, how to compel life to yield them what they wanted without selling their beliefs for it.

Then one night there came a storm that is still remembered in the islands for the son it brought to Sentinel and the son it took away from Waldron Island.

The wind came howling out of the north, with icicles in its whiskers. With each terrific gust the tent seemed to lift, but it always came down again. All around was the sound of crashing trees. They say that atmospheric pressure during a storm will often bring a baby early. Mine was born in that one. Between pains I read aloud instructions from a government bulletin, while Farrar scurried about, building a fire.

At daybreak he got down our big boat and went to Speiden for Ma Chevalier. At last they returned. Ma said that Dad was chopping ice off the deck of the *Alice,* trying to start the engine. Hours later he chugged down our side of the island, took a look and said he was on his way for the doctor.

Together, Ma Chevalier and Farrar delivered the baby, while the storm beat down, seeming always about to tear the tent from its moorings, but never quite succeeding. And out on the water a young man from Waldron went in the early morning to re-anchor his boat, let go of the oars for a moment, and the boat was whipped over by the wind with no one near to hear his shouts for help.

When, at four in the afternoon, the doctor came leaping up Sentinel, North was tucked away in his chicken crate behind the stove. Ma Chevalier had spanked him to life and everything was all right. The doctor took one look at me and said, "Ten dollars, please."

Sunny days came. Farrar put up fir-bough shelters outside and the baby and I were moved out where we could watch the wind in the trees and the tides tirelessly ebbing and flowing. Later, we scooped a little place in the hill on the south side where the sun stayed the longest, and North lay for hours on fir boughs, his eyes sheltered and the rest of him in the sun.

There are fierce northeasters in the Puget Sound country and the boats go about for a day or so sheathed in ice, and top-heavy. And gales blow. But winter never lasts long up there. Spring is edging in all the time.

In January the pussy willows were out. Alder catkins unfurled overnight. There were radiant warm days. That year, spring came early, and North and I were out of doors most of the time.

In May, word came that Farrar's mother was dying. Could we come? She wanted to see her only grandchild. They didn't know we had spent all our money and had no way of getting there. We sold everything we owned to Dad Chevalier for a hundred dollars, but left Nanny and a new mate we had bought for her on the Island to shift for themselves.

And so we left Sentinel for the second time, this time not knowing where the future would take us. But we had won our homestead. Because of Farrar's two years of naval service, we had only to live on it for seven months and show certain elementary improvements, which our shack amply fulfilled. Thus the gumdrop became our own. And Farrar says it is the taxes on Sentinel that keep his nose to the grindstone. They are a dollar and a half a year.

XIII. AMERICA BY CART AND DONKEY

AFTER Farrar's mother died in Van Buren, we were stranded. We had no money, no home, no plans. But we were confident that adventure lay in wait for us. We still saw no reason for abandoning our plan of retiring first, seeing America while we were footloose, and bringing up our children to school age in the very lap of adventure. There would be years, decades of time for settling down, when North was seven and had to go to school.

North was strong and well. We fed, slept, bathed, and handled him by the book. I stood fiercely by my conviction that my children should have perfect care, no matter where we went, or what we did, and perfect care meant schedules and an awful lot of soap and water.

The baby, then, was ready for whatever turned up for us. We talked of going to South America, or starting on our long-dreamed-of covered-wagon trip over the United States, stopping beside the rivers we loved, camping in hickory-nut groves in the south, sugar-maple groves in the north, white-oak, tulip-poplar, beech, long-leaved-pine groves wherever they were. It was impossible to dream hard of Africa or Spanish America, or even the South Sea islands, when we longed to see again and again the woods and rivers and hills we had known as children.

"But we have no money," said Farrar. "We haven't a horse or wagon. I'll have to get a job until we can outfit ourselves again."

"We can sell the ivory collection," I said, and struck fire.

Farrar went up to St. Louis to exhibit the collection, and made talks in a department store there about the Eskimos. The St. Louis *Post-Dispatch* ran a big story about the Alaska year, and Farrar sold the two white fox furs we had brought out, for enough to outfit us, without having to break up the rest of the collection.

Meanwhile, I got myself into one of my own special scrapes. In Van Buren, the heat was affecting both the baby and me, and I decided to join Farrar. It was a simple matter for us to board an early-morning train for St. Louis. I had exactly fifty cents. When the conductor came for my ticket, I told him that my husband would pay at the other end of the line. At least, I hoped he would. I didn't know then whether or not he had made the sale.

"But I only go halfway," said the conductor. "There's another man the rest of the way."

I hadn't thought of that. The conductor was worried about the outcome. "I tell you what," he said. "I'll lend you the money for the other half of the way. The other conductor would never let you through." Which he did, and by the time I reached St. Louis, Farrar had sold his furs and could return the money.

I shall never forget how Farrar looked at me when he learned that I had come without any money. Even he hadn't dreamed that I would do a thing like that. From then on, I was a kind of stranger whose actions he couldn't predict.

Meanwhile, I had been re-reading Stevenson's *Travels with a Donkey*, and I was all for reducing our covered wagon to a cart for the baby, and buying a donkey which could live on grass along the way while Farrar and I walked across America.

We had seventy-five dollars with which to buy cart, donkey, camping equipment, and clothes for ourselves.

Farrar went to a mule market in St. Louis and found a big jennet for which he paid fifteen dollars. We named her Sally Fanny, and set out to find a two-wheeled cart. At last we turned it up at an old blacksmith shop, had oak bows made for it, and a canvas cover with a tight cupboard built on behind with a lid that let down to become a table. Buckets, tools, and our sacks of ivory hung down below the bed of the cart. Not the entire collection of ivory, however—we left most of it in storage with our clothes in St. Louis, taking along only rough ivory for trading on the way. We also took an army pup tent with the regulation mosquito netting to fit inside it for sleeping right on the ground.

What a sight we must have been, jogging out of St. Louis! Farrar and I walked ahead to set the pace for Sally Fanny, who would have ambled like a somnambulist if we hadn't, except when she took a mischievous spell and wanted to run away. Behind us the mouse-colored donkey clopped happily along, silken ears moving as though they were on swivels. She was listening for sounds from the cart, I think, for after a few days she seemed to know when the baby was sleeping or sitting up and looking about, and adjusted her pace to his rhythm.

June, holding North, and Farrar with the Donkey Cart.

Behind the donkey, the canvas-covered cart cluttered with buckets and tools—a peripatetic bassinet—the big-eyed baby sitting in the cool shade of the top, his hands grasping the sides of the cart bed, his head bobbing.

Idyllic days. I think we had never been happier, and never have been since. The baby made it more romantic, somehow—he was the kernel, the very nucleus of the adventure.

We made about ten miles a day. In the morning we fed and bathed the baby, prepared breakfast and extra bottles for the day. Farrar tidied camp, took down the tent, rolled up the bedding and made the cart ready to receive its occupant. By the time we were ready to leave, the baby was ready for his morning nap, jogging along the road.

At noon, the baby had his vegetables and a sunbath for a few minutes, after which he would play on his tarpaulin under the shade of a tree while we had lunch and rested. We stopped early for evening camp, and then I did the baby's daily washing, boiling everything within an inch of its life in the silly notion that we might be picking up all kinds of strange germs. We kept that baby so nearly sterile it is a wonder he didn't catch everything, having no chance at all to build up natural immunity.

Sally Fanny did her grazing in the evenings, too. We would stake her out wherever there was grass and she would snip, snip until long after we were asleep and would be snipping away the next morning when we awoke.

What nights of sleep! At first the ground seems a hard bed. But after two or three nights, the body seems to achieve a catlike ease of relaxation. The earth absorbs pains and infections and ailments. Go to bed however weary or dispirited and the earth will take it out of you. You sink down and down into a sleep that is like a rebirth, and awaken refreshed and healed.

Because we had no money, we stopped every now and then while Farrar did a day's work for enough to carry us for a few more days. We needed little for we bought things at farm prices. But if there was some especially good digging to be done, we would stay for two or three days, and Farrar would make as much as nine dollars. He loved to do road work with pick and shovel.

Once we camped for two or three days in a little public grove just outside a town. A little dog came sniffing up to investigate us.

"Come in," Farrar said. "You'll like it here. We live the nicest dog's life you ever heard of."

The curly-haired black dog stayed with us all that day, and then a man came to take him home. The next day he was back again and again the man came. On the third day the man said, "His name is Teddy—you can have him," and giving the little dog a last friendly pat, he went off and Teddy stayed with us.

After that, we had a little black dog running along beside our gangling jennet. The baby liked him, but Teddy didn't like the baths he began to get. Farrar called me the washingest woman he ever saw. "You'll wash away all their natural oil," he said, and I laughed. If the baby was going to play with Teddy, I thought, the dog had to be sanitary.

Now, I'd let them both alone and save myself a lot of trouble.

Illinois and Indiana are riverful states. Every little while we'd cross a beautiful, clear stream, often so shallow there was no bridge across it. Whenever we could, we made camp on the bank of a stream and I would do my washing in it, the cool water running over my feet.

June washing the baby's diapers.

It was midsummer—high slack tide of the year. The ground was hot underfoot, the air hot, the sky poured heat down over us. But it was nearly always cool in the shade, and at nights we often slept under cover.

Of course, a good many people stopped to ask us questions. Once a man and woman in a big car went past waving gaily at us. After awhile, they came back. They stopped. They had returned to ask us if we wouldn't sell our donkey and go with them to California. We looked so happy, they said—a boy and a girl, a baby and a dog—they wanted us to come and be their family.

"But we're happy because we live like this, not in spite of it," Farrar told them. "If we went with you and changed our ways, maybe we'd be lonesome, too. You sell your car and come with us." But they couldn't quite see that.

All that afternoon they stayed with us, talking and reasoning. The surer we were that we knew what we were doing, the more they wanted us for that very sureness. They left, along about dusk, driving off again in the direction in which they had first been going.

Once we camped over Saturday night in a beautiful grove around what seemed to be an abandoned building of some sort. It was so nice there that we decided to stay over Sunday and do our weekly wash and dry it on bushes everywhere.

We were just starting the next morning, when someone drove into the grove. Then another car came, and a surrey. Everyone came straight to our campfire to see what we were doing there, and we found out that the building was a meeting house. Services were to be held that day, they said. We certainly couldn't hang out a washing now. But we could stay. There was going to be a returned missionary who would preach or talk. Why not stay and listen to her, they said.

By ten o'clock or so, our campfire was surrounded with people. Then the missionary arrived. A spare, tall, thin woman. She took one look at the crowd around our fire, the laughing faces, our shabbiness, the donkey and cart and—a helpless baby—and marched over to set us to rights.

The poor zealot jumped to the conclusion that these shabby people were poor in spirit; that the man with a guitar was a shabby character at best; that a woman who would traipse around like this with a baby couldn't amount to much.

The cards were stacked against her, of course. We were the underdogs and the crowd was with us from the time of man. But because she goaded me, I put her in the wrong, ever so gently at first, then more obviously and cruelly for I knew the Bible as well as she and could meet her on her own ground—I am ashamed to remember how I stripped her naked there in front of her own people. She went away at last, into the church, walking defiantly like a hurt and bewildered child, and the people laughed and thought how clever we were. It took me years to understand that I had behaved precisely as shabbily as I was dressed.

After the quarrel, we had a host of invitations to go home with people for dinner. But the grove had lost its sweetness for us and we left.

It never rains but it pours. Not long after that we stopped in a town park, I to rest while Farrar went to a store for a few things we needed. As always when we didn't keep moving through a town, the people began to cluster around. There must have been a lot of missionaries or "good" people in that town, for pretty soon we found ourselves about to lose our baby. They seemed, with one accord, to decide that we weren't to be trusted with a baby. I talked as I'd never talked before, and if they were a chastened lot at the end, I was a badly frightened woman, sick and shaken.

In Terre Haute, Indiana, Farrar found a job that paid so well, he decided to work at it for ten days and make enough to last us without stopping again. If we were going to reach Washington before winter, we would have to travel right along. We decided that I would go on with the donkey and baby and dog, while Farrar stayed behind. I'd probably get as far as Indianapolis in ten days, and he could overtake me on the interurban trolley between the two towns in two hours or so.

There is something about aloneness that gives new flavor and color to an experience. Walking alone in front of Sally Fanny, I felt like a different person from the one who had walked with Farrar. Alone, I went to farmhouses to ask permission to camp in groves, or to buy milk and vegetables, and felt curiously naked. Alone, I pitched the tent and made our camp, looked after the baby and the animals, and felt like a pioneer.

Walking alone, I had a sense of identity with the trees and grass and fields and fences and streams. Aloneness closed me in, wrapped me around with a kind of shroud yet—pleasure was deeper, too. I was drawn closer to everything. My senses had time and leisure to take in the beauty afforded at the tip of every blade of grass, shaken down from every leaf.

Once, though, a man followed me for miles along the road. He was in a little store where I had stopped to buy some things. The storekeeper had asked all the usual questions, and I had given the usual answers, explaining that my husband had stopped in Terre Haute for a few days.

When I went on, the man was walking along beside me. He said he was going over the next hill to see his sister. When he didn't stop there, I was surprised, but he said it was the next hill, and we went on. After miles of this, I decided something must be wrong. "It's just down there," he said, pointing to a grove of trees, and we went on down still another hill. There was no house there. I stopped. I was frightened. Beating him to whatever draw he was about to make I said, "I have an ax back here. I'm going to get it just in case," and he moved on off into the grove and left me trembling beside Sally Fanny.

Just then a girl came driving a horse and buckboard. I stopped and asked her whether she would drive slowly for a few miles. I was frightened. It was by now nearly dark. She said of course she would, and asked me to go home with her and camp in their grove, which I did. That is the nearest I have ever come to any kind of personal danger in my life, though I have been in lonelier places than that, with loggers, fishermen, hunters, foresters, Coast Guardsmen, miners, even drunks.

It had taken us over a month to get from St. Louis to Indianapolis, a distance of less than three hundred miles, where after ten days in Terre Haute Farrar rejoined us. The next morning we couldn't find Sally Fanny. We searched everywhere. Finally a small boy came along and said his father had heard the trolley hit something in the night. Maybe it was our donkey. Farrar began to search the ditch on the other side of the tracks, and there lay Sally Fanny. Our great adventure was over.

No, not quite. Farrar said he'd pull the cart and baby. It ought to be easy. So he cut off the shafts and rigged up the harness to fit himself. We started off and he pulled the cart within twenty miles of Dayton, Ohio-nearly a hundred miles. "I made better time than the other donkey," he said.

But the highway was tarred and graveled instead of paved. We struck a long stretch of heat-softened tar. It stuck to the wheels. It stuck to our feet. All Ohio seemed to be uphill. The fun turned to hardship and we didn't know what to do about it.

Once a big truck came along and the driver gave us a lift. We were with him half an hour but we gained two days in distance.

One day we stopped beside the road in the shade. Pretty soon a little boy eased out of the bushes across the road and over to us. He went up to the cart and examined it.

"A cart!" he said. "I've wanted a cart all my life, for my pony."

"Well, sonny, the cart's yours," Farrar said and startled the little boy. "I mean it. I'll get our things out and you may have the cart. All you have to do around here is wish, and it comes true. What else do you want?"

"I'll have to ask my grandfather first," he said. When he came back, he had fifty cents. "My grandfather says you must take this for the cart. He says I mustn't take it for nothing. And you are to make me out a bill of sale."

So Farrar made out a bill of sale for the cart and harness, and away went the little boy, pulling Sally Fanny's cart behind him.

Now we felt better. We were free. But our things were piled up around us and we had no idea how we were going to get any further.

When along came Texas Slim and Montana Nell. Two enormous vans drove up alongside us and stopped. They were show trucks. "The Champion Knife Throwers of the World," said the banner on the front van. They took us in, baby and baggage, and we rode with them to Dayton and spent that night in their big truck,

We had about sixty dollars, with the money Farrar had earned in Terre Haute and ten dollars he had got from the railroad company in Indianapolis for our donkey. We decided we had better spend our money for tickets to Washington. There Farrar could get work until he earned enough to pay the express on our trunks.

It was September when we reached Washington—ordinarily a summer month there. But not that year. It was cold. And it was night. We were so nearly broke we dared not go to a hotel. And in our state of shabbiness we were ashamed to go to our friends.

We took a streetcar out to Glen Echo, struck up into our old familiar woods, and in the pitch dark made camp there in a white-oak grove. The baby was asleep, wrapped in everything we had to put around him. Farrar and I had no coats. We wore summer-weight camp garb, and our teeth were chattering.

When we crawled out of the pup tent next morning we were surrounded by our old familiar Maryland woods—tulip poplars, white oaks, beeches, sycamores. There was the brook, still singing. Just around the next bend was the slope on which the laurels had bloomed three summers before. We made our campfire breakfast beside the brook, the fragrant smoke rising, yellow leaves falling, the baby crowing happily and eager for the new day.

XIV. IN WHICH WE KICK OVER THE TRACES

OUR old cabin in the woods was occupied and North was two years old before it was vacated and we could move into it. Farrar got a job at common labor until we could send for our things. When they came, we took turns going in to the city to see who could get a job first. I won, by a hair, and Farrar became what he called a house-husband. He stayed home and took care of the baby.

We found a cottage with a fireplace near Bethesda, a suburb of Washington, and here Farrar held carefully to the schedule of diet, baths, naps, and washings.

It was our first taste of working at separate jobs, one of us in business, the other at home. It was fun, at first, but after a while Farrar said that being a house-husband wasn't using his mental energies while it took too much of his time—the ancient complaint. He voted for an apartment in town with a nursemaid; he was going to find a job, too. First, however, he decided to go to New York and sell the ivory collection and three-tusk walrus head, so as to clear decks for the next adventure and put aside some money for the birth of the next baby.

In New York he found a newspaper job on the Brooklyn Standard Union and for six months or so we stuck out our separation for the purpose of recouping finances. But they didn't recoup worth a cent. New York and Washington are expensive cities to live in. Farrar and I made the same amount of money and when he joined me in Washington, we had saved equal amounts—nothing, and had used up the proceeds from the Alaska collection beside.

By that time the cabin in the woods was vacant and we moved in. I gave up my job to prepare for the second baby. North loved the cabin as we did, going with me to the spring, helping to milk old Chloe, digging in the garden, bringing in wood, eating so many blackberries he began to look purple all through.

Our second son was born in one of the best hospitals in the country—where he got an eye infection which lasted several years, for our expensive pains!

From the first both children objected to coddling, and seemed poised for flight from the home nest before they had a feather to their names. When he was still a little fellow, our second child even rejected the name we had given him and one day, for no reason at all, said, "I will be called Bobby," and Bob he has remained.

North was twenty-nine months old when his brother was born, and asking the eternally unanswerable baby questions. Where is tomorrow, now? Try to answer that with careful honesty so that a two-year-old can understand it. Where has yesterday gone? Why is this a cabbage and that a tomato? Scientists have nibbled at that one since time began. I said, "In five thousand years, nobody has discovered why. When you are a man, perhaps you will find out." When he asked, "How long is five thousand years?" I rattled some pans so as not to have heard.

Farrar and I had fallen into bad ways. He got a job selling advertising for a daily in Washington. We began to read advertising books by the score. At night we would write sample ads for his prospects and the next day Farrar would land them. That led us, naturally, into studying all kinds of businesses: clothing stores, markets, retail selling in general, merchandising problems, the automobile business, management of banks and real estate and optical firms.

We plunged into it so wholeheartedly that we became excited over this new subject of business. Why, men weren't simply after money! There was adventure in business! We moved back to town, we began to spend money, we went into debt. The books said you had to get into debt to establish your credit—for that is the kind of thing they published in the twenties. We swallowed it all. Farrar's forty dollars a week ceased to be adequate and dwindled to the merest pittance. I had to earn money, too.

I began to write sales letters.

The editor of one of the national advertising magazines took an interest in me, gave me advertising space, and I began to get a few clients. But we were going into debt faster than we were earning money. Once start going down hill like that, and it is a lot harder to get back up to zero than it would have been to stay at zero in the first place. Fortunately, while we were going into debt, we were really learning something about business methods. We had grown so excited over this new game that we decided to plunge in for a few years, clear off our debts, and show our families that we could make money if we had to. But chiefly we determined to have the time of our lives at this new adventure. We didn't say a word about what would become of the children. Not a word about our plan of living rich, simple, free lives as long as we could.

Somehow though, we didn't plan to plug away at the jobs we had—to make them grow and grow and yield success. We picked California as the greenest field, the farthest away. There, we would go into business.

I wrote a series of collection letters for a jeweler in South Carolina, got a hundred and twenty-five dollars for them, and set out with the babies for California. Farrar hitchhiked, leaving Washington without a cent and arriving in California, sixteen days later, with five dollars in his pocket, which he had made by singing and selling one of his songs along the way.

Farrar had taken a freight car across the desert, and for three days and nights he was without food or water. His car was sidetracked out of Sacramento and he went on in to the city. He bought a glass of milk and was standing on a corner waiting for his strength to flow back when a newsman, seeing his emaciated, hollow-eyed look, offered to buy him a meal. Farrar explained that he had money but must wait a while to eat all he wanted.

Meanwhile, in San Francisco, I had the fabulous luck of being asked to speak at an advertising convention on the art of writing sales letters. Advertising men from all over the country would be there and, if I spoke well, it probably meant the offer of the best job I had ever had. And so it turned out. I became copy chief of a direct-mail advertising firm in San Francisco.

Separated again. This business game didn't always seem to play fair.

But we were making eight thousand dollars a year, and I stayed where I was until we had cleared up our debts back East, and were up to zero once more. But I didn't propose to go on being separated. There was no fun in anything unless we could be together. Farrar was making more—he was manager of the biggest food market in Sacramento—so I joined him to become his advertising manager at no salary. (When he is running somebody else's business, he goes Scotch with a vengeance.)

What a good time we had, running that market! Fragrance of coffee, fruits, vegetables, fish, fowl, flesh, bakery goods, ice-cold buttermilk, cheeses, pickled fish and strawberries, sacks of feed for the farmers. Farrar used to stand at the rail on the mezzanine, looking down over his market, making a sing-song about the countries from which all that food came: nuts from Brazil, tea from the hills of Darjeeling, Cuban sugar, potatoes from Idaho, corn from Iowa, Virginia peanuts, California peaches, Texas beef, sardines from Norway, coffee from Guatemala and Costa Rica, and perhaps Arabia.

We published a little weekly leaflet in which I did a great deal of original experimenting with ways to interest the customers. I believed and proved that people will read a paper that is all advertising if it is written for them instead of for the product. I filled that paper with colorful, intimate details of the market, with nonsense and information, with personalities and news of new foods. We had fun with that paper, and gave it a lot of credit for taking the market out of the red and putting it over into the black in two years.

I was asked to come to Denver to speak to a national convention of advertisers. For the little paper had got a lot of publicity. That invitation was the straw that broke the back of our business camel. It was momentous. If I went, I was committed to advertising and business. I'd get another good offer which I couldn't turn down. Farrar would be committed, too, for I planned to talk mostly about his achievement at the market. He had put into it all his common sense, his genial ability to get along with people, his immense fund of new and fresh ideas. If I could have carried out all his ideas, I would still be talking at advertising conventions and Farrar would still be taking red businesses and making them black.

Characteristically, I accepted the Denver invitation first and thought

June and Farrar and their sons in Sacramento.

about it afterwards. What were we getting out of this business game? We were again making about eight thousand dollars a year, for I had taken on one or two other accounts in Sacramento. But what had we to show for it? A housekeeper-nursemaid. A comfortable house. Farrar had had some of his songs published. The children were well dressed and so were we.

Was this, then, the great life we were going to live? Were we giving the children what we had meant to give them? Had we anything to show for the time we had put into this money-earning business after the debts were paid off?

We wondered whether we hadn't given up more than we had gained during those two years in business. (We didn't count the three years in Washington, for those had been jobs which were necessary for our living while we waited for our second son.) We were tending to judge people by a batch of false standards now. We were neglecting our children. Somehow we had gone off the track for this money-making game before we really needed the money, and when we did need to give our time and leisure and attention, all the warmth and glow of our spirits to our children.

The upshot was that I wrote to Denver and asked them to find someone else to take my place.

It wasn't possible, however, to throw over the market in that cavalier fashion. The owners depended on Farrar. He must find some trustworthy, capable manager to take his place before we could be free again.

That year, in March, I took the boys up to Puget Sound to live in a cabin on Johns Island, near Sentinel, while Farrar worked himself out of his job. He hunted all over California to find the right man for the market which he had grown to love. When he did find his man, managing a small market in San Francisco, the prospective successor thought that anyone who would give away a five-thousand-a-year job to another man was strange beyond belief. He sent his wife to Sacramento to find out what it was all about. But she reported that all was well and the new manager took over his job. He is there yet, contented and prosperous.

For seven joyous, laughing months the boys and I camped on Johns Island. We were like children out of school. Farrar bought us a little motor

June's cruiser, the San Juanderer.

North rowing, Bob on rear seat.

cruiser, which six-year-old North learned to run, as he had learned to row the summer before. We went all over that country in the little white bird which we named the *San Juanderer*. We were so happy I couldn't contain it all. I queried the newspapers around the Sound, asking whether they would like me to write adventure stories in a daily column called "Puget Soundings." With one accord they turned it down.

Later on, when I got my chance at it, the column ran for three years, bringing in thousands of new subscribers to one of those very dailies, and tens of thousands of new friends for it and for me. Then, with one accord, they all wondered how they could have failed to see the possibilities when I had first presented the idea to them. This canny, non-gambling instinct in people robs them of a lot of good things. To take your chance whenever it bobs up is the way to run a business, as it is the way to live.

In September, Farrar wrote that we were to return to Sacramento. He had found his successor and he had a surprise for us. We put the cruiser in storage at Bellingham against our return to the islands, and the boys and I hurried to join Farrar.

A very dream of a little house on wheels.

He had built a house car! A very dream of a little house on wheels, built by a cabinet maker, but designed and painted and finished off by Farrar. It was an old 1922 Dodge. Farrar had the seat backs hinged to let down and become a lower bunk at night. For the upper bunk there were slats to go across the windowsills with beaver board over them to hold the boys' bedding. The attic, on top, held all bedding, tent, suitcases, odds and ends, beaver boards, slats. There was a lean-to on behind to hold camp equipment, typewriter, files, manuscripts and letters, and a correspondence course for North who was nearing seven and should be in school. This time we were going to leave nothing in storage.

Canvas-covered boxes on the running board held Farrar's seven thousand songs, for he was going to sing his way around the United States, selling his songs for a living, and hoping that some day a music publisher would hear him and say, "Come with me, young man."

The doors of the car were blue, the car bright yellow, the running boards the color of concrete, the chimney painted to look like bricks, the roof green. It was a fairy-tale house. Over the hood he built a front porch on which he was to stand and sing. Flower pots below the porch bloomed with artificial poppies, or something of the sort. On the eaves he had written, SINGS AND SELLS HIS OWN SONGS, and across the back of the lean-to, BURN'S BALLAD BUNGALOW.

The chimney was hinged so that it could be unhooked and lie flat when we drove under low bridges. Often, though, we forgot to unhook it, and then we would hear a great thump and know the hook had pulled out again and the chimney was down.

It was mid-September when we left Sacramento, two years and nine months since we had left Washington, D.C. We were practically down to zero, but that was the precise degree of riches that suited us best. We were on the right road again, bound for adventure, with sons old enough to enjoy it.

We planned to spend a year showing the boys their own land before they had to knuckle down at school. North had gone to kindergarten and I planned to teach him his first-grade work on the way so he wouldn't be behind the other children when he got back. As a matter of fact, individual instruction is so rapid that he was up with the third grade when he got back, and consequently gained rather than lost a year.

XV. BURN'S BALLAD BUNGALOW

FREE again. The good earth flows past our windows now. At night we stop wherever clear water runs and trees offer shelter. Down California's coast highway we go, our top-heavy little house swaying like a drunken longshoreman. Off to get acquainted with two little boys. To introduce them to their homeland. We would show them rivers and brooks, groves and hills, and—what they wanted most—snow.

I had had them inoculated against diphtheria, typhoid, typhus, and other things which I have forgotten now. They were both robust, though North had an oddly frail look. I believe he was what the books call an introvert, while Bobby was an extrovert like his father. North had a thin, wistful, sensitive face, while Bobby had a round, sunny, confident countenance; the one very slender, the other plump and sturdy. North would be seven in December, Bobby had been four in May. Both of them loved the earth in a personal way. North's interest took the practical form of learning to row a boat, cut wood, plant gardens. Bobby was utterly indifferent to work of all kinds. His delight was passive, but no less genuine than North's. It is nonsense to say that one must work for a thing in order to enjoy it. It is idiotic to suppose that we would treasure beauty or air to breathe or love more, if we had to sacrifice for them. It is the free things which are most precious. Even money itself. An inherited fortune can give more pleasure, find its possessor more prepared to enjoy it, with more leisure for that joy, than an earned fortune can do. We have rigged up that falsehood to trick ourselves into working when we don't want to.

How beautiful that California coast! The road runs along the top of a high bluff above the roaring surf. The Pacific Ocean charges in against the bluff, white mane tossing, blue hips amorously pushing, the continual wind screaming at them both like a jealous fishwife. Once in awhile the bluff suddenly disappears and you are driving almost along the beach itself, and become a part of that elemental turmoil.

Sometimes at night we stopped at auto camps for fifty cents, for we slept in our own car and didn't need to take a cabin. We didn't need to be economical this early for we still had something like a hundred and fifty dollars in the bank, but camping indoors wasn't one of the ways we liked to spend money.

Wherever we found a stream, we camped beside the road. And whenever we came to a National Forest, we would stop near a spring, under tall redwood trees, or pines, the boys eagerly hunting cones and all the woods treasure which children know about. If the camp were beautiful, and all hands were enjoying it, we would stay for several days, and Farrar would paraphrase an ancient Chinese song:

> *When husband, wife and children are one*
> *'Tis like the harp and lute in unison.*
> *When a family lives in concord and at peace*
> *The strain of harmony shall never cease.*
> *The lamp of happy union lights the home*
> *And bright days follow when the children come.*

June and North homeschooling.

"Our children have come and the bright days are with us," he said.

In the mornings, before we started the day's journey, I taught North. He was learning to write, to spell, and to do sums. We would sit on a log, hunkered over our books, or behind the car, using the door of the lean-to as a table. Bobby was never far away, looking on wistfully, for he wanted lessons, too. I thought then that he was too young, but now I am sorry I didn't give them to him while he wanted to learn. For by the time we let him go to school, he was inexpressibly bored by the simpers of women teaching small children in the "Now, children" manner. He was years finding himself. How little we understand our children. And when we begin to catch a glimmer, it is too late—the damned too-lateness of things in general.

In dazzling San Diego Farrar drove out to a carnival and made his first money, selling songs—two or three dollars—and brought it back like a foxtail, as a trophy.

Now we were seeing the orange groves of California, blossoms, ripe fruit, green fruit, all on the trees at the same time. There had been orange groves not far from Sacramento, but we hadn't seen them. How fragrant the air of Southern California! You move in a golden bath of sunshine, perfumed, sweet. People, movies, planes, automobiles, trains, lizards crawl obscurely over that land and still the desert shimmers there, mysterious and unmarked.

The desert of the Southwest is more than a thousand miles across, as the crow flies. Except for the towns, irrigated strips, valleys of rivers that do not dry up in summer, and the mountains, it is all desert; some of it blinding white sand dunes; some of it gray volcanic ash, alkaline and harsh; some of it miles of broken rock with greasewood clumps between. There were times when we longed to spend the rest of our lives wandering in and out of barren ranges of upheaved snags of earth at the desert's edge.

The fascination of the desert doesn't lie in beauty of the ordinary sort. I think it lies in the sheer scarcity of things. Each drop of water is precious, each flower so quickly gone that you fairly fling your heart around it. In the desert you would tend and cherish one geranium, hoarding water for it, watching it blaze against the dry whiteness all around it. You would love the cool sunrises, drinking in their beauty before it turned to a blinding glare. Each thing of beauty there stands out separate, to be wholly loved, never taken for granted, like a bride, or a baby, or sight after long blindness.

In 1928, the road across the desert was unpaved. We drove over dim tracks in the sand, hoping they were the right ones. Sometimes they weren't, and we would have to go back and hunt for other tracks to follow.

Camping on the desert was pure delight. If there was no wood, we broke off clumps of greasewood and kept a fire going long enough for a meal. We needed the fires, for it was always cold at night, however hot the day had been.

The boys scouted around for miles, once bringing in armloads of surveyors' stakes which they had pulled up along the new highway. Farrar, once an engineer, was troubled at that, but we burned them and they warmed us.

We killed many rabbits. They came out at sundown and Farrar took the handsome new twenty-two special, which he had given me for use up in the islands, and stalked out after game, the boys and I following at a little distance to watch.

In Phoenix, Arizona, Farrar made fifteen dollars, driving his car around the city to advertise a show at one of the theaters. Then, under the momentum of success, he sold twelve dollars' worth of his songs to one of the chain stores. We drove out of Phoenix in triumph. Ever since we have remembered it as one of the loveliest cities in the world.

It was toward the end of October that we went to Grand Canyon. The greenery on those skirt-like ledges of the big ditch had taken on fall colors, the summer mists had gone, the keen, clear air was like a sharp lens to magnify the grandeur. Because it was so late in the season, there were few people there. The rock wall hadn't yet been built.

On that first early morning when we walked over to look down on splendor such as we hadn't imagined, North said, "This must be the most beautiful thing in the world, Mother. We might as well drive our car into it and die right here." I had been thinking the same thing; it startled me to hear him echo it.

We had driven on up the Canyon to the east, and camped overnight

On the road in the Ballad Bungalow.

beside the rim, near what is now the observation tower. A group of horsemen came along to look at our car and talk awhile: geologists, photographers, scientists, nearly a score of them. They had come from Bryce Canyon in Utah, to explore still unknown reaches of Grand Canyon. We liked them and they liked us. The next morning they invited us to store our car and go with them. They would get four more horses and we could join forces.

"Are you serious—you'd take us—small children and all?"

Yes, they said. They would enjoy the children. They would like to have Farrar's guitar. And they would love to have a woman along to do the cooking. I'd certainly get the heavy end of this deal, but it was I who most wanted to go. Horses down a canyon bed, exploring. The very guts of earth. Oh, I wanted to go! But I didn't say so.

We told them that we would join them next year, and they said the invitation would still hold. But by the following year another adventure had pushed that one off the boards and we have never seen them since, though I dream of finding them yet and going exploring.

If I live as long as the Wandering Jew, I shan't forget our camp on the Painted Desert, below Grand Canyon, or find words for that beauty trembling over the earth from horizon to horizon. The road seemed to wind over dunes and down dunes, over rocky plateaus, into soup-plate depressions where the colored air, above varicolored sands, thickened and darkened to richer purple and rose. The petrified forest wasn't far away. The sands came in the beautiful colors of those flint logs. The children were eager to see wood that was rock.

The sunset was a bouquet in the sky, the colors washing us and all the world around. On top of one of the curious rocky plateaus we pitched our camp for the night. As we stepped out of the car, North picked up a rock that had once been a chip. "Here's some petrified wood, Mother," he cried, recognizing it at once in the prescient way he had. He and Bobby set to work gathering wood for our fire that might have burned fifty thousand years ago, while Farrar and I scouted around for a few contemporary sticks. We never failed to find something to burn, if only dried cow pats.

All around us the world lay still and dark. We made a fire, had something to eat, put the children to bed, and sat talking low, watching the stars come out in the soft purple blackness overhead.

Then we heard a great noise, coming like waves over the desert. "Whoop! Whoop!" the cowboys shouted at their herds. A thousand cows lowed plaintively, calves bawled. They were hungry and tired. We couldn't see them, but after a while we knew that they had stopped in the wide, round, valley-like depression below us. Presently campfires gleamed in the dark. Then they died out and the herd and men slept. Late that night a coyote bayed us awake, and we looked out to see a moon-washed land, eerily white and still.

Farrar's original sheet music.

All over that country the Navajo Indians grazed their sheep. We couldn't see much grass for the animals to eat, but once in a while we saw an Indian on a pony standing perfectly still on top of a knoll, as though posing for one of those railroad pictures, his stilly grazing sheep looking like clumps of gray sagebrush over the undulating desert.

By now, of course, we had run out of money, though we did leave a few dollars in the bank for some unguessed emergency. And the boys had a few dollars in their bank which they were saving for a dog when we should find him.

At every town, Farrar sold enough songs to carry us on to the next one, though he hadn't the courage to stand on his platform to sing.

We lived a life of easy hardship all that year. It is a curious thing that physical hardship is so often spiritual ease—short of desperate want, of course. There must have been plenty of quarrels and disagreements, but for the life of me, I can't remember them.

There came a stretch of desert and mountains and no towns at all. At least the towns were too small to be interested in wandering minstrels.

Farrar's (aka "Bub's") original sheet music.

Our engine developed trouble. We leaked gas and oil for a long time before we discovered it. On top of a hill somewhere in New Mexico, we ran out of gas. We hadn't a cent. There was no town within miles. But we were on top of a hill. We could coast down. No telling what might lie at the foot. So we coasted, and our momentum gave out within pushing distance of a gasoline station in a pocket of the hills.

"You may have our money, Dad," the boys said at once. We were saved. We filled the tank, replenished the oil, stopped the leaks. We could make the next town where Farrar would make the next batch of money. And we did.

We had many close shaves like that. And shaves are a lot closer with a car than with a self-supporting donkey. In New Mexico there are a good many small towns, but they were so full of Mexicans to whom guitar playing and songs were everyday things, and who were so poor anyway you couldn't have sold them a song to save your life. We scraped through that state by the skin of our teeth.

Another time when we were flat broke, and no money in the boys' bank either, we drove into a government camp on the Great Divide. It was November and snow and ice covered the ground. We drove in under the pines, parked the car under a maple tree with beautiful leaves that kept falling, and which the children gathered with delight to show us. We had a few potatoes, some canned tomatoes which I kept on hand for the children, enough butter for supper and canned milk and cereal for breakfast. Then our food would be gone.

It began to sleet. Farrar cut some rich, pitchy chunks out of a stump and built a good fire. We ate buttery potatoes and tomatoes and went to bed, cozy and secretly happy, the way you are when you know that things can't get any worse and therefore something has got to happen.

In the morning it was still sleeting but we didn't pitch the tent. Farrar made another big fire and I made the mush. We ate the hot food and began to put our things away for traveling. North was still scratching around among the colorful leaves under the maple tree.

"Here's a dollar," he said casually.

Farrar made a leap and grabbed the dollar before he remembered that it wasn't his.

"We're saved," he shouted. Gasoline was three gallons for a dollar at the ranger station. Three gallons, added to whatever we had in our tank that read zero, would take us on to the next town.

Farrar went up to the station for some water. Bobby went with him. "Norshy found a dollar," he told the man.

"Did you really find a dollar?" the man asked, and Farrar ruefully admitted it.

"A man from Spokane, Washington, lost it. He hunted it for half a day. We promised to send it to him if it was ever found."

Farrar breathed again. "We'll borrow it," he said, and took the man's name. We carried that name clear around the United States and meant to drive into Spokane some day and surprise the owner with his dollar. But by the time we reached Spokane, we had lost the name, and to this day we are still borrowing the dollar. Are you there, man from Spokane? Speak up and claim your dollar!

Advertisement for the Burn Ballad Bungalow.

XVI. WINTER SUNSHINE

IN TEXAS, the desert grows wilder and rougher, less sandy, more rocky, the old brown bones of earth jagging up everywhere. Pencil cedar flourishes here and the air is fragrant with its incense. Towns appear more frequently and the people begin to seem like kinfolks. Bow-legged cowboys swagger across the main streets of little towns, with that innocent look which cowboys have.

Pecos, Texas, was a small town, but it was lively. The theater there booked Farrar for the evening. We made ten or fifteen dollars, bought supplies and moved on.

About thirty miles out of Pecos, we had a flat tire—one of hundreds. While we stopped on the side of the road, the boys and I strolled ahead, hunting pebbles. Two cowboys, who had been hunting wild horses, rode up to talk to Farrar who was bending over the spare tire, hammering in the rim, which hadn't been put on securely at some garage. Suddenly the cowboys yelled to me. I turned to see Farrar staggering to the car, with blood streaming from his head. The tire had blown out, driving the rim into his head.

We got out clean rags, staunched the blood, and one of the cowboys flagged a car going back to Pecos. Taking along the tire and a water bucket Farrar got into the car, his wound gushing blood at every movement of his head. Back in Pecos, he walked from the highway to the hospital, found a doctor who was just finishing an operation. "Don't take your things off, doctor. Sew me up," he said.

With his head sewed up, Farrar walked back to the garage where he had left the tire, filled the bucket with water and waited for a car going his way. What agony he must have suffered when the numbness was gone and he bounced back in the car, holding the bucket of water off the floor so it wouldn't slop. That night we camped on the side of the desert, and drove on the next morning. Ever since then Farrar has worn a scar over his right eye.

What a big state Texas is! Like California, it offers desert and lush valleys, hills, tropics, temperate zone, marshland, and nearly anything else to order.

We crossed from mesquite to pecan groves, turning north at Dallas to visit some of Farrar's relatives in Oklahoma. It was November and the pecan harvest was in. There were bushels of the sweet, rich nuts. They were not like the rancid, sharp nuts which are sold, polished and waxed, in the stores. The dull, gray-colored ones are fresher. They haven't been treated to hold in the moisture.

Not far from Hugo, Oklahoma, we found one of the things we had come to see. One evening, at camping time, we drove into a likely-looking grove. Hickory woods. Few of the leaves had fallen, for this was low country. But they were a bright, clear yellow. As we entered the grove, the sun burst through an opening, struck fire from the golden leaves, and the

Camped beside the road.

four of us were drenched in a shower of color. The children shouted and ran wildly around as they do sometimes in a summer rainstorm, excited and happy. Under the trees we found hickory nuts, and when the quick, complete dark of the woods swept in on us, we built a fire, watching the leaves tossing about overhead where the heat of our fire set up air currents.

In Texarkana, on the line between Texas and Arkansas, our car broke down completely. It had been giving us warnings for a thousand miles, but we hadn't heeded them. Now the whole rear end of the thing dropped out. How on earth could we sing and sell enough songs to buy a new universal? From a bank there, Farrar borrowed on his bonus, and we camped in a beautiful oak grove while the car was being fixed. Then south again, driving toward New Orleans, which I had never seen.

Below Baton Rouge, Louisiana, we entered a world utterly new to me. Land of gray-beard trees and a silent, sneaky river like a brown ocean just over the levee. We drove along below the river's level. I could feel it there licking its chops. The levee had a look of melting softness. "I'd hold my finger in the dike like the little boy in Holland," North said.

We had come again into a country where people swept their yards as we used to do in Alabama, instead of mowing them as people do in California. Here there is so much water the ground is sour with it, slick, bare, not a sprig of grass to be seen, though an occasional rag of a poinsettia hangs on a stick beside the steps of a shanty. I am speaking of the yards of the poor, of course. Well-to-do people live much the same everywhere. It is by the customs of the poor that you tell the towns apart.

In many Louisiana towns we saw patent-medicine men plying their ancient trade, selling dollar bottles of tonic to laboring men who only made a dollar a day in the sawmills. It seemed incredible, having just come from California, that men with families were working for a dollar a day in booming 1928. They needed the tonics. They all looked emaciated, sallow, stooped, with barely enough ambition left to laugh at the medicine man's humor.

We had forgotten that this could be in our America. It was the first time I had ever met labor exploitation face to face. I was shocked to my roots and so were the children.

We'd sell no songs in this land! Sing to them, if those dull ears were thirsty for song. But not for money. Pawn the new gun. Pawn the fine camera and get out of here. Get out before you explode.

Farrar remembered New Orleans from his boyhood, as some fairy dream. And I remember it like that now. For here poverty was tucked away in its separate part of town. Anyhow, it wouldn't have been the lonely poverty of little towns. People in cities do manage to live better, more healthful lives, with more normal fun and companionship than people in company-owned small towns, whatever may be said of small-town life in general. We saw no hopeless-looking people along those bowered streets.

Parks and bayous and bridges, giant oaks, with long whiskers to their knees. And that river. While Farrar sold songs, the boys and I wandered into the "Quarter" and on to the river to watch bananas coming off the ships on the endless chain that is a line of Negroes going in at one opening of the ship, coming out another. We tiptoed around those mysterious docks, in between bales of things, keeping out of the way of the workmen. We felt the river, we saw the ships, we smelled and tasted the old romance.

We camped about five miles out of New Orleans in an auto camp built near a farm where freak circus animals were kept over the winter. Dirty, unhappy-looking monstrosities with six legs, two heads, extra odds and ends of things hanging off them anywhere. That glutton-bellied river went its greasy way a full ten feet above us. The levee was bank full. It rained and rained.

The Mississippi is no father of mine, but an evil, bleary-eyed old roue of an uncle, forever going on a drunken spree and raising Cain with peaceable folks. The rivers of the South, red with the loam of dying farms, silently, inexorably going along, paying no attention to anybody— deep, muddy, spooky rivers—are horribly fascinating, but who could love them? Give me the ocean and brooks and merry mountain rivers, man-controlled, serving man.

In New Orleans Farrar got a job playing Santa Claus for a music house. Nobody ever looked the part better, with his jovial, red face. In costume, with the little house to give him background, he went to the schools and up and down New Orleans streets for ten days. He got a hundred and fifty dollars. We could have Christmas, too.

At Thanksgiving we had been so broke that we had eaten one can of hominy for dinner, searching the woods for pecans. The children had had their canned tomatoes as usual, but they were beginning to look a bit thin. Now we were able to let them hang up their stockings, knowing that Santa Claus would fill them.

From New Orleans to Alabama the highway skirts the gulf. We drove to Mobile, Alabama. Here there were Negroes, ships, bananas a dime a dozen, and sunshine—a lovely city with a shade of nostalgia to sharpen its beauty. Alabama is my own state and I had not seen it for sixteen years. I hadn't remembered that people looked hungry in Alabama. Concave people, concave faces and bodies. The Negroes merry over nothing, the white people pale for all the sunshine pouring down on them. A woman sweeping her yard with a bundle of sticks tied together. I had done it often enough in my childhood. Why did it look so pathetic now? Perhaps it was the contrast between the well-fed, healthy North and this unremembered poverty of the South that made everything here seem sad. It is strange, though, that happiness plus sorrow is keener than happiness alone. Why should it be? Is sorrow, then, our native element? Does our soul remember it as our blood remembers the sea?

Swarming memories almost crowded me off the Alabama ferries. We would drive along a red-clay road, slip and slide over the brow of a steep hill that was the bank of a sudden river. It would fall away straight down into the water, and the boys would catch their breath. But there, tucked up against the bank, would be an engineless ferry with its gangplank out. We would drive aboard, the ferryman would change the angle of the boat in relation to the current, and the river itself would push us across, the ferry secure to the overhead cable.

My mother ran a ferry like that when she was a little girl. Her ferry didn't have even this spool of cable that wound now one way and now the other, with the current doing all the work. She had to tiptoe up to the overhead cable, hang on for dear life, and manfully pull the bateau across, hand over hand. She told me that once she had a baby sister with her when the river was high and swift, and how difficult it was to hang on to the boat with her toes and the cable with her hands, so as not to let boat and baby go racing downstream to their death while she was left dangling from the cable.

We went to Pa's old place to see the walled spring where so many happy things used to happen. The acres had eroded down the gully we used to play in, until only the pink, sandy skeleton of the farm lay bleaching away, a pine or two to mark where the orchard had been. Not so very many years ago the farm had been a lush haven. Gone down the branch, my aunt said. Who was farming it now? Someone who lived down on a riverbank where the topsoil had come to rest? Or maybe Pa's farm kept going out into the gulf, some of it still reddening some river so pregnant with loam that it waddled down its valley like an old cow near her time.

One Saturday night we drove off a pretty sandy road into a pine and hardwood grove to camp. Here were open spaces for our campfire, and trees and bushes so much like the woods of my childhood that I went out to hunt for a sweet shrub bush. I found plenty of black gum, that sweet wood from which snuff dippers make their brushes. We found sassafras trees and nibbled their aromatic bark.

It was a perfect campsite, quiet, far from any house. And there was a hint of another road going through the woods, off to some unguessed place.

On Sunday morning, we woke to warm January sunshine. And we knew then that we must go to Florida.

XVII. AMERICA—ROUND TRIP

EVERYONE had warned us not to go to Florida. The aftermath of the boom had left it a bitter state, they said, and we would starve to death trying to get around the great loop. But we wanted to see our only tropics. After all, we could have stayed in Sacramento if we had merely wanted to have things easy. So we turned south from Georgia and our little house rolled into Tampa.

Oh, Florida! Sunshine so bright it is white, flocks of great white birds barely showing against the sky. Water everywhere. Marshes. Big luscious flowers, growing in a cluster of spikes high in the crotch of a tree, as inaccessible as the moon. Birds singing. Frogs croaking over the land. Grapefruit ten cents a dozen—big, heavy, dark ones, dripping with juice. Snakes weaving among the grass out in the water. A huge black nose—a crocodile—easing toward the highway, dragging itself up on the warm concrete, lying there like a dead thing.

Three-sided houses on piles in the swamps, and Indians living in them: a floor, three walls, one side open to the sun, no furniture but a log to sit on, an open fire to cook on, a dry floor and a blanket for a bed and the out-of-doors for living.

Florida was supposed to be the state where a man would go hungry, but Farrar made more money there than he had done on the whole trip. He wrote some advertising parodies, sang one at the South Florida Fair and the other in Miami, averaging fifteen dollars a day. He made so much money, in fact, that we all bought new clothes.

The Tamiami Trail is adventure every step of the way. It ended on the blazing beaches of Miami. Returning north, we skirted the outer coast of Florida, Georgia, and South Carolina, turned inland through North Carolina and Virginia and entered Washington from the west instead of the south. We had never before seen this magnificent country of the Atlantic Seaboard or known what a land it is, spring flowers popping out everywhere.

We had meant to follow the blossoming spring up the coast, but it had been so hot in Florida we couldn't wait, and by the time we got out of the tropics nothing was in bloom but little tender things like bluets, anemones, and bloodroot. The tough old shrubs hadn't dared to poke out so much as a bud yet. They were like old men who keep their creaking bones well-wrapped while the babies run about stark naked.

In Washington, we took the boys to the Easter-egg rolling on the White House lawn, and though they dutifully rolled the eggs we had colored that morning, they didn't enjoy it much. It was a confusion of noise, broken eggs, shells, anxious mothers, and shrieking children.

By this time the pear and cherry trees were snowing in all the orchards. Pennsylvania wore a halo of them. Driving through these orchards, it was hard to believe in Pittsburgh.

By the time we reached New York, we were broke again. While Farrar took his songs to the publishers, I got a job at $60 a week, writing advertising copy.

"If you could only write hillbilly songs, you'd be made," the publishers told Farrar, and talked grandly of a thousand dollars a week and sending him out over the vaudeville circuit.

"I can," Farrar said, and that same day wrote the kind of song they wanted. That fixed Farrar. If he could turn out a folk song in one afternoon, with the authentic, plaintive tune of the hills, he was a find. Victor wanted him.

Just then four things happened in the same week. The advertising agency I worked for went broke and we lost our income. The executive at Victor's with whom Farrar had been dealing was called to California, and asked Farrar to await his return. Helen Woodward got me an entree with a woman's magazine and the editor gave me some work to see whether or not I could handle it. And we got an invitation from Dr. Clara Barrus,

John Burroughs' biographer, to camp for a few weeks in Burroughs' old orchard. Wouldn't we love camping under one of Uncle John's apple trees, she wrote.

Would we! We had spent the late spring and hot summer in New York while we were after the flesh-pots and the children had been exceedingly bored. I could do the work for the magazine just as well out of town and await their decision up there.

So we set off. New York is a beautiful state. Its great river, moving quietly, laden with history, never goes on a rampage. We drove north, following the Hudson, and then west to Roxbury where John Burroughs used to live, delighting in the stone fences, the tidy New England villages, and the rolling hills within pasture fences.

We found Roxbury, turned up a country lane to the unpainted house on the hill and the orchard across the road from it. There we pitched our tent under an apple tree and made our campfire at the edge of the orchard overlooking rolling fields of ripe hay.

The campers under the apple trees.

One day a funny little incident occurred there in the orchard. A wealthy neighbor, who had formerly come to the old house to pay her seasonal respects to John Burroughs, and now came to see Dr. Barrus, dropped by to see the campers under the apple trees. She was somber, rather condescending, and very lonely. Like the missionary back in the days of the donkey, she was concerned about our souls. Were we saved? Did the children go to Sunday School? She gave us some tracts which we burned when she had gone. We didn't like to expose the children to anything like that quite yet.

But she was a nice person and she meant to be gracious and kind. She sat on a cushion from the car and all of us talked around the fire. After a while I saw a man standing by the hedge. He was looking toward our fire and I invited him over. He hesitated. I saw, then, that he was in uniform, the woman's chauffeur. Having no experience with the very rich, I thought I might have created an awkward situation, but the woman turned to her servant and asked him to come over.

He came then and stood across the fire from her. After a while he forgot himself in his eagerness to hear Farrar tell how you can take life in your own hands and live it to the brim. The woman stirred a little, too, and seemed to have a dim feeling that she too had been handed a tract.

One night there was a heavy fog. In the morning the valleys were full of blue-white mist, the hills sticking up out of it. It might have been water and islands. Farrar and I looked at each other.

"Reminds me of Puget Sound," I said, as casually as I could.

"Yes, it does," Farrar said. Then he bit again on the sore tooth. "I can almost see the salmon jumping down there. That's Speiden, and there's Pearl Island—and Battleship. North and Bobby," he called to the boys who were busily gathering wood for the morning campfire, "what does this make you think of?"

"Puget Sound," North said at once. "I wish we could go back there." Not askingly.

The boys never asked for things. They expressed their opinions and we could take it or leave it. They had learned, before you would expect children to know, that we operated on hair-triggers and if they asked for a thing they promptly got it. We would turn around in the middle of any road and go somewhere else. It put too much responsibility on them and they rejected it by ceasing to ask.

It was that fog between the foothills of the Catskills that robbed Farrar of what might have been his big chance. Every morning for a week the fog was there like an ocean between the hills, and the hills were like islands above the fog. We gazed at it hungrily, dreaming of fair beaches, of our little cruiser in dry dock, of our own island, of Dad and Ma Chevalier on Speiden, waiting for us.

One morning I said, "Let's go," and there was shouting and dancing around the campfire. Dr. Barrus said one would think we had been let out of jail.

"We have let ourselves out," Farrar said. "We're always getting in but we always get out, too."

Farrar has never heard from Victor since. But I had already mailed my sample work back to the woman's magazine and their telegram, bidding me report, followed us clear across the country and was waiting for us when we arrived in Bellingham, on Puget Sound, where we planned to put the children in school.

We saw the rainbows in Niagara Falls and felt the heavy blow of that roar on our eardrums. Sometimes the gods use heavier drumsticks than human ears can bear and you run from the pounding. But we had one unforgettable experience there: Farrar sang from his platform for the first time.

We were camping in the general public space reserved for campers and people were crowded around us. One man asked all about the car, and wanted to know what the platform was for. Farrar told him. "Well, get up and sing on it, then," the man said, and Farrar did.

"How do you make a living at it?" the questioner asked him.

"I sell my songs," Farrar said.

"Hell," said the man, "we're on vacation. We don't want to buy songs to lug around. Why don't you pass the hat?"

"I never thought of that," said Farrar, ashamed to admit that he simply couldn't do it. So the man took his own hat and went around the circle. He collected eight dollars or so which we sorely needed and that was the beginning of a brand-new technique for us. From Niagara Falls on, Farrar sang from his platform and people paid for the entertainment without having to buy songs. He made a lot more money!

Farrar with guitar and slide whistle.

In Michigan we found our dog. One day we drove past a sign that said "Collies for Sale" and the boys raised a clamor for Daddy to stop and back up. In a dirty, lonely pen a big ungainly collie pup paced up and down. He was about six months old, as awkward as a calf, with huge feet, and a piteous, pleading look in his soft eyes. The boys took one look at him and they were his.

The owner came out to bargain but there was no bargaining to be done. The boys had saved just seven dollars and that would either buy him or it wouldn't. It did.

By this time the car was on another rampage, and we were kept broke looking after it. When we entered Yellowstone National Park, we gave the gatekeeper the last money we had. We drove into that gyrating wilderness with enough food for a few days but with no idea how we would get out. But we were adept by now at leaving tomorrow alone. We found our camping place and set out to see the park.

Color in the sulphurous overflow around the geyser holes. Delicate wild rose, forget-me-not blue, cowslip yellow, lavender and old lace. The canyon of the loping river. The great forests. To many people, Yellowstone seems so full of horrors, rumblings, and spoutings that it is a nightmare. But we loved it, though we were broke and the car was leaking oil, and we were driving it with everything grinding itself to pieces before our ears.

Then one day we drove into a clearing among beautiful, tall trees. Behind us came a caravan of sightseeing buses. One of the tourists came over to the car and asked us to sing. North and Bobby who, by now, had learned a great many songs, responded promptly, and then Bobby gravely held out his hand. What had we done that this baby should expect pay for a song! I protested, but Bobby was firm. "Of course, I didn't sing for nossing," he said, and the man laughed. He was amused at the baby, at me, at this study in American vagabondage and its effect on children. He gave Bobby a coin. "The laborer is worthy of his hire," he said.

Now the people crowded around, demanding songs. Farrar and the boys and I all stood on the platform and sang and sang. The tourist took up a collection in a business-like way and we had nine dollars. Then the bus driver looked at our car, discovered a bolt gone from the engine base and a hole through which the oil had been leaking. He found a bolt and plugged the hole and we drove off to a service station, filled the tanks and oil cups and were off again.

When we got to Pendleton, Oregon, it was nearly time for the annual round-up and the town was full of cowboys. Many of the Indians had already arrived and set up their tepees. Pendleton is set within a nest of rounded blue mountains, with wheat fields rolling off in every direction. You have a feeling of open, far-flung country—as though you could go on and on, and never find your way barred by a fence or a wall or a sign marked "Keep Out."

The Columbia River is a lover of adventure. It runs wild and free through all sorts of country—mountains, deserts, forests, barrens—now cutting its way straight through high ranges, now gouging out a canyon right in the desert for no reason at all.

At the Dalles, Indians were dipping up salmon from the river. The fish were on their way to the spawning ground and only the Indians are allowed to catch them during the run. Then the beautiful river slipped through the Cascades and into the lush country of western Oregon and Washington, and we took deep breaths of the sweet, moisture-laden air of home. This was our own country, the Pacific Northwest, unlike any other section of the United States.

Now forests darkened the sky above us but they gave a deep sense of security, too. Trunks of trees, four, five, six feet through, rose straight and tall, lifting feathery crowns a hundred feet, two hundred, higher still into the sky. Where the forest was virgin growth, uncut since the time of man, there wasn't the tangled undershrubbery common to second-growth woods. But there were huckleberry bushes even here, ripe for our picking.

North, now, to Puget Sound. The highway ran along a bluff overlooking islands and boats easing along, towing their wakes. They had built Chuckanut Drive since our homesteading days, and we followed that curving, winding, horseshoeing, palisaded drive to Bellingham.

It was September sixteenth, a year and a week since we had left Sacramento. Farrar made a talk in Bellingham to the American Legion. He took along a huge map of the United States on which we had marked our ten-thousand-mile course around our land with a heavy blue line, the ends nearly meeting on the West Coast.

"You can see," he told them, "we were headed for Bellingham all the time."

Part Four

PUGET SOUNDINGS

Farrar with axe in front of newly built Study Cabin.

*I am having the time of my life with my daily column
and Farrar is building houses on our hill and
gardening as he has never gardened before.*
June Burn

XVIII. WE LIVE IN BELLINGHAM A MILLION WORDS

OH, BUT you can go home again! People are always retracing their steps, finding home over and over. Not the same buildings and trees and roads. Perhaps not even the same people. But whoever loves the earth in all its changing shapes and ways never goes too far away. The Puget Sound country is one of our homes—perhaps the dearest. A haven secure against want and trouble—a fortune cached away which none can thieve.

If you come over the mountains from eastern to western Washington, the first sensation is of moist coolness after dry heat, or, if it is winter, of warmth after freezing cold. There is a change in color from summer-yellow or winter-white to everlasting blue-green; a change in shape from rolling prairie to broken mountains and hills. As you descend the western side of the Cascades, following some glacier-fed stream, always white instead of red like the rivers of the East, you think it is twilight, no matter what time of day it is—for you have plunged into the forests. After a while you emerge into the more open farming country, with its feeling of prosperity all about, for no matter how poor the farmers of the Pacific Northwest may think they are, they have never experienced poverty as it is known in the South or the East.

Suddenly, you round a curve or top a hill and there is Puget Sound before you, glittering in the sunshine or misty gray in the rain. There are ships coming and going in every direction, sidestepping the myriad green islands that pattern the Sound. Behind you are the mountains you have crossed, snowy white, and another range to the south, and another to the north. You are encircled by snow-capped ranges. You have come home!

But Puget Sound is changing. The land trembles under the blows of greedy axes, felling trees much faster than they grow. In twenty years, at the present rate of cutting and burning, Puget Sound virgin forests will be gone, the watersheds eroding, floods threatening.

Fishermen—purse seiners, trappers, gill netters, reef netters, "salmon derbies," beam trawlers—are stripping the sea. Just as the Okies destroyed their homes by skimming the soil without making honest return to it, so Puget Sound may be destroyed, if farmers do not withhold the tractors, plow under legumes, return humus and minerals to the soil; if loggers do not cease their ruthless cutting; if fishermen do not ration their takes.

I wish I could help the forces of conservation in the Northwest to protect Puget Sound from that death. Words are the weapons with which we can fight, if only one could find the right ones.

Before we had left John Burroughs' orchard in New York, we wired a friend to sell the cruiser and buy us some land near the training school in Bellingham which the boys would attend. Our friend had found two acres at the foot of Sehome Hill, one a little fir-clad knoll, the other a level acre of meadow and garden. If we had hunted America over, we couldn't have found a more perfect place.

We decided that while Farrar built a log house on the Two Acres, I would find a job. I knew what I wanted to do—write the column I had tried to sell the year before. I wanted to go into every nook and cranny of Puget Sound and write about it.

North and Bob with the Kitchen Cabin in the background.

The *Bellingham Daily Herald* finally agreed to let me try it. They could pay only thirty dollars a week, but if the column was successful, I would get more, they said. As a matter of fact, the crash came two months later and I never got more; instead, three years later, when the Depression was badly felt out our way, I was cut to twenty dollars, which precipitated a crisis and another way of life, whereby hangs another tale.

Farrar began to build the kitchen cabin. He cut down trees from our own knoll, peeled them, and put the cabin up alone, looking after the boys when I went after stories, and milking the cow which we bought as soon as we could. Meanwhile, we lived in the car, camping out as we had camped all over America. Farrar put up a brush windbreak around the campfire, and I sat on a box, with the typewriter in front of me on another, and wrote my daily column, sometimes in a drizzle.

At times the delivery boy from the grocer's would find

June and Farrar at June Acres.

me typing in the drizzle and feel sorry for us, and Farrar and I would laugh when he was gone. Once the boy asked us how long we had been there and Farrar replied, "Only ten thousand words." Later it was. "We've been here a hundred thousand words, now," and when we had been at it three years, he called it a two-million-word stay at one job.

By Thanksgiving we moved into the kitchen cabin. The door wasn't in but we hung a blanket over the doorway and began to entertain our friends there instead of around the campfire. By now we had a swarm of friends, made through the man who had found Two Acres for us, and gradually the column was winning us more.

Kitchen Cabin, built of peeled ten-inch logs, was twelve-by-fourteen, inside dimensions. It had one door and five windows. There were double-deck narrow wooden bunks on each side of the doorway; the closet, cupboard, sink, and work space along the left-hand wall; bookshelves, a work and dining table, and corner table with shelf underneath it, on the right-hand wall. At the far end, between the tables on each side, were the cook stove and woodbox. There was a long bench in front of the table, and shorter ones at each end. The table could seat eight in a pinch. It was fixed to the wall, under big windows overlooking our meadow and garden and the road below. It was like a diner on a train, the windows looking out below and beyond. Trees grew all around the cabin. It was so sheltered from the road that many who passed below never saw it at all.

When Kitchen Cabin was finished, Farrar set to work on a study for me which was also to be the family living room, with a tiny bunkroom partitioned off at one end where two of us could sleep. It was a graceful little cabin, with a hemlock-bough flare to the roof, eight windows, an arched blue door, built-in seats and shelves and cupboards. It was so compact that I could work at the desk and reach for everything I needed, without moving from my place.

North moved his studying down there. Then we found a little Estey organ and Farrar moved his music down. Nobody could expect Bob to study all alone in Kitchen Cabin. The Study grew to be home and we never built the big house we had planned for the top of the hill. We were afraid, if we made ourselves too comfortable, we would not tear ourselves away when another adventure called.

The cabins cost two hundred dollars all told, including hardware, windows, lumber, shingles, tarpaper for lining, flooring, cook stove, and heater. Just as each cabin was built, taxes were lowered. Every time the tax assessor came out he would say, "Well, I see you have another cabin. Your taxes will be lower this year."

The Study Cabin.

Interior of the Study Cabin.

All this time, I was roaming about Puget Sound, gathering stories as one would get water from some limitless artesian well. I took a tugboat to the Olympic Peninsula and spent eight days in logging camps, guided by the bull bucker. He showed me logging from cruising the timber, building the railroads and rigging the spar trees, to cutting, bucking, dragging, hauling the logs down to the waterfront where they were made into rafts and towed to the Bellingham mills.

The men staged a special spar-tree topping for me. I sat on a mountainside and watched a man go stalking up a tree, stop below the feathery crown, and begin to make his undercut. The blows rang out in the cold mountain air. The woodsman leaned back against his belt to rest. Then he sawed for a while and took up his ax again. The tree cracked.

The high rigger gave his resounding cry, "Wa-a-tch ou-ou-t!" Another blow and another. "Timber-r-r-r!" Another crack, one more blow, a mighty kick, and the soft green plume hurtled down into a ravine far below. Above, the high climber was hanging on. The trunk of the tree was swinging back and forth from the force of the kick of the falling crown. When the sickening pendulum slackened, the man came stalking down again. We hurried over. Someone lit a cigarette for him, put it into his mouth. He was casual but he was trembling with fatigue.

This fabulous Peninsula is still almost pure wilderness, the wildest and perhaps the most interesting in America. Cougars, mountain lions, deer, elk, bear, whistlers, conies, grouse live in the mountains, and come down to the natural prairies to feed.

There are towns, resorts, hotels, lakes, farming communities, schools on the Peninsula, but they could all be dropped down some huge crevasse of a glacier, and the wild, rough country would scarcely show where they had been. The surf would pound the rocky bluffs, rivers would roar down from the mountains, snows fall, rains beat, forests again cover the earth, wild goats and eagles dispute the crags, and the wilderness return to itself.

The logging camps are lonely places in the mountains, like ships at sea, cut off from the world. The men live in bunkhouses and eat in a raw, plank dining room, the tables piled high with bread, pies, cakes, canned fruits, boiled potatoes, meats, tea and coffee—but the camp pigs die of it, and so do the deer if they aren't kept away.

The men come stalking into the dining room, whose floor is gouged from their hobnails, throw a leg over the bench, reach out for food, and are half through their meal by the time they get the other leg over. They wear what they call tin pants—waterproof ducks that are metal-stiff, cut off just above the top of the loggers' boots, the cut ends hanging in a rough fringe. The boots are well-oiled and hobnailed. They wear tin jackets, too, over woolen shirts. Fine looking men. Young engineers just out of college, maneuvering the railroads through the hills so as to get at the most timber with the fewest possible expensive bridges and tracks. High riggers, tall and lean and blond. Foremen who have come up from the ranks, intelligent, practical men, smart enough to know everything that goes on and to keep their mouths shut when lady journalists come around for stories.

Not that I was after damning facts. I didn't know then that there were any damning facts to be after. I wanted to tell the story of getting giant logs out of inaccessible mountains, the story of the men, the curious nomenclature of the woods. It didn't occur to me then that there was careless, wanton waste, without a thought for the good of the land, for the prevention of erosion, for the protection of the rest of the forest from fire, for the safety of the men, even for the future of the Peninsula.

The series of columns on the logging camps established me on my job. The old-timers liked it. Schools used it. I had letters from people all over the Northwest, saying they had never before known the whole story from growing tree on the Olympics to sawn lumber in Bellingham. After that my column became a fixture on the front page of the morning and the editorial page of the evening *Herald*.

XIX. A BURN'S-EYE VIEW OF PUGET SOUND

BEFORE long, people began to tell me of stories I could get for my column—stories of the men and women of Puget Sound. A young banker said he had been up in the mountains, evaluating some property. He was climbing an obscure trail in the snow when he saw tracks coming from and returning into the hills where he knew there was no house. The tracks were extraordinarily far apart, such long strides that he thought at first they must have been made by a very tall man. Then he realized that the man had been running. Someone must be in trouble.

The banker turned off the trail and followed the tracks up and up, on the chance that help was needed. Farther and farther into the forest he went until he came to a ravine. Down below he heard someone working. He went to the edge of the ravine, looked over, and shouted to the lone workman splitting out shake bolts. A little old woman looked up.

"Whaddayawant?" she shrilled up at him, not very hospitably.

"I saw tracks of somebody running," the young man called back to her, "and I thought there might be trouble. I followed the tracks to find out."

"Naw," she said, "I just went out to get me a box of snuff."

There was a big woman, full of bosomy laughter, who owned a rural telephone company, managed her business, made her own repairs, climbed the poles herself, and, with her sister, ran a freight boat on a lake behind a waterpower dam. She conducted an orchestra, too, playing for dances or just for fun. Highly cultured, strong, interesting, and brimful of fun.

In the shoestring valleys of the Skagit's tributaries there live many hill people from Kentucky and Tennessee. Here you will find old grist mills with big millstones, fields of tobacco, and even little patches of sugar cane in some sheltered nook. These people remember crafts that date back to Elizabethan England. They sing the songs and tell the folk tales of a time long past.

Someone told me of an artist who went into the hills and found a community of these people, almost all of whom were on relief. Discovering that they knew crafts as old as America, she began to revive them, to find a market for their baskets and pottery. Within three years she took that community almost entirely off relief.

They are hardy—these river-farmers. Boys who had grown up on the Skagit would travel twenty miles down stream to Sedro Woolley by finding a cedar log or plank or shake bolt that would bear their weight and riding to town on it, standing ankle deep in glacial water. Sometimes the river-farmers take their hay to market on plank rafts supported by two canoes lashed to the raft underneath each side. They row back, upstream, their boats towing the raft, bringing back supplies of staples for their households.

Far up the Skagit there is a family which is almost entirely independent of the outside world. They grow their own sugar cane and make syrup and crude sugar as Pa used to do in Alabama; they raise their own tobacco, cornbread, meat, vegetables. They raise their own wool and weave their own cloth. When they need thread, salt, or lightweight garments, they trade turkeys for them.

When my column threatened to go stale, I had two favorite

June gathering stories for her column.

things to do—take a boat to the islands, or the "galloping goose" to Sedro Woolley and thence to Mountain Katy's. She was a wild free one from whom I got many of my tales, and she and I were forever setting off together after new adventures.

There was a government fish hatchery at Birdsview where I once watched men in hip boots catching the weary, heavy salmon, collecting eggs and sperm, tending the miniature sockeye, returning them to the stream to find their perilous way back to sea.

There was a soapstone mine in the steep side of a hill above the river. We reached it in a truck driven across the upper Skagit on a railroad bridge. Our wheels straddled the rails and there were no side walls on the bridge, which was covered with snow and ice the day I went. There were not six inches to spare between our port wheels and the rocky river bed far below, but the driver hardly slowed down. "You'll go when your time comes," he said.

The Skagit is Puget Sound's most interesting river. It rises on a glacier on a mountain in Canada, cuts down through wild country, drains a vast mountain wilderness, gathers more and more white glacier water as it runs, stops at Seattle's Diablo Dam to fill an immense lake, turn a few big turbines, and roars down, snatching bits of soil wherever it can, depositing them on the rich level acres of the famous La Conner Seed Flats down where the Skagit flows into the sea. That land is so rich and valuable that the taxes alone are sometimes as high as fifteen dollars an acre.

A pioneer who had come to Skagit county and had helped to reclaim the tide flats from the sea and build the dikes, gave me his diary in which the whole story of the river was told. It filled my column for days. He was one of the last of the old-timers and he died shortly afterwards, but not before he had seen his story in print and had the rare satisfaction of knowing his job had been completed from the dream to the recording of the accomplishment. Today they are still growing cabbage, turnip, radish, beet, flower, and cauliflower seed on his flats, and the Skagit still drains his acres, but it is controlled now and no longer brings down quite as much silt as it used to do.

Most of the rivers of Puget Sound come down through National Forests because there are National Forests on most of the mountain crests. The

Nooksack and the Skagit both flow through Mt. Baker National Forest. Mountain Katy and I often went into that forest for stories, wading the wet underbrush, pulling ourselves across the mountain streams on go-devils, eating huckleberries and blueberries until our tongues were black, stopping to swim in icy water or to lunch on some river's white beach.

Once I decided to go up to a lookout station and find out how foresters locate fires and set up the machinery to fight them. Katy and I checked in at the head ranger station and got permission to climb the thirteen miles to the lookout station. Then Katy went off in another direction to visit her husband and I tackled the climb alone, always a richer adventure than with even the best of companions.

But the forest is so threaded with fire-fighting telephones that the ranger soon discovered Katy wasn't with me and he sent a man on horseback in pursuit. All day long I walked. Up and up, through burned-over desolation where some careless camper had left a spark to flare and burn a thousand trees whose snags now commemorate his passing. Through cool dells where water ran fast. Over curious marshes on the mountainside, weaving in and out of the forest up to the timberline.

Just as I approached the open flowery meadow which marked the end of the forest proper and the beginning of the almost treeless mountaintop, the man on horseback overtook me, leading his tired beast. And down from the lookout station came another man. From here on I was to be well guided. Since one of the lookout boys had come, the man with the horse decided to remain in the meadow overnight where his horse could nip the grass. He would take me down the mountain next day.

At the foot of the mountain I had been hot, but I was cold now. We entered the snow and in no time my feet were soaking wet. Huckleberry bushes emptied bucketsful of water into my boots. We followed the telephone line up and down, until at long last we came to a little tent on the very peak of a pointed knoll at the top of the world.

Inside the tent two boys were preparing a feast. The supplies had come not long before. They cooked everything and we ate it all. I wondered how they would solve the problem of putting up a woman guest but it didn't bother them for a second. They hung a tarpaulin down from the ridgepole of the tent, unrolled their sleeping bags on one side of it, and mine on the other. We lay there, talking across it, for hours. One of the boys could sing, another told stories, and the third remembered all the poetry he had ever read.

Just as we were falling asleep, the fiercest thunderstorm I have ever experienced broke over the mountain. The lightning kept up such a steady flash it was like daylight for minutes at a time. It cracked inside, along the telephone line. And how it thundered! During all that racket the telephone rang and had to be answered. The wind blew a gale. Thunder spattered against the mountain like a giant repeater. I love thunderstorms but that one was enough to last me for a long time—until now, in fact, for I have never seen another as spectacular.

Next morning, when the boys went out to the sundial-looking contraption set level on a hemlock stump atop the point of the mountain to look for fires, there wasn't a flare in all the forest. If there had been one, they would have taken an azimuth reading, other lookouts would have taken readings, the fire would have been precisely located and men sent to put it out.

A crown fire, started by lightning, may leap from treetop to treetop, and set up a roaring inferno that will destroy great sections of forest before it can be controlled. Ground fires, caused by cigarettes or campfires or careless logging operations, are more easily controlled if they are caught in time. But because there are so many more of these, they are the most frequent cause of burning down the forests. Sometimes fires are set by the unemployed so that they may get work fighting them. Sometimes they are set by farmers who want to clear more grazing land for their animals. Greed in some form or other is at the root of many fires. But wanton carelessness in logging operations has burned down too much of our forests and sent up in smoke enough timber to employ thousands of men for many years, to build tens of thousands of homes—to say nothing of water conservation, flood control, and beauty.

An unfailing source of stories were the tribes of Indians on Puget Sound. Several reservations were scattered along the coastline, for ours are chiefly waterfront Indians. Every January the Lummi Indians hold a peace celebration to commemorate the peace treaty between the Indians and the whites which had restored to the native Americans a few acres of their land and a few of their ancient fishing rights. I spent twenty-four hours with them during one of those celebrations.

One morning I took the stage to the Reservation, waded through mud up the road to the big "Smoke House," and entered a windowless, floorless, barnlike hall where two huge campfires burned, the smoke finding its way out through two holes in the roof. The dark forms of women moved around the fires, preparing for dinner. Ducks hung on sticks, roasting. They were so high that they didn't need to be cooked for tenderness. At the edge of the fires huge coffee pots were steaming, pots of potatoes boiling. Salmon, split in half lengthwise, were impaled on sharp sticks and browned at the fires. Children played quietly on the seats around the huge building, and old men sat on benches, talking of old times. In and out of the house moved young men and women, sometimes bringing in cordwood from piles outside the door.

By dinner time hundreds of guests from other reservations had arrived. The dinner was good and time after time the tables were seated. As each group finished eating, they stood around their table and sang a kind of grace to their hosts.

That night they danced. All night long, while children slept in coats and blankets on the wide top seat, their fathers and mothers, even the great-grandfathers, danced their individual spirit dances.

Before one dance would end, someone else would "get his Tenana." That is, his spirit would come surging inside him and he would want to sing his own song, dance his own dance. He would howl and moan and sob and shake. He would bend over, head in his hands, yielding himself to the hypnotic spell of his own urgent rhythm. When he had worked up to a state of excitement, he would leap into the sawdust ring and start his dance, around and around the huge fires, the sweat pouring off him until he was all but exhausted. Then he would return to his seat, his sobs and moans gradually tapering off.

Before a woman danced, her friends would unpin her hair and take off her extra garments so that she was stripped for action. Her hair would fly around as she danced. When she returned to her seat, her friends matter-of-factly pinned up her hair again, while she shook and sobbed and slowly recovered from her hysteria.

There were group dances, too, with beautiful masks and gorgeously beaded costumes. Violent dances which no white man could endure but which the oldest man of the tribe went through as madly as the rest. They would dance around that hundred-foot-long room in a squatting position, head flinging to right and left, moving at a double-quick tempo. It is incredible what power the body has when the mind is half-hypnotized with excitement.

A curious feature of these dances was that each person helped to beat time and to sing. They each had two trimmed fir sticks about sixteen inches long which they beat together with a steady clacking that accentuated the excitement of drums, voices, moans, crackle of fires, blowing of noses.

At ten o'clock that night the whites were ushered politely home. All but me. A group of Indian women with whom I had made friends let me hide behind their ample bodies in a corner where I could not be seen. I was to stay all night and watch the secret dances.

Toward midnight a group of scientists from the University of Washington arrived. They wanted to see the tribal dances, and particularly to see the secret dances. But they were disappointed. The Indians went on with their individual, moaning dances until the university people left at two o'clock. About an hour later I fell asleep, overcome by the heat, leaning against some warm fat body.

When I awoke the secret dance was just ending so I could not report it. However I did see the sick man, whom the secret dance was to cure, being helped off the floor. He had come there prone, and now he was moving about.

Lying on his cot he begins to get his Tenana. He sobs and moans himself to his feet. Friendly hands help him into the ring and drummers gather around him. The sticks clap violently. People begin to sing his song. The song mounts. The drums beat. The sticks clap. At last the sick man shakes off his sickness. He dances, around and around the ring, the drummers following close behind him, sticks clapping. That racket would raise the dead, I think.

Once around the ring. Twice around. The sick man is strong again. He staggers back to his place, sinks down exhausted. But he has danced.

And who knows but the stirring of his blood, the hysteria and heat and excitement have helped him?

At dawn we breakfasted, tireless women serving coffee, bakery rolls, duck, and potatoes. Children awakened and came stumbling down the step-seats, waiting quietly in the background for tables to be cleared again and again, so that they could eat.

It was raining when I left the smoke house that morning and the mud was deeper on the road. Cars were hub-deep, standing around in the woods.

Bellingham looked strange and new when I got back, and I went to the *Herald* office to see whether it was still there. It was hard to believe the world was still the same after twenty-four hours in that house, with the din of primitive racket in my ears and the smell of roasting ducks and salmon in my nostrils.

XX. I HUNT FOR STORIES

FARMING is the most important industry on Puget Sound. It is almost as romantic and exciting as logging. Farmers do not top spar trees, but they often come upon kitchen middens or burial mounds in their pastures, and sometimes dig up ancient skulls. Once a young farm woman wrote that they were finding skulls and shinbones in their pasture and they were so excited they had stopped the spring planting to continue digging. Would I come over and see their Neanderthal man? I went.

They lived on an island, and the pasture, now a hundred feet above water, might have been down on the beach when these men and women were buried, which would make the bones very old indeed.

Unlike the Okies, the farmers on Puget Sound never stop learning. County agents and teachers from the State's agricultural college hold field schools, meetings, and conduct teaching tours. The Home Demonstration Agent keeps the women abreast of progress in food processing, vitamin discoveries, household economy of all kinds. Four-H clubs keep the young people on their toes, producing garden produce, crops, cows, poultry that take prizes.

It is amazing what people have been able to do with progressive farm methods. One woman took her big farm out of the red in four years, compelled it to pay, discovered what was the most profitable unit of operation for her farm, and was successful after having struggled with poverty all during her less progressive husband's lifetime.

A young couple, who managed to save something from sawmill wages, bought a small farm which the wife ran while the husband went to town to work during the first years. They are now independent and prosperous for they studied their problems, learned how many chickens they could raise profitably without hiring help, devised homemade brooders, kept careful books, and managed to educate themselves as they went on. From ignorant sawmill laborers they have made themselves influential, well-to-do, intelligent people.

The most interesting thing about farming on Puget Sound is that the farm women take annual vacations. They go off to camp for a week of fun, sleeping late, tea parties, talks, and games. Not all farm wives go, of course, but hundreds of them do. One of the big consolidated high schools of Whatcom County is used for the camp. It is near the mountains in beautiful country, and the small fees which the women pay enable the committee to buy cots, hire entertainers, and plan all manner of fun.

Fishing is the third largest industry on the Sound, and surely the most interesting occupation in which men can engage. In the old days, old-timers say, spawning salmon worked their way up the streams in such numbers that you could walk across them. "Why, I've seen 'em so thick at the mouth of a stream, just starting on their run, you couldn't row a boat among 'em. Their fins would be sticking out of the water like a mat of thorns," one of them said.

In the early years of trapping, fishermen would allow milling thousands to come into the trap until they were piled up almost solid and often died before the buyer's boat came to take them out. At last the people were aroused at the senseless waste, threatening loss of a great industry and a few years ago passed a law forbidding traps. Nowadays the big fish-cannery operators speak bitterly of the fish caught and eaten by seals and bears. And, in truth, man has so long wasted the salmon that the comparative few taken by seals and bears do make a difference in the pitiful remainder now. It may be necessary, before the salmon industry can be restored, to outlaw the purse seine boats, too, for a few spawning cycles; and to outlaw forever the "salmon derbies" whose waste serves only to attract tourists. Puget Sound is not so poor in resources of beauty that it must attract tourists by such artificial means.

Before I realized all this, I loved to go out on a purse seine boat, watch them spread the immense net "purse," pull the drawstring, and haul a netful of shining salmon aboard. It was fun to go to Stuart Island and watch Dad Chevalier's men reef-net fishing in their long narrow boats, set in pairs near a shore where the fish always passed at the turn of flood tide. There was a tall platform at the bow of the boat where men stood to watch for the fish. When they saw them, far down in the green water silently flowing toward the boat, they gave a signal, the men grabbed the edges of the net and began to haul in, drawing the boats together, gathering the top edge of the net together, hauling the dripping meshes into the boats with ten, forty, five hundred shining big salmon tangled in them. Sometimes they would haul one lone fish aboard, and the women on the bank would give derisive hoots. But I have seen the boys standing hip-boot-deep in fish, the boats sinking lower and lower in the water until no more could be hauled in. Then a fish buyer comes along, the fish are pitchforked into his hold, and the long narrow boats ride high and light again, ready for the fish on the next tide.

North and I went to Alaska with the biggest salmon-canning company in the world. The ship was taking men and their families to the summer cannery camps where they were to stay until the last boat of the season took them off again. Farrar and I had gone to Alaska by the outside route, and this time North and I saw the famous Inside Passage, with its steep forested islands and mainlands, the swift rivers, the little towns of Southeastern Alaska that come down to the seashore on stilts.

Between Vancouver Island and the mainland of Canada we nearly scraped islands to port and starboard, the channel making sharp turns into new island vistas every few minutes. That is the way to see a land—slowly, stopping often, going into all the towns and villages, hunting flowers—smelling, tasting, feeling its craw.

At every stop we went ashore to see totem poles, to find a waterfall the captain had told us about, to hunt wild flowers in the woods or on the tundra—a stone's throw from the main street of any town—or to go fishing.

We went out the Aleutians as far as Dutch Harbor. Everything on the treeless Aleutians looked small and lost in the vast tundra. Step out of your door onto that yielding springy tangle of a million roots, go a few yards behind the prostrate willows, sink to your waist in the curious furrowlike depressions, plunge into a marsh and in a hundred yards become one with earth. For you are lost. Trails must be constantly tended here if they are to survive. Get off the trail and you will have no sense of direction or distance. The sun won't help much for it rides higher up here and makes a different swing across the sky. You can't find your way by the moss on the tree trunks for there are no trees. Or by the direction of the wind—for it may change at any moment. It's a big land, this Alaska!

How sweet and small my own land looked after that month in Alaska. Always before I had thought that Puget Sound was on almost too big a scale for me. John Burroughs used to say that he liked a river to be small enough to flow through his heart. I felt my heart wasn't big enough for Puget Sound. But after Alaska it looked exactly right and always after that I could feel it fitting easily in my heart.

At one of our stops two Aleut girls, who spoke English and seemed unusually intelligent, asked me whether I would take them outside with me. They wanted to go to school and were willing to work for no wages at all if someone would take them.

I wired the company and got permission to bring the girls out. One of them would do our work so Farrar wouldn't have to, and a friend of mine offered to take the other. The girls were overjoyed.

My friend met the boat and took her quiet, homesick little Aleut home with her. My girl was older, gayer, more eager. She showed no signs of homesickness at all. At Two Acres we walked across the meadow to our little hill and entered the study. My Aleut took one look around, her face fell, she looked for a moment as desolate as a young girl can look. What was the matter? She had thought we lived in fine big houses outside. This was smaller than her home in Alaska, and they had running water in her house. Where was she to sleep? Oh, woe, woe!

I should have thought of that. It would take more primitiveness than this half-breed girl had, or more civilization than she would ever have, to enjoy our log cabins. She wouldn't be happy here. What to do?

I telephoned a wealthy friend who said she would be delighted to have our Rachel. She would drive over at once. And away they went, over the hill, to one of the most beautiful houses in Bellingham where Rachel lived happily ever after. She is still in Bellingham, clerking in a store, and as content as she was meant to be.

The history of Puget Sound began to interest me more and more. Old-timers sent me stories of the early days and I began to collect diaries. I heard from sea captains who had run the first steamers in the country, old prospectors who had gone there during the gold-rush days in Alaska, people who had gone into the hills forty years before with packs on their backs and not been out since, people who had lived in an old Bellamy socialist colony which flourished back in the depression of 1893. I collected books and pamphlets, histories and anecdotes. And at last I wrote a series of historical articles which ran for weeks, trying to be gayer than the important histories, but more accurate, too. It was fun to write and it led to many other projects, one of them taking me into the Caribou country of Canada, settled during the gold-rush days of 1858.

The Fraser River is in Canada, but its history is tangled up with ours. They were largely Americans who struggled up that river into the Caribou country during the gold-rush of 1858. One day Bellingham was a little sawmill town at the foot of steep hills rising above the bay. The next it was a tent city of some ten thousand souls all bound for the Caribou. They didn't all get there, but their struggles and the trail they built from Bellingham Bay up the Fraser into the Caribou country all made Puget Sound history.

With a party of friends whose grandfathers had helped to build that trail, I set out to follow it—along improved highways and with the comforts of an automobile. At last we reached the very outposts of a mining camp to find men still panning gold in the rushing creeks, still picking away at white granite streaked with yellow. We visited a gentle, gay old lady who had been less gentle and more gay in her youth, and now was thoroughly respectable, with granddaughters in college. At a hotel we saw an Englishman in boots and tweeds and a monocle who lived up in the hills with a wife who was not permitted to show her face, while he came silently out of the woods, stalking grandly about to buy his supplies, and rode silently back into the forest the next day.

Even ten years ago, young people came out of this far northern section by packhorse to go to college. But not now. I met a nurse training in Seattle not long ago who had come from beyond the Caribou country. It was her first trip outside. What did she like best, I asked. Oh, the automobiles, she said. Didn't people have automobiles in the Caribou?

No, she said, there were no roads—only trails. Then she had come out by pack mule.

"No, I flew out. Everybody up there has an airplane."

Whidbey Island, Washington, is the second largest island in the United States, the largest of 172 islands in the San Juan Archipelago. Some of the San Juans are nameless, treeless rocks jabbing through the blue channel, literally mountaintops in the sea. They are very high, the valleys between them sometimes measuring hundreds of fathoms down. There is a maximum tide rise and fall of about thirteen feet in the islands. This incalculable quantity of water rushes around among the islands through very narrow channels, causing dangerous whirlpools, tide rips, and currents as fast as eight knots. At Deception Pass, between Whidbey and Fidalgo Islands, all boats of ordinary size wait for slack tide rather than tackle that devil's caldron. At slack tide, all the passes are as calm as millponds.

Schools are a problem on the Islands. Often there are only two pupils, sometimes only one, who in that case must either go to another island to school, or wait until a teacher brings another pupil with her to keep school. On Waldron one year the teacher advertised for an extra child, for the law requires that there be at least two pupils. If the teacher is any good, the children are well taught and should make at least two grades a year; if they are bright, they can reasonably be expected to make three grades in a year, thus saving the township some money.

Once I set out to walk around all the larger San Juan Islands, and on one such walk I found the place of my dreams and went home to lie awake nights, wondering what it would cost, afraid to ask lest I couldn't afford the extravagance even of dreaming about it any more. I talked about it so much that Farrar went over to see it, too, and he too loved it.

About then the first half of the world war bonus was paid. Farrar would get six hundred dollars. Perhaps we could make a down payment on that island place with its half mile of white sandy and graveled beaches, its spring and well and lush swamp for a garden. Then we could dream to our hearts' content.

Farrar went to Friday Harbor to see the man who owned the twenty-two-acre point on Waldron Island and found that we could buy it outright and have enough money left for twenty-two acres more on the same island, but on another point. We bought them both in a hurry.

Now we owned not only Sentinel but forty-four acres on Waldron where we had beaches, water, daily boat service, sandy roads, a school, store, and nearly fifty other people.

We felt like millionaires. We were secure now, whatever might come. We could take our cow and tools, make a garden on Waldron, build cabins there, fish, and live practically on nothing at all.

As soon as we had bought the acres on Waldron we began to get restless in Bellingham. I'd come back from the Islands fairly stuccoed with romance. It was all we could do to hang onto our jobs. We began to dream about a trading boat for the Islands, carrying books and magazines, small items, perhaps a barge for dances and a stage for community theatricals, and later on, movies. We'd add a printing press and publish a peripatetic journal of the Sound, making the rounds of the Islands every two weeks. We wouldn't be in competition with the stores for we'd carry entertainment, mostly.

And while we dreamed, I went on with the column. There wasn't a phase of life on Puget Sound that it didn't cover. Sports; basic industries—such as coal and gold mining, cement and sugar making, canning, the pulp mills; ships coming in from all over the world bringing silks and tea and pineapples—going out with fish and lumber and paper pulp; tides pouring in at Juan de Fuca's big gate, washing us clean twice a day; rivers—the Nooksack, Skagit, Hoh, Stillaguamish, Snohomish; seabirds and land birds, flowers in all the summer dells. And rain. Soft rain quick to heal the scars we make with our too-greedy tools.

XXI. CAMPFIRES IN THE HOUSE

IN 1932, when the depression struck Puget Sound, my salary was cut to the bone. It occurred to Farrar and me that we could live on Waldron on no income at all as easily as we could live in town on a small one. And anyhow, we wanted to try living on our island farm before the children were out of grade school. This was our chance.

For a year, Farrar had been going to Waldron at every opportunity. Now, at the close of school, the three of them moved to the Island, taking the cow and two heifer calves and everything on the place that was moveable. Farrar had built a summer-camp cabin for himself and the boys where I visited them between story-gathering forays.

I had made so many commitments for stories that I could not give up my column until October—three years after starting it. But at last I closed the cabins in Bellingham and took the little *Chickawana* for Waldron, where the boys were already in school.

Now, Waldron is unlike the other islands. Indeed, the Islands are all as different as though they were continents. Each has its own individual characteristics. One is rocky, mountainous, craggy, full of wild, sweet nooks. One is open farm land, spread flat under scurrying clouds. Another is full of prehistoric fossils, its unusual rock formations drawing people from long distances to see them. Waldron, six square miles in size, nearly four thousand acres, is level save for one hill, and it has sandy beaches.

The Islands differ in other ways, too. One is strongly co-operative, independent of the outside world. Another is a tourist island, sophisticated and urbane. A third is strongly commercial—the shopping island. Waldron is like some hill community in the South, with a strong family or tribal spirit against outsiders.

The day I went to Waldron to stay, Farrar and the boys and I took a walk along our beaches, over slick rocks at low tide, up sandstone bluffs, through salal jungle, to the highest bluff of all. It stood fifty feet above the water, looking out over Canada, over islands near and far, over passing ships and lighthouses, over tides moving up and down the channel forever. We went through the woods out to the edge of the bluff. And there, tucked against the mossy bank, was a little cabin.

June's Study Cabin.

"Your study, Mother," the boys said.

All summer the three of them had worked on it and they had thought of everything. The cabin had a fireplace, a high bunk with two layers of huge cedar-shake file cases underneath it, a little closet at the end. There were two windows, one of them above the work bench, with shelves in the corner for books. The other window was larger and looked out over the water.

Though it was only eight by nine, that study held far more than the larger one in Bellingham. It was more compact than a ship's stateroom. For seats, Farrar had brought up water-smoothed log ends from the beach. A high one for the work bench, two low ones for "hobs" beside the fireplace. The floor was of sandstone, covered with a grass matting which the sea had washed in one day from a China ship.

My study was so far from the living cabin that it became an island joke. "Have you seen June this week?" people would ask Farrar when he went down to the dock without me. He slashed a trail above the beach, around the edge of Fishery Point from the living cabin to the study cabin. But once in a northeaster, spray dashed over it, ice covered the trail, and the wind blew fiercely. After that, Farrar slashed another trail across the point, through the woods. I could walk that second path and imagine myself in the deepest heart of Brazil. Then suddenly I would come out on Study Bluff and the world opened like a rose.

A half-mile around the point, at the other end of our waterfront, the living cabin sat flat on the ground behind a shelter of fir trees. If you came to visit us by boat, you would land on a beautiful sloping beach that curved without a break for two miles or more. Pull your boat up on the white drift logs that make a ring around all the Islands. Walk across deep white sand to the belt of woods and there, behind a group of virgin firs, you'll see the low cabin huddled close against the ground. Bend your head a little for the door is short for a tall man—Farrar found it down on the beach. Lift your foot to clear the sill log, step in onto four-inch-thick planks found on the beach and laid flat on the sand to be our floor.

You will turn left instinctively as you enter, for that is where the fireplace is. The fireplace that cost twenty cents. See how the immense flat

The Living Cabin.

sandstone blocks protect the logs of that corner from the fire. Farrar found them on a bank up near the study, brought them down in the rowboat, set them on edge, and secured them by spikes driven into the logs and bent over. Then he plastered the cracks with blue clay found down the beach in the other direction. There is a whole bluff of fine blue clay on our second place.

The twenty cents went to buy a piece of rusty old metal lath. It lines the corner of the cabin from floor to roof and the little pole chimney up on the roof. When the metal lath was nailed on over the logs, Farrar plastered it with the blue clay too, so there is no danger of fire.

There is a quarter-section of a lampshade over the corner of the cabin above the fire. A big lampshade, to be sure. It is the hood needed to make sure that all the smoke goes out the hole in the roof instead of into the house. When the first cabin was built, Farrar hadn't discovered that he could go out into the woods and find a limb curved to his need for the lower rim of the hood. He cut two poles, toenailed them together, nailed long cedar shakes parallel to the ground, taking them up to the roof where the chimney joins on and so fashioned his hood. But for the other cabins he cut limbs from trees, curved just right, nailed his shakes up and down to make beautiful flaring hoods.

Living Cabim with kitchen addition.

It took a gale to make the fireplace smoke. It wasn't a fireplace, really, it was better than that—a campfire in the house. The fire was built right on the ground, with the floor planks coming up to a row of stones around it.

We cooked our meals and did our canning on that fireplace for more than two years. In the second year, Farrar built a big kitchen onto the living cabin, with a secondhand range to cook on, and wide shelves for storage and handy tables. I think we used that kitchen three times. It was so much more fun to cook at the fireplace.

Farrar found a flat piece of iron which he laid across the stones above the fireplace. This was the hanging rod. With heavy wire he made loops around the iron, secured it to an old stove apron on which we could set

June playing the organ in the Living Cabin.

our pots, and we had a cooking platform. Other wire loops hung down to hold pots with handles. (After nine years that same stove apron is hanging there on the same wire loops, with blackened pots on nails for coffee or mush or whatever you want to cook. But when you go, be sure to take the old box off the chimney on top of the house. It keeps out the rain when we are not there. Once, someone forgot to take down the box and smoked himself out of the house and clear off the island.)

The seats are log-ends found on the beach. One of them is very wide and rather narrow—a perfect settee. Table, organ, long canvas-covered seat under another window, made of cedar shakes to hold bedding and camping things when we are not there, shelves all around the walls—that is the living room. The bedroom just beyond is a later addition. That first year we had two double bunks in the main cabin, one above the other, and the four of us used to lie there together—the best togetherness I have ever known—and watch the fire die out at night, shadows flickering on the walls.

The living cabin is built of peeled logs and has a shed roof, which is the most adaptable kind there is. It makes its highest joint with the roof at the corners and thus makes Farrar's corner campfires possible. It is sightly, too, when you have added on a shorter bonnet in front to cover a porch. You can have the gable type for looks and the shed type for convenience.

By now we had a living cabin, a study, a barn for the cow with a lean-to for the calves. We still wanted a cabin for the boys and one for Farrar so that every member of the family might have a private retreat. Farrar never built his own cabin but what fun we had building one for the boys. It was to be their Christmas present that first year when we had no idea what else to give them.

Along toward Christmas time they began to wonder what Christmas would be like without any money or toys or Christmas dinner. We promised them that with Christmas trees growing at our very door, rose hips and snowberries to make chains, they would remember this as the happiest Christmas of their lives. As a matter of fact, friends sent many gifts for the boys so they would have had something in any case.

On Christmas Eve we took the boys up to the study cabin to spend the night. We built a fire for them and left them tucked up in that solitary place, feeling a little timid, I think, though they wouldn't say so. They were to come down next morning when they heard a whistle. They had a clock so they wouldn't get up too early.

Early next morning Farrar moved the Christmas tree up to the new cabin we had built. We built a huge fire in the fireplace, decorated the cabin with fir and cedar boughs, cones, moss, snowberries, great clusters of madrona berries which lasted, that year, until after New Year. The cabin was beautiful. The bunks were made up, one on each side of the door. We had built the cabin with five sides so that the fireplace could be in one corner and still leave the cabin exactly divisible by two.

At seven we whistled for the boys and I went up the trail to meet them, blindfolded them, and led them about the brush for awhile, telling them they were going into a secret cave. At the door of the cabin we got down on hands and knees and crawled into the cave. We took off their blindfolds when they were seated on their own bench beside the fire.

The boys blinked at the light and color. "It's our cabin," shouted North. "Oh, Bobby, it's a cabin for us! See the bunks!"

It was the happiest Christmas of their lives.

XXII. LIVING ON NOTHING A YEAR

WE CALLED our place on Waldron, Sundown Farm, though it really wasn't a farm at all. True, we had a cow—after a few months, two cows. But we had no pasture and no fences. We rented a pasture a mile down the beach and Bob took the cow down every morning before going to school, sometimes in pouring rain, sometimes in a northeaster that all but froze his breath.

Both boys helped with the cooking and the dishes, took care of their own cabin, and helped with the washing on Saturday. None of us liked to wash, but we didn't mind too much when we all did it together.

Farrar cleared ground for a garden. We planted spinach seed in the fall, hoping to have greens early in the spring. It came up in February and the first of March we had our first raw spinach salad, made of leaves so small and delicate it would have been a shame to cook them. With dressing made of heavy cream, egg, and cider vinegar it was perfect with our hot hoecake.

Early in the spring, all hands worked in the garden which came up around stumps, between rocks, among the logs. It wasn't the garden we had had in Bellingham, but it served.

In February wild nettles came up. We wore gloves and used scissors to gather them so as not to be stung. We ate nettles every day for two months or more, for if you keep them trimmed down, they do not run to seed but continually put out tender new shoots. Nettles have a slightly medicinal flavor which we grew to like very much. And they do not sting, of course, after they are cooked.

People constantly asked how we managed to live on an uncleared place without money. Occasionally we had a little money from work on the road or from selling a fish. And we had laid in a stock of supplies before we gave up what income we had in Bellingham. We had tons of hay for the cow, sacks of grain for the chickens, sacks of ground-wheat for us.

In addition to the wheat, wild greens, and garden things, we had fish. We gathered apples from an abandoned orchard, too, and they lasted until long after Christmas. Milk, butter, a few eggs, dozens and dozens of cans of vegetables I had put up from the Bellingham garden, and, the next year, canned fruit and vegetables from the McNaught gardens and orchards. Those lean Scotsmen practically adopted us and we them. From their well-tended, fruitful acres we had all we wanted, except, of course, of their income crops like eggs and cream. No thrifty farmer gives away his cash crop; but they let us have all the cherries, apples, pears, carrots, cabbage, peas and beans we could use. The Scot is the most generous person in the world anyhow. Thrifty, canny, industrious, he always has something to share; big-hearted, friendly, kind, he shares it.

Whenever Farrar got work on the road, we replenished our staples—salt, sugar, rice, and, oh, blessed event, coffee! Listed like this, it sounds like high living, but at times we were close to bedrock. At the end of two years we figured that four of us had lived for twenty-six months on two hundred dollars.

One of the secrets of living inexpensively is standardized meals. People used to commiserate with me about cooking on the fireplace. I could never convince them that it was fun and no harder than their cooking. Sometimes, when they came to our island, they used to make fun of the time we spent in getting our food. We began to think about it. It was true, we spent nearly all our time getting enough to eat. Going after the cow and taking her back to pasture. Cutting wood. Milking, fishing, gathering hay, rowing around to the McNaughts for vegetables and fruit, gardening, canning, cooking. But we had the evenings for reading and talking. And there were always a few hours a day to sit by our fires and talk and read and dream. About six hours a day went into hard physical work whose only purpose was getting something to eat.

Then we reflected that that was the purpose of all work. The people who laughed at us spent eight hours a day in offices and laboratories, and had only food and shelter to show for it. They, too, could not sit about their fires to read and talk until their work was done. When we thought about it, it seemed that everyone worked simply for something to eat, and that most of them worked at jobs they didn't enjoy, while everything we did on Sundown Farm was rich pleasure. Even the boys understood that.

But to get back to standardized meals. We ate practically the same meals every day and never tired of them. For breakfast, we had a huge pot of ground-wheat mush, faintly smoky, eaten with all the rich cream we wanted. Glasses of whole milk, over six percent butter fat. For lunches, hard scones of ground wheat, unsalted butter, an apple, perhaps a boiled egg. For dinner, which we called supper, hot hoecake swimming in butter, fresh greens, salad of dandelion or miner's lettuce, or sorrel, or our own garden things. We often had fresh salmon or canned meat, canned fruit after the second summer, or raw apples. We never tired of anything we had.

Of course, we were lonely at times. The Bill Chevaliers lived down the beach and their children and ours went to school together so the boys weren't lonely. Every morning I wrote in my study and Farrar worked on the place. In the afternoons we worked together. In summer, there was fishing, gardening, canning, fruit-gathering. Farrar and I still had so much to talk about that the longest winter evenings were too short for us. Yet running through those rainy winter days there was a sense of waiting. We never called it loneliness. Country people think of it as waiting for spring. But it is a kind of loneliness.

During the second summer one of our old forest-ranger friends came with his family and bought the place next to ours, and after that stayed for six months during the summer, building friendships which will last all our lives.

"I wouldn't live on an island," people said, "so far from a doctor—no way of getting help when you need it." Isolation is sometimes fatal when there is serious illness, but the deaths due directly to city congestion account for far more deaths than isolation ever causes.

But, of course, when you need a doctor, you need one. Bill Chevalier had the only motor boat on Waldron, and when anyone was ill, Bill would either bring the doctor to the patient or take the patient to the doctor. Or, if Bill was not at home, someone would row across to Orcas Island and telephone to the Coast Guard.

The children made fine progress in the little island school. Of course, they missed the extras—organized play, music, drama, good books. But they gained in the sense of non-competition. Some children are stampeded by competition. All children, I think, are harmed by it, taught to put values on grades instead of on the acquiring of new disciplines. Grading systems are anachronisms and ought to be scrapped forever.

We discovered that if you give a child a chore he values it. If you demand a chore from him, he hates it. If he neglects his chore, simply take it away from him, without words or upbraiding, and he will not neglect it again. That chore represents to him his belongingness. It is his proof of being a part of the family unit.

Children are proud and naturally courteous. They are extremely aware of all the currents of emotions and thoughts around them. With everything open and friendly and co-operative in the family, they are happy. They discipline themselves. Once, when North was twelve, he went to visit some relatives who quarreled a little. He was surprised and wrote home to ask, in amusing seriousness, whether we knew that grown men and women sometimes quarreled as he and Bobby did?

Community life on Waldron was full of interest. Someone from every family went to the dock to meet the boat, bring home the mail or supplies, and so we all kept up with the island happenings. On the dock, school affairs were discussed, road work decided upon, parties planned. Fishing or clam-digging jaunts were talked about. Someone promised to help his neighbor with the haying. Another offered to cut some wood for the schoolhouse.

At Christmas there was always a program, a tree, and inexpensive gifts for everyone. At the dock we drew names and bought gifts for those whose names we had drawn. Occasionally we had a dance in the schoolhouse, with everyone bringing a lantern to hang on nails around the room. The women made cakes or sandwiches or brought coffee. We always took the cream—it was the only thing we could take. At midnight someone would make coffee on the big heating stove and we would have supper. The music was furnished by a squeaky old phonograph with worn records.

Even during our two years, the island pattern changed a lot. Young people grew up and went away to Normal School or CCC camps, or to Alaska with the fishing. Families moved away, others came, a few died and were buried in the little acre plot cleared from the forest and fenced and kept neat by the community.

When the first white woman to come to the island moved away we wrote to an engineer friend of ours who was stationed in Central America, telling him that the hundred and sixty acres could be bought for a song. He sent the song and we bought the place for him. Late that summer his younger brother and his bride came to Waldron and began forthwith to change all our lives. They set out to turn that old, worn-out place into a modern poultry farm; and they are doing it, scandalizing us with their speedy achievements.

In no time at all, they had a chicken house and boxes of chicks shipped from California. Then they had another chicken house and another. They were using so much lumber, they decided to build their own sawmill. Then there were more chicken houses, a truck, and a tractor. How much water the chickens drank! They needed water piped into the chicken houses, and they did it. Puget Sound days are so short in winter, and the hens go to bed so early at the very time when egg prices are best, that they put in a plant so they could generate electricity for lights to lengthen the days for the hens.

They added a threshing machine, another truck, an old car. It would be nice if there were a beautiful log store on a bluff by the dock. It would pay its way and perhaps make money. Anyhow it would enhance the value of their property. They built it.

The poultry ranch is now complete, with our engineer friend sending checks all these years to support its rapid growth—no mere hens, even the sixty percent laying kind, could do that. For eight years, he has financed the ranch. Sometimes the net income from the hens has gone as high as two hundred dollars in a single month, but improvements and building and labor have been twice as high as the income. The engineer may be said to support two families and he has enabled many other Waldron families to earn their groceries for months at a time. He says that even moderate incomes like his are not taxed in proportion to the indirect taxes which the poor must pay, and he makes up for it by paying out his salary in wages for others, living very simply himself. He maintains that if all conspired to keep money in circulation the great problem of unemployment would be solved.

True, he and his manager brother are rapidly achieving a farmstead capable, in time, of supporting them all. From their seventeen hundred hens, Waldrona Farm ships 630 dozen eggs a week. They keep books on all their activities from the eggs to the store. The figures during these eight years make an amazing story—a modern Growth of the Soil.

During these later years, others have bought on the island. We decided to sell our second twenty-two acre place. We had paid $125 for it and sold it for $500. We sold it through one of those friendly little personal ads in *The Saturday Review of Literature*. A number of people answered, for we spoke of mountains and salmon and ships, of beaches and virgin trees and a high, overlooking bluff. One man telephoned from Philadelphia but we didn't want to sell sight unseen. We wanted congenial neighbors—though, of course, we needed the money, too. There was a letter from the wife of a university professor in Ohio which was just right. We invited them out. They came, we saw, we loved. They went over to Waldron and bought the place.

Waldron has grown from a population of forty to a metropolis of sixty or more in summer. It is pleasant to have neighbors on all the farms, with no land lying idle, no white beach without its bonfire on summer nights, boats out in the channel going up and down, up and down, after the leaping salmon.

We seem to do things, and find out why, later on. After we had been on Waldron awhile we discovered that the discipline of chores, the rapid progress made in a non-competitive school, primitive living which required a maximum of activity and skill were so good for the boys that we must have gone for that. But we could spare only two years for it, for North ought to return to his own school for the last year in the grades. At least, we wanted to return to town and that sounded like an excellent reason.

We had rented our Bellingham cabins to an artist who had sketched and painted them from every angle, and she had piped water up the hill into one of the cabins. We had not received rent from her but had let her apply it on the improvements she made on the place. She left Two Acres in far better shape than she had found it, and now she had so grown to love life in this simple style that she had built herself a cabin much farther out in the wilderness.

Our Bellingham cabins were vacant then, and we decided to return to them in time for school in September. The boys were as strong as young oxen. They could wield an ax like woodsmen, milk a cow, plant and cultivate a garden, wash clothes. Bob could cook and North was an expert house cleaner. They could row and sail and fish for salmon. They knew the technique of felling a tree in any direction they wanted it to go. They could build. They knew the edible wild greens, the names of trees and shrubs. They were happy, well-disciplined and sure of themselves.

It had been a fruitful two winters and three summers. A golden age. Salmon leaping below my study bluff, ships from Japan steaming up the International Boundary beyond Skipjack Island, lighthouses throwing their long gleams down the starlit channels. Three log cabins and remembered hours beside their glowing fires, close family togetherness such as we will never know again, I think.

XXIII. WE GET A BEAR BY THE TAIL

FARRAR and I seem to have a genius for plunging ourselves into difficulties of our own making. Shortly after we returned to Bellingham, we deliberately took a bear by the tail and in no time at all, the wolf was at the door. We started a weekly publication of our own which we called *The Puget Sounder*.

June and Farrar's publication.

To others who have been beguiled into that venture, the story of the next few years would be no surprise. We could neither chase off the wolf nor turn loose the bear. For once you have started a journal, taken subscriptions and sold advertising contracts, you are in for it. You can't fail, for there is no money to return the subscriptions or to pay advertising damages. And you can't go on because you have lived on the money that came in, instead of paying it to the printer. Soon you are deep in debt.

My old column had not been forgotten, and before we went to press with our first issue, we had 750 subscriptions to the new publication, which was to carry "Puget Soundings" as one of its features.

Luckily, we had a printer who could afford to carry us. At the end of the first six months we saw that we were on the verge of failing and called him into conference. He suggested that we change to a monthly instead of a weekly and said that he would carry us a little longer. We gave him a deed to Two Acres in Bellingham for a thousand or fifteen hundred dollars—I don't remember which. "The place isn't worth fifteen hundred," we told him. "Never mind," he said, "your bill won't be, either." And we left it at that.

From the beginning, Farrar sold enough advertising on *The Puget Sounder* to keep it free of debt. But we still needed some way of supporting ourselves and we hit upon radio. We called in two of our most faithful advertisers and suggested that they co-operate with us on a half-hour weekly radio program. I was to write the programs, and Farrar and I were to produce them. We expected that both circulation and advertising would improve once the radio program was under way, but they didn't.

The program was fun to produce, however. We called it "Little Tours of Puget Sound." We really took the tours, for I never could write imaginary episodes as well as actual ones. I always managed to get down real conversations out of which to build the dramatized script the next day. Farrar and I wrote the scripts, commercials, did the announcing, directing, and took our parts in the show every Wednesday evening.

We went to the famous Oceanography Laboratories in Friday Harbor and got one of the scientists there to come to Bellingham and appear on the program. We went to Diablo Dam, on the Skagit River, where Seattle's Electric Company gives a spectacular week-end tour of its own. We waded in hip boots on the mudflats to see the oyster beds where Japanese oyster seed were scattered, grown to huge sizes, harvested, canned, and sold. We visited the wonderful gardens of the Sound country. We covered the land like locusts.

By the second year, *The Puget Sounder* had two thousand subscribers but it wasn't making a living for anyone. We thought we might do better if we moved to Seattle. We had used up our fifteen-hundred-dollar credit with our printer and if we left now, we would be clear of debt. We had climbed up to zero again.

In Seattle, marketing The Puget Sounder, *Farrar said, "Whenever I have this hand in mine I always feel like eloping off for some adventure."*

In Seattle we found another printer and this time we almost kept abreast of our bills for awhile. We kept most of the Bellingham advertising and gained some new Seattle accounts. Then we found a sponsor for Farrar's radio program of homespun philosophy, songs, and nonsense, who paid us almost enough to live on while I conducted another radio program in behalf of *The Puget Sounder*.

On the new program I interviewed most of the famous people of the Northwest. The great anthropologist, Dr. Ales Hrdlicka, on one of his annual trips to Alaska, appeared on my program. Father Hubbard, the glacier priest, came, too. Seattle is filled with interesting and colorful people. There is the Flower Lady, a gentlewoman of seventy-five who does her own gardening and sometimes gathers baskets of flowers and takes them into town, giving them to anyone who looks sad or tired. There is the Flower Man, who grows immense roses and makes perfume from them, as they do in France. There is a merchant who experiments with fine tomatoes on the roof of his pickle factory.

Meanwhile, *The Puget Sounder* was running along as usual. We filled its columns with pictures of this scenic land and with articles and stories by all the writers and leaders of the Northwest. Esther Loomis, a landscape architect, wrote Puget Sound Gardens; Edith Hardin English wrote about the alpine flora of the Cascades, on which she is an authority; J. M. Edson, about the birds and mammals of the Northwest; Dr. T. G. Thompson about his Oceanography Laboratories, the work of the university's famous research ship, the *Catalyst,* and about the effect of the Japan Current on life in Puget Sound. The State Planning Council wrote one entire issue, the Forest Service another, the schools another. One of the university professors became fiction editor. An advertiser agreed to sponsor that department, giving a small check to each writer whose story was published. We were going to discover the new writers of the Northwest.

Once a funny thing happened to me. An advertising agent asked us to take a whiskey advertisement and I refused. They insisted and finally we agreed that we would run that ad if I could write an editorial against it in the same issue. The makers of Hudson's Bay Whiskey have a sense of humor. They agreed to place a full page ad in spite of my editorial. When the paper came out, the advertiser liked the anti-whiskey editorial so much that he ordered five thousand extra copies of the issue, had a big red arrow printed over the face of each copy with "See Page 4" on it, and used it as a mailing piece all over the state. I got into trouble with the post office over that, for a publication with second-class mailing privilege may not sell extra copies in that way. But the damage was done and we got new subscribers from all over the state.

It was still nip and tuck, however. The boys had paper routes and made enough to buy their own clothes and provide themselves with spending money. Farrar sold real estate. I wrote freelance advertising copy. We had our radio programs. Still, we couldn't keep that journal out of debt. It hung like a dead weight around our necks.

I was forever getting *The Sounder* into somebody's bad grace. We fought for the cause of conservation, the most vital economic issue of the Northwest, though not the most popular with the business men. But even there it often happened that I did not believe in specific planks of the conservationists' platform. Thus, in one breath, I would get Mr. Ickes down on me, though I admired his courageous stand; in the next breath, the Forest Service which I loved; and the lumbermen were against me all the time, for though I thought they should be allowed to continue operations, I believed they had betrayed their land.

I had a genius for getting into trouble. I would work with sportsmen and purse seiners to help outlaw the salmon traps, and then I'd try my best to outlaw the sportsmen's wasteful "salmon derbies."

Once Farrar had a big market practically signed up with an advertising contract. Simultaneously, I had done a story about the market. It was beautiful—a colored photograph of those meticulously arranged stalls would rival the Grand Canyon. But try to buy those perfect vegetables. You'd be given faulty ones from a pile behind the counter. I didn't know Farrar was getting a contract from them and that there was talk of a radio tie-up. Anyhow, I ran the story and Farrar did not get the contract. He never blamed me for it. He said if we couldn't make the journal pay by telling what we thought was true, we'd fold. We folded.

I don't mean to suggest that ours was a heroic failure. Conservation was the only heroic cause we upheld. No, it was a good, hearty failure—but not heroic. We poured all our time, energy, and hope into that publication,

WE GET A BEAR BY THE TAIL

but it wasn't enough. It had been a merry-hearted little journal that often made people laugh, and sometimes made them angry, but too often it left them indifferent, and that was fatal.

We flung nearly all our possessions into it—the Bellingham place, the "strip" on Waldron. Farrar even mortgaged our homestead island—Sentinel—to keep us going. Sundown Farm itself was threatened. At last, we saw that it was hopeless, and began to let the circulation dwindle.

In 1938, North entered the University of Washington.

Bob was in high school. The time had come to settle down. And so, with the March, 1939, issue, *The Puget Sounder* was no more. We were going to miss that bear, and we still had the wolf anyhow.

Now what! What do wild, untrained, wanderlusting people do when they want to make some money? Farrar had grown to be in considerable demand as an entertainer and public speaker. When his brother Bob became so popular, Farrar's speaking engagements became so heavy he had to charge for them. A talking tour of Washington netted him three hundred dollars in one month.

We had some radio experience to go on, and I had done a great deal of advertising copy writing. But how could we co-ordinate all that into a plan for making steady money? We did not know.

We decided, at last, that Farrar was to go to New York and try to turn

Farrar, singing his way to New York.

his entertaining and radio experience to account. He would barnstorm across the country, as he had done around the state, and make enough to keep the family going as he went.

So one morning Farrar drove east. The next day he got a fifty-dollar engagement for three days in a boom town, and from then until he struck North Dakota he sent back more money than we had had in a long time. I paid all our small bills, leaving the big ones until later. For the first time in years I bought a new dress and hat. It began to seem that Farrar could go over the United States, talking at theaters and clubs, amusing people. He called his talk, "How to be Happy, Anyway."

To save money, Farrar camped out. He would make his talk, drive out of town until he reached a likely-looking place, drive off the road and, in the dark, get out sleeping bag and turn in. When he struck the cold country in November he slept in the car, curled up on the back seat. He would empty the radiator into a gallon water jug and use it for a hot water bottle and still he nearly froze. I had made him a huge sleeping bag of two virgin wool homemade comforters. He had extra blankets, an extra comforter, a canvas. And still he froze.

Farrar, sitting by his campfire.

But in the mornings, when he crawled out of the car, built a campfire and made coffee and bacon and toast, he was whole again. And he loved it. There is something about a campfire to revive you no matter what is wrong.

In Minneapolis, Farrar forgot to drain the radiator and it froze, the engine burst, and he sold the wreck for ten dollars. He took a train to Chicago and stayed there nearly six months, getting so many club dates, with an occasional week on the radio, that he would be there yet if he hadn't thought he ought to come on to New York and try for big time on the radio.

Farrar at WINS radio studio in New York City.

Part Five

THE CAMPFIRE BURNS

June and Bob before setting off on their trek.

"You mean just walk out the door and be off?"
Bob's eyes were shining. "That's what I mean."
June Burn

XXIV. O AMERICA!

NOW I come to a part I dread to write. It was one of the richest adventures of my life, but it wasn't conventional. It wasn't making money as I should have been doing. It wasn't—but I might as well tell it.

After Farrar left, I did my best to find a job but there was deep depression in Seattle and no openings to be found. One evening I said to Bob, "How would you like to do your studying on the road with me for the rest of the year?"

Bob's face lit up. He and I had grown up on adventure stories, he in his generation, and I in mine—stories of boys going out for to seek their fortune, their possessions tied in a rag on a stick slung over their shoulder, stowing away on ships, sleeping on park benches, great hardships, great expectations. From Horatio Alger to J. B. Priestley.

"Fine," he said casually. He had heard so many wild plans, off and on, he refused to get excited. "When do we start?" he twinkled at me.

"Next Monday," I said, and he began to wake up. "You really mean it? Where are we going? What for? How will I keep up with my class?"

"Yes, I mean it. I'll never find a good job unless I look for it. There must be money somewhere for us. Maybe South America. Or Mexico. We may go there."

"But how will we travel? We haven't any money to start on."

"The Chinese say the longest journey begins with one step. We can take that, can't we?"

"You mean just walk out the door and be off?" Bob's eyes were shining.

"That's what I mean."

I had written the department of education at Washington for a list of universities which give high school correspondence courses, and from one of them I had got their course in Algebra, and one in Spanish. And before I forget it, I should say that Bob's grade averages were so high and he so well mastered self-discipline that he has gone to the top in all his studies since the trip. There are advantages to study and school with one's fellows around one. But for speed and real mastery of a subject, individual instruction is certainly superior. Then add the beauty and freedom and happiness of the open road, and a child learns so fast you can't believe it.

Before Bob and I left, we found North an attic room, just off the campus, where he could live alone as other college boys lived. His windows overlooked a ravine with trees so near that squirrels flowed down the branches to sit on the windowsills and beg. The boys and I painted the room, furnished and decorated it as gaily as we could. It was a great success. To save money, North would make his own meals on a two-burner electric plate. He had a tiny radio, plenty of lamps, tables, bookshelves, a couch with many cushions and one easy chair.

Friends persuaded Bob and me to have typhoid injections which delayed us two weeks and then, one rainy morning in early March, 1940, Bob and I shouldered our packs and set off down the highway. We meant to hitchhike to California, so as to get out of the bad weather quickly, and then to walk all over that radiant state. Two weeks later, we were in San Francisco.

Along the way we rode with people of all kinds, from every stratum of American life, and caught significant echoes of the preoccupations of troubled people during troubled times.

A truck driver—"They'll have to take me feet first into the next war."

A farmer from up in the hills—"If England lets Finland lose, it's good-by England and France."

A lumber company executive—"Things will begin to pick up soon. The war is bound to bring a boom."

An attorney on his way to fight his company's case against the NLRB—"Oh, we're bound to get in it. We can't keep out."

A truck driver—"What gets me is the way Hitler treats old people. I'd fight about that. You ought not to treat old people like that."

A Pentecostal preacher—"Are you saved?"

A mining engineer—"We'll surely get in it. It ought to bring a boom. But if I were a young man I'd refuse to go, just the same. It's the big boys' war."

A farmer—"If I had my way, I'd conscript all the young men in America and give them military training. Nothing like it for discipline."

An unemployed man hunting a job—"I don't like to see anyone walking when I got room."

A lot of America was drifting along the road. While we rested under a tree, a man came by carrying no baggage at all. He wore two shirts and an overcoat.

North, student at the University of Washington.

He was going home to Kansas after twelve years of trying to find steady work in the sawmill country. He seemed kind, humorous, tolerant. "I'm going home to Kansas," he said, "and I can hardly wait to get back."

When you walk, you are somewhere at every step. In a car you are somewhere only when you stop. How good to walk after a ride! Walk long and hard. Feel your heavy packs. Feel your body. Feel yourself moving over the earth.

It rained and rained. It poured. But Bob and I always found somewhere to get into shelter during the sudden downpours. Once we stopped in a barn where men were sacking oats. Huge percherons waited, harnessed, their hoofs making echoing noises on the floor of the barn when they shifted position. Their breath was sweet, mingled with the smell of dusty oats, smell of the rain outside, acrid smell of an oak tree just coming into leaf.

Tiny wet balls of gray wool are dropping in a field. Even in the rain they turn into lively dry balls of snow-white wool as we watch. It is lambing time on this farm.

Daylight is a blessed thing. Tired brains can conjure up such horrible things at night, but the daylight always dissipates them and you see a good, safe world after all. But when night comes down again, there is the same unease waiting for us. I think it is the sense of doom that has fallen on all of us. Ever since Munich we've had it. More since Poland. And most of all since Finland. We feel helpless. And to feel helpless is dangerous. It is the most dangerous thing of all. Everyone should be able to take up his cards and say to himself, "I will play this one now. I will do something about it," in full confidence that there is still something to be done. 0 America! I think my generation grew up loving her as no other has.

Looking up the Rogue River from Agness.

Myrtle trees are in bloom. Along Rogue River manzanita and sagebrush are blooming. Meadowlarks send up little spurts of golden sound. Southern Oregon is a new, different, more spacious world. We come into Northern California country while we are still in Oregon. Long leaf pine, madrona, manzanita with its little pink bells.

We are living on fifty cents a day for the two of us except when it rains and we sleep in auto camps. Out of Ashland, Oregon, we pass a long string of hitchhikers, a very picket fence of thumbs leaning toward California.

Eleven miles to the summit of a Coast Range mountain dividing Oregon from California. Klamath River, Shasta River, wind blowing across the sagebrush. As we descended into California we began to see more and more signs of gold mining. Mines perched on steep hillsides. Masses of gravel where dredges were going down a valley scooping up the rocks and gravel, washing off the gold, piling the tailings in a row like a miniature range of mountains.

Marysville is in the very heart of California. A wrestler with eyebrows like John L. Lewis and a dry, shy wit brought us from snowy mountains in Oregon to this radiant sunny lowland on what may have been a magic carpet, for it was night and we hadn't seen the slow transition from mountain to valley.

The first thing we noticed about the sun-laved town was the number of derelicts on the streets. Seattle doesn't get them so much because our climate is not hospitable to the homeless. Out at the edge of town, along the bright banks of the Yuba River, we saw our first Okies. Their ramshackle camp stank in the sunshine. They had dug holes in the sand, stuck up four poles, stretched gunnysacks around the poles and called them privies. Shrubs along the bank waved signs of the recent flood from their bare twigs. People said we would hate the filth of Mexico, but I knew I would not mind it as I did this. For this was home. One sees the dust on one's own mantelpiece with agonizing sharpness, but hardly knows if his neighbor's house is deep in dust.

What bursting sunshine! Peach orchards in bloom, larks singing on every fence post, acacia trees yellow, fragrant, soft as downy ducks. Fleeces of clouds sailing along, blue hills in the far distance, green fields near. A car full of Okies stopped. They could not offer us a ride but they asked if we were all right—whether we had food enough. It was not long since they had made that trip from the dust bowl to this sweet land and they knew what poverty and hardship were. Hoboes on a passing freight waved gaily to us as we sat by the side of the road, resting. After every ride we walked until we were tired and then rested until somebody stopped to give us another lift.

Here came an old man pushing a two-wheeled cartfull of rags in gunnysacks. "Oh, I don't want no rides." he said, scratching himself. "I ain't goin' nowhurs. Whur'd I be if I did git a ride? I go along easy like, sell some rags, bum me a meal now and then. A lady gimme a piece of fresh meat this big awhile ago. An' I sold $1.58 worth of rags a-Sattidy. That'll do me a long spell with bummin' in between. It's better than relief. I wouldn't take relief if I died for it! Me, I'll bum like a gentleman!"

Peach orchards, a very dream of rose-purple. Trees pruned down to the blunt, angular branches, the new twigs hanging down from them like weeping willows. It is these slender twigs that are in flower. My eyes are thirsty for the sight of them heavy with fruit.

In Sacramento, one of our friends made a speaking date for me at the Lions' Club and at a festive meeting of the employees of a big insurance company there. The ten dollars with which we had left Seattle had lasted so far. Now we would make what seemed like huge sums of money. It was great fun making the talks. I had forgotten how pleasant it is to hear people laugh at one's nonsense.

In California, March is like May. Everything begins to bloom. The orchards foam with white plum and pear, purple peach and yellow mustard and poppies scattered around below the trees. Once we camped in an orchard under ancient, gnarled prune trees. Black, angular branches, pruned for decades, stuck out at crazy angles. Blooms hugged the stems and turned them into soft feather boas that stood on their tails in grotesque arrangement.

The full moon shone on the orchard by night and on other flowering hills falling away in every direction. Not far from us there was a famous gold mine in the middle of a peach orchard. Its early-morning whistle mingled with the bird songs. Petals from the trees fell down into the deep dark shaft and onto the tops of the cars parked around the mine.

A Pentecostal preacher and his wife were camped in this orchard. They were lonely and said if we would stay in their orchard another night they would take us to a Pentecostal meeting on a nearby Indian Reservation. The preacher was sure we'd be saved if we would only go. I had known revivals and camp meetings as a child but it would be a new experience for Bob.

The little white church, with flowers and a well-tended strip of lawn, was as pretty as a picture in the moonlight. Inside, the preacher knelt by the altar, praying in a rather musical, nimble succession of syllables which he meant to be the "unknown tongue" of the Bible.

The preacher's wife and little son also prayed at the altar, their voices rising and falling as accompaniment to his. It was incongruous to see him take down one of his uplifted hands to push back his glasses and look at his watch while the syllables went right on.

After awhile a woman went onto the platform to lead the singing and the congregation sang heartily in ragtime style, song after song, fast and slow, sometimes keeping time by clapping.

Then an old woman led the testimonial meeting.

"I want to praise the Lord because I am His and He is mine. Glory Hallelujah!"

After each testimonial the preacher's wife would strum a chord on her guitar and they would all sing. Sometimes the preacher joined in with his saxophone or his nice baritone.

"I want to praise the Lord because two years ago I was a drunken driver and now I am saved . . . I want to praise the Lord because I am not one of them modern dancers . . . I want to praise the Lord because he saved my soul and what a wonderful world it seems to me now . . .

XXV. RATTLESNAKE IN THE BUTTERCUPS

EXCEPT for rainy nights, Bob and I slept out of doors. Late in the afternoon, we would stop in a town to buy bread, butter, bacon, fruit, a vegetable, two potatoes, some fresh meat and milk, and set out along the road until we came to a good camping place beside a stream or under a tree in a pasture. We could carry a quart of water in our canteen and we were therefore free to stop anywhere.

At camp, we would build a fire and cook supper, using Bob's Boy Scout cooking outfit. One of us used the frying pan for a plate, and the other used the plate that comes with the set.

Sleep, flat on the ground, sleep under stars, sprinkling down their beauty through the leaves; sleep in deep soft grass, or on pine needle beds; in oak leaves—and sometimes, when we made camp after dark, in poison ivy.

In the early mornings I used to lie looking up into the leaves, thinking about my boys in a world gone mad. What would become of my sons—of young German, English, French, Russian boys? Lying there, so close to the ground, my sons became all sons, I one mother, with the pity of every boy, whistling in this dark, tearing me to bits.

For Democracy, we say, to give us something to hold onto. We couldn't endure it otherwise. Finland going—for nothing. The beast of Germany rampant—for nothing at all. Germany a hollow suit of armor on the march, half men inside. And we being whirled faster and faster into the vortex. How could we bear it? Our sons, this generation, brought up so bravely to hate war as the coward's way. Are we to say now, "No, we taught you wrong. It is the hero's way, after all."

Old men, old women, too, congressmen, industrialists, munitions makers rigging up something great to tell the people. For, let the real cause of war be what it will, the people fight only when they believe the cause to be something great and splendid. And that is the noblest comment on humankind. You have to give them something grand to fight for, or they won't fight.

I thought of my brother, Clive, and how his heart was broken after Versailles, his body broken before that. Now were my North and Bob and all the other young sons of America to be broken body and soul on the same old barbaric wheel?—Oh, there is the morning star. It is dawn. The leaves tremble in the first daylight breeze. Now the tips of the grasses stir—birds begin to chirp. A few feet away, Bob opens his eyes.

We make breakfast of toast, butter, bacon, and coffee and put up a lunch of whatever is left. Then, at lunch time, we sometimes stop to buy more milk and raw fruit; thus we balance our diet.

Now for lessons. We let the fire die, and as the sun comes up I write in my journal while Bob studies. Then I look over the paper which is going to the university and hear him recite his Spanish. It is eleven o'clock and after before we start our day's travels. There is no hurry. Bob lifts his heavy pack and I hold it while he puts his arms into the straps. Then he lifts mine and holds it for me. We put on our hats, mine an immense Mexican straw which a friend in San Francisco had given me, to keep the glaring sun out of my eyes. We see that every spark of our fire is out. Now for the highway.

Sometimes we walk for miles before a car comes to a stop beside us and a voice says, "Want a ride?" Sometimes we barely reach the highway before we are picked up.

Bob wanted to see snow—deep mountain snow. We decided to go up to Lake Tahoe, that jewel of blue water rimmed, now, in high walls of snow. We rode with the driver of an orange truck, selling oranges grown on his ranch in Southern California. After he let us off, we climbed and climbed up a beautiful mountain road, through pines. After awhile, just as we were wishing someone would come along, a big orange truck came by. It was the same man.

"I was afraid nobody would come along, on this road," he said. "There isn't much travel this time of year. I can just as well go your way."

When we had planned to go to Lake Tahoe, we overlooked one thing: that there would be nowhere to camp. Everything was covered with snow. It was deep in all the forests, rimming the water. Auto camps were not open, nor were the Government parks. Snow plows had kept the road open and we walked between walls of snow, green trees above us, green water on our left. The blinding sun had melted the snow from around the base of the trees, but when we waded knee deep to some of these bare spots, we found the ground wet, no wood for fire, no possibility of camping.

We came to an oil station which had been boarded up for the winter. The sun had melted the snow from the front porch of the little cottage. We decided to spend the night on that porch, without a fire, with no supper but crackers and cheese and fruit.

Just then a truck came by, driven by a caretaker for one of the big summer places on the lake. He said we would freeze if we slept out in our light sleeping bags that night. We must come home with him and camp in their little boat. We could have a fire in his tool house and cook our supper there.

Thus we saw the beautiful lake by moonlight from the portholes of a yacht, rocking ever so gently on the quiet water, Mt. Rubicon over us, mountains all around, deep snow everywhere, pale green water spreading out under a nearly full moon, a tiny island not far away—stars, trees, and silence. Bob drank from the lake. He said, "On a walking trip through the mountains we leaned over the side of the boat and dipped up a cup of water."

We left Tahoe as fast as we could. We had walked and driven its full length on the California side and we decided to return to the temperate zone by Highway 50. People had warned us that we wouldn't get any lifts that way but we didn't care. It was lovely in the mountains. We could walk thirty miles a day—walking all night, if we had to, so as not to freeze.

People were right. There was no traffic on this highway. All day long we walked between head-high snow walls, down a mountain highway that curved around the great blue lake, looked out over snowy mountains, big trees, white valleys embroidered with black shadows. Pines, firs, cedars, manzanita. Huge brown stems of trees rising from the snow everywhere. A silent world.

After miles of snow walls we came to Upper Truckee River. We had had only one lift, of about three miles, and we were too tired to go any further that night. We were almost without food, too. We saw a roadside stand with smoke in the chimney, and bought a loaf of homemade bread.

We had found a camping place that was comparatively dry and built our campfire for the night—the first in two days. It was like news from home, that fragrant smoke curling up between the trees. Then the woman who had sold us the bread came through the woods, hunting us. She said we would freeze, sleeping outside. She had a guest cabin which was in disorder, but there was a stove in it. Wouldn't we come over and sleep there that night?

Next morning, clouds had come up. It was going to storm again. We had to get out before new snow blocked the way. I was really frightened.

That was a wide valley, level as a floor. Pony Express stations along the way. Up, now, to the summit. Up, endlessly, between walls of snow, walking on the shady side, for white snow reflects heat. Only six cars passed all mornmg.

At every curve of the road a new view opened up, now a creek's canyon far below, the tree trunks standing out separately in the snow; now Lake Tahoe not very far away, silvery blue. Some of the Sierra peaks were fir-tipped, others pure white with snow meadows opening out between them.

The summit was still miles away. We'd die if we had to walk all that way, we said. We'd find ourselves camping out at seven thousand feet yet, if we didn't look out. The snow walls were so high now we could not see over them. Our only view, straight up, was of the exquisite pointed crowns of the silver-green long leaf pines against the blue sky.

The summit! At Echo Summit Lodge, completely buried in snow, we doffed our packs and walked up to the roof where others had climbed before us. There we commanded a 320 degree view of Tahoe, canyons, Sierras, meadows, trees. How did the pioneers cross these divides? What drove them to it? Adventure? Failure? Gold?

Down now. The snow had become a white prison. The clouds were boiling up again. The storm would catch us yet.

Walls of snow. Mountains. Silence sharpened by the small roar of water under the snow walls. On and on and on. Bob's left foot is blistered. Skiers fly by in their cars. If the storm doesn't catch us, we can get down to Placerville in two days—it is only fifty miles away. I watch the darkening sky.

At last a truck rounds a bend coming down a slope. It roars by—no, it stops—it backs up! It is full of young people going home to Placerville. There is plenty of room for us behind. The truck swoops down to the town, forty miles away. Down and down, out of the snow to the land of little creeks and rivers. Down to the orchards again—why, they're in bloom! Did you remember that, Bob? Down to myriad flowers, yellow, blue, white, purple. The pink bells of the manzanita, rich golden poppies, a white flowering shrub. It is sprouting spring all over the place!

At Placerville we buy some food. We will camp in the open again tonight. It will be warm. The air is fragrant. Water runs fast toward the Sacramento River. A few miles beyond the town we come to an open spot in the woods.

We killed a rattlesnake that night. Bob was pulling out some rocks to make a fireplace. The snake lay behind the rocks. Bob killed him but he decided not to build a fire place after all, and that night we spread our sleeping bags closer together than usual.

California is a well-pruned state. In the Lodi country, the black, witch-like stubs of grapevines are like eerie hands reaching up out of the ground, each spread finger holding a bouquet of young leaves. Marysville for peaches, grapes at Lodi, pears at Placerville, apricots in the valley on the way to San Jose, and prunes all around San Jose.

Once a car let us out on the edge of a town in "the valley," which always means San Joaquin Valley. As we stepped out onto the highway and were lifting our packs again, an old man came out of his house and invited us to stop in their backyard cottage that night. "I can't bear to see people on the road," he said. He was a Frenchman. He had served in the First World War and had seen refugees wandering homeless over the earth. Now he couldn't bear seeing anyone homeless. Once, he told us, he had kept a mother and several children in that little cabin for a month, giving them food, too.

What will post-historic man think of the tiny terraces on all these bare hills around Stockton? Will he know that they were worn there by the feet of cattle and sheep going around and around the hills, never up and down, as they graze?

Toward the coast, the hills begin to wear trees. There are soft groves in all the hollows. Men are plowing the land, the even rows going round the hills with the contour. On the very top, the plowman must get dizzy making his small circles.

We were on our way to the Coast Range mountains where the mercury mines are. The war had brought up the price of mercury, or quicksilver, and all the mines were running again. We passed curious little mercury "stills" along the side of the road where farmers were eking out their incomes by burning a flask every month or so, boiling it out of the rocks, drop by drop. We passed larger operations with rumblings going on and "Keep out" signs at every approach.

We followed a little dirt road over the hills to Almaden, making a loop through the mine country. Farther on there was a big hole in the middle of the road, a mercury mine that had fallen in on itself—the fourth mine we had passed that day.

How soft and open those hills, yellow green with deep clover, grass foaming with flowers. Pink wild hollyhocks, yellow pansy-like violets, dusty blue flowers, rich scarlet flowers like tiny birds.

We were walking along a main highway when a car came to a stop beside us. "Hey, you kids! Where do you think you're goin'?" When my big hat turned around and he saw it was a woman and her son he wasn't a bit daunted. "Get in," he said.

We got in and landed at a saloon where he bought us soft drinks and himself a stiffer one. We told him about our disappointment at missing a mercury mine.

"Hell," he said, "I'll take you through the very gizzard of the biggest mercury mine in the world. It's older than the United States. It's the place where the Indians used to get their war paint. Cinnabar ore is red, you know. There are five hundred miles of tunnels in that mine. Some of the rock is so rich the quicksilver drops out without cooking. Sometimes a guy can't work it at all, it's so rich, because his hot drill vaporizes the mercury and the poison gets in his lungs."

Back we went with the miner. He took us through the mine and explained every step of the process. The cinnabar ore is dug out, burned to release the mercury vapor which dribbles down a pipe, condensing again into those round silvery balls that never flatten out. They were liquid but would wet nothing. They were solid but you couldn't pick them up. And now those silvery drops were worth almost their weight in silver.

We went into the dangerous caverns where huge drifts of rock rolled ominously down two-hundred-foot slopes. We looked into the shaft down to other levels. "Don't touch that arch above your head. Stoop low. Might bring the whole world down on you. You shake hands with God every time you come down into this damn hole," he said.

Almaden mine wasn't officially running. These were out-of-work miners, getting rock out by hand, hiring Mexicans to carry the heavy sacks of ore from the workings, miles deep in the hill, out to the retorts. Once in a while someone would find a "picture rock" so rich with the red streaks of cinnabar that it would net its finder fifty dollars for a day's work. The miners paid a percentage of their take to the estate that owned the mine, another percentage to the one who owned the retorts, another to the man who burned the rocks for them, and still made good wages. The mine is running full blast now, no doubt, and more dangerous than the day we took our lives in our hands to see it.

XXVI. WE RIDE A FREIGHT

WE MET lonely people.

There was a woman who picked us up, a solitary woman whose husband was dead. For eleven years she had managed a ranch alone, hiring help. She was tired of it but she, too, had a bear by the tail. You can't neglect fruiting trees or fail to give employment to families who depend on you.

A homeless cowboy, who had been a widower for eight years, stopped to talk to us. He was going north. "But I'd just as soon go south," he said. "Couldn't I come along with you? I'm lonesome as the devil. I want me a wife. If I came with you awhile, we might find out if we hit it off."

A little man in a shabby car picked us up. He was so lonely it took us two days to get rid of him. He was a scissors grinder who stopped at every town, gathered up scissors from beauty shops, barbers, and hospitals and sharpened them on a fine emery wheel attached to his engine under the hood of his car. He traveled slowly, making very little. He was so gentle and pathetically lonely that we had him join us for supper the first day and allowed him to camp nearby so that we could go on together the next day.

As the spring advanced we thought it might be safe to double back up to Yosemite.

That is a strange valley, almost entirely encircled by sheer, thousand-foot bluffs. A mecca for the Indians in the old days. But I cannot share John Muir's enthusiasm for it. It is as though things on such a big scale insisted too much on their charm. You rebel against anything that is pushed at you—even a great book. The rock walls spout water at every turn, the falls hurtling down in white sheets of flame, or drifting in thin silvery mist, or blowing out in feathery plumes, snaring rainbows. Melting snow fed the waterfalls, which fed the Merced River, the clearest, greenest stream I ever saw.

We walked more than a thousand miles in California, criss-crossing the valleys, strolling the hills, tackling the mountains until, at last, we came to the formidable desert. The desert flowers were at their peak, surely. The majestic yucca with its stems three or four inches thick, ten feet tall sometimes, ending in a huge spike of large creamy bells. Fragrant white primrose-like flowers, bushes, weeds, and low harsh-leaved trees in bloom. Flowers of every color and kind, not in sheets as on the Coast Range, but in precious sparse clumps that are tiny oases of color over the gray-green desert. It was flamingly hot. "But this isn't hot," a driver assured us. "Wait until August. The real desert is across Cajon Pass." And presently we topped the four-thousand-foot plateau which is, officially, desert. There it was, springing wide open from horizon to horizon. Spiney Joshua trees in bud. Greasewood yellow with tiny blossoms. Sagebrush, manzanita, dark green juniper, mesquite.

"Why don't you ride a freight through the desert?" suggested a man who took us fifty miles along the way. "That would be adventure. Certainly it wouldn't be much of an adventure to die of thirst crossing it, would it?"

He offered to leave us at a town where the freight trains stopped for water. He told us to go down to the watering tank and ask a brakeman which train to take. Then all we'd have to do would be to sit tight until we reached Nevada. We were headed for Boulder Dam. He left us in a tombstone factory near the tank where the train was to stop. Bob went into town to buy two quarts of milk, a half dozen oranges, four bananas and four tomatoes. We had some bread and filled our canteen with water, for we were told we must take plenty of liquid.

A hobo came by to chat with us. He said we'd better take the Union Pacific to Las Vegas, not far from Boulder City. "Hunt you a gondola or a refrigerator car," he said. "Throw the top back and crawl in. It will be cool and clean. But look the train over before you select a place. And don't talk to nobody."

The train thundered up to the watering tank. Bob and I strolled down the tracks, trying to look like old hands. There were no open doors. What was a gondola, anyhow? I knew what a refrigerator car was, but not how to board one.

A man jumped off the train. "There's an empty car ahead," he said. "The door is open on the other side. I'll help you across." He pushed us up the steep steps, across the car couplings, down on the other side.

"That's it. There's a man in there. He looks all right, but don't talk to him. Ever ride a freight before? . . . I thought not. Don't talk to nobody."

The floor of the car was as high as my head. I took off my pack, and then, as though he were helping me onto a horse, our new friend took my foot in his hand, gave me a quick push upward and I was in.

The other passenger was a boy from Illinois on his way home after three years of hunting a job. He was kind, reserved, courteous, a lad in his twenties. At stops he told us a little about himself but he asked no questions. "Don't talk to anybody," he warned us. We never did find the ones we ought not to talk to.

We rocked along at what seemed a terrific speed. The noise was ear-splitting. The car bounced and rolled. No one could hear a word above that uproar. We held our mouths open to keep our teeth from cracking together, bent our knees to take the jolt off our backs, and felt the flying dirt tangling in our hair.

But we loved it. We had the big car to ourselves, space enveloping us, both doors open wide now to the desert. It was still terribly hot, but we had all the wind there was. The white desert flew past. For a while we followed a stream, the Mojave River, I think. A line of cottonwoods streaked alongside. Little isolated houses, barns, corrals, looking lost and pitiful. Wild solitary rolling desert covered with sagebrush. Flowers in purple-pink masses. Hills that looked like crumpled metal, the pure sea of the sky with a few white sails becalmed on it.

Our wild white ride ended at midnight in Las Vegas. Amazingly dirty, as sore as though we had been breaking broncos, hungry, thirsty, tired and sleepy we tramped through the brightly lit town out into the alkaline desert on the other side.

In Boulder City we stayed with a friend who refused to let us go on to the Grand Canyon as we planned until he was sure we had a ride across the desert to Kingman. There were no houses, no water between the two places, he said. He consulted the chief of police to see if he could arrange for someone to take us.

In all our four months and four thousand miles, that was our most interesting ride. We made it in a truck with a cowboy and his wife, wild burro hunters, who made their living in those jagged-rock hills of the desert, roping burros, taking them by truckloads to Los Angeles to be sold.

"If you got any fear in you, you'll never catch a wild burro," the cowboy said. "You've got to ride so fast you often catch a spill, jumping four-foot-high rocks, the jumping cactus after you all the time. That's choya—round balls of spines that fly off at a touch . . . horse'll buck you off, but you don't hardly notice it . . . them burros is like a goat for speed. They're always above you. If you see 'em on a ledge an' you ride there, they'll be up higher when you get there. Once my horse was pelting down the hill and come to a ditch that brought him down against some rocks. He skinned his face right off. I sort of tied it up with the string out of my tobacco sack, but it's still crooked. He's all right, though. We only lost two horses in nine years . . . once we caught sixteen wild burros in three days. My wife she got three cracked ribs that time.

"A fellow might get old out on this desert, and dry up and shrivel up, but he ain't got something wrong with him all the time. He'll die healthy. Out here you have to dig for wood and climb for water. It's up on them dry-looking rocks that you'll find a spring sometimes and the only wood is the roots of big brush. The burro trails'll take you to water. We've found lots of new water holes by following burro trails to the top of hills.

"There's some of the best range in the world along this road. This dry stuff along here's called filleree. There's lots of things folks can eat here in the desert, too. Fis weed greens are the best in the world. There's a kind of yucca you can eat, too, when it's little. Squaw berries, little and red, they make a nice drink. Pine nuts, mashed up and boiled in water, make good soup. Like oyster soup. Have to strain the hulls off.

"Ever hear of lazy woman's bread? We make that in the desert over a campfire, for it don't need no pan. We criss-cross some baling wire into a kind of rack, then we pat the bread out thin and spread it about a quarter inch thick across the wires and bake it right over the coals. It's like a big thin cracker.

"Sure, we rope anything. Bobcat, lynx, coyote. Roped a badger one time but he kept digging out and we had to turn him loose. Hardest thing to rope is a coyote. When we want to have some fun we stop roping wild burros and take out after a coyote. You never heard such hollerin' in your life.

"Once we seen a bobcat in a yucca with eleven coyotes barkin' at him from the ground. They had the bobcat treed in the yucca but the bobcat didn't mind. The yucca was six or eight feet high and the coyotes couldn't quite reach him. There he was, eatin' a rabbit as peaceful as you please, with all them coyotes howling down below. It was a sight.

"These burros come from the ones the old prospectors turned loose. They was brought from Mexico. They started runnin' wild. We caught one that was sure twenty-five years old. There used to be around 2,500 around here, but we've caught them all but about 300 now. We're roping ourselves out of a job all the time."

Within the Grand Canyon there was cool shade. There was water. The days were cool. Thunderstorms came up to give the air its daily bath. There were long easy hours for lessons and writing, for walking and dreaming, resting and sleeping.

Then word came from Farrar that he had signed a contract to tour the Middle West with his happy-go-lucky talk and a new song he had written. The war was steadily growing worse. It was a time for families to be united, not separated. So Bob and I agreed to go to New York instead of to South America and continue our adventures with Farrar in some rattletrap which he would buy for his tour.

From the Grand Canyon to New York we hitchhiked. We rode with dozens, scores, hundreds of people, from a self-confessed murderer to a famous surgeon, from a rich playboy with nothing to do, to a concert tenor who was taking a year off for his health.

As we came into the wealthier east we began to ride in bigger cars, driving faster and faster. Salesmen. Salesmen. Salesmen. Jolly fellows.

THE CAMPFIRE BURNS

Sober business men who picked us up as though we were baggage, said little, set us down again. Doctors who talked a mile a minute. Two middle-aged Jewish refugees from Czechoslovakia who practiced their English on us. "Oh, wonderful country," they said. "We can say what we like here."

At Harrisburg, Pennsylvania, we are picked up by a car which will take us to New York.

For the last time we take off our packs and climb into a car. New York tonight!

New York City, Seventh Avenue, looking south from 35th Street, 1935. Berenice Abbott, photographer.

XXVII. FROM NOW ON, EVERYTHING IS GRAVY

I NEVER thought to love a city so much—as I love Speiden and Sentinel and all the islands of Puget Sound. New York is not unlike a virgin forest: the buildings, tall trees to shut out the sun; people, the undergrowth of salal growing close and tangled; the traffic in the streets, the rivers, but with no go-devils to cross them.

Farrar's contract had fallen through by the time we got to New York, and here we were, all three of us, sans job, sans contract, sans everything.

Bob found little to do here, compared to fishing and boating and building on Waldron. He got restless for the West and one day he said, "I believe I'll hitchhike back to Puget Sound and visit North before school starts;" and he did. We gave him ten dollars and went with him on the subway to 242nd Street—the end of the line—and watched him strike out up the highway all alone. He was sixteen, strong and self-reliant. In six days he was on Waldron with five of his ten dollars still in his pocket.

Meanwhile, Farrar and I haven't landed that real-money contract—it's always just around the next corner—but we've had a grand time almosting. First, we lived down in Greenwich Village. We thought it would be cheaper there, but it wasn't. It wasn't quieter, either.

The first night in our basement room we were disturbed by a woman's shrieks, of "Help! Help!" A man leaned from an upstairs window. "Do you want me to call the police for you?" he shouted.

"Now see what you have done," the woman's companion growled. "Shut up or I'll. . . " and we heard a slap. And then nothing more.

A week later police cars began to arrive at the door of the house where we lived. Presently we heard wild cries for help. I lay on the bed and covered my ears. At last the cars drove off, carrying the girl who had subsided into helplessness. They were taking her to Bellevue because she had been drinking too much. Still another week, and the police came again. We began to feel we were living in a haunted house. This time one of the upstairs tenants had committed suicide because she was going blind.

Our new landlady is like nobody else in the world. We have a big sunny room with an old fireplace which our landlady built herself, a bathroom whose plumbing she put in herself, a kitchen whose shelves and table she built. She painted the floor bright blue, the walls cream, the fireplace chimney a dull red. In the middle of the room she made a long table under which the bed pushes halfway by day to become a couch, with the cushions leaning against the side of the table. It is the pleasantest room we have seen in the city. When it rains, our ceiling leaks, but we put pans under the leaks. Farrar says, "If we were in the woods we couldn't get out of this rain at all. Here we just push the bed under the table."

Our landlady furnishes fireplace wood free, getting it from two Negroes who are paid to haul wreckage away from buildings. She pays them to dump the wreckage here. Sometimes it is bed slats, planking, old chairs with hits of upholstery still hanging on, doors and windows out of which she must break the glass. Sometimes it is walnut banister railings or mahogany shutters painted ten layers deep and hard to burn. Once her Negroes were sick and we ran out of wood. The landlady heard of a woman who was selling her furniture at wrecking prices. She trotted over there—a tiny, sixty-year-old, courageous woman—and came dragging old bureaus and tables and washstands across the street. Then she took her big hammer and broke them up. That night we burned seasoned oak wood.

The wonderful thing to me about New York's skyline is that it is made up as much of a lacy tangle of bare twigs in winter and soft leafing trees in summer as of angular buildings, for there are parks everywhere. And the city is full of blacksmith shops, their silver-tongued anvils sounding much as they did in Dickens' time. And through the Village and up and down East Side and West Side go the pushcart peddlers, the chestnut roasters, the hot-dog venders. Or sometimes a little tin box on wheels goes by, steam pouring out of it, smoke going out a one-joint stove pipe. It is the roasting ear man. He boils sweet corn in his tin tank. A customer calls out from the sidewalk and the roasting ear man pushes up to the curb, forks out a hot ear, spreads it with butter from a dish open to whatever is blowing about, and gives it to the customer in a tiny sheet of waxed paper. The customer goes along the street eating it.

Whenever we get flat broke, Farrar goes out barnstorming and always manages to make enough to tide us over. Once Farrar got a long-distance telephone call to go to Philadelphia to interview a lecture bureau. We spent our last money on bus fare to Philadelphia and then had to take to the woods and camp there until time for the tour. Beautiful hardwoods, red leaves falling, blue haze over the hills, squirrels gathering hickory nuts overhead. You'd be surprised at the number of hickory nuts those dainty, graceful squirrels could eat. One of them could cover our sleeping bags with bits of hulls and shells between daylight and sun-up. We watched them coming to the hickory tree under which we were camped. There would be a swift gray movement down the trunk of a tree across on the next hill and in a few moments movement along the intertwined branches overhead. The squirrel runs out one limb to its tip, flies lightly across leafy space to the next, until with a sound like wind it makes its flight into the hickory nut tree. Sometimes three or four of them come at once and then there is a half gale in the tree.

It was the first time in many years that we had camped for more than a night in deciduous woods and we loved them as one only loves the gone things. A black gum tree turning its rich crimson shook beautiful leaves in a breeze and thirty years fell off me and were dead leaves on the ground. And I longed to go over the land, wherever people meet in their still free ways, to show them freedom. It comes from inside themselves and is to be won by self-indulgence, really, instead of by self-denial.

In one way and another, we have just managed to get by this year. It is almost as if we were homesteading again, the oar slipping off octopus backs right through the boat every day or so, geysers almost big enough to drown us, spouting up.

The other day Farrar said, "We could get a little houseboat, or even a bateau, and float down the Ohio into the Mississippi to the Gulf. We'd go to Pittsburgh and start from there. I'd play the towns along the way and make talks and we'd make more for the boys than we ever will here."

But that was only spring boiling up in him. Out in Puget Sound, they are doing their spring plowing. We imagine we see the swelling of the leaf buds in the parks here and we get restless. When the boys are educated and we don't have to make any money, Farrar and I will go back to our island. We may have to pick sluckus with the Indians. But even if we don't make any money at all, we have had a grand life. From now on, everything is gravy.

When the boys are educated and we don't have to make any money,
Farrar and I will go back to our island.
June Burn

POSTSCRIPT

June and Farrar travelled to the University of Missouri in a covered wagon.

SEVENTEEN YEARS LATER

Not long after this book was first published, when I was teaching at the University of Washington and Farrar was in New York on radio, there came a young naval officer to my door one day.

He had come, he said, because he had read this book and wanted to meet the author. I was pleased of course but more casual than I'd have been if I had known that he was going all over this neck of the woods searching out people and places I had written about. Or that *Living High* was and is that young man's favorite book! I still can hardly believe that, but it must be so, for on his own not large income he has set up publishing partly because he wants to reprint this book.

But this boy does more than reprint a book he loves. A few years ago there was an island of virgin timber off Maine about to be sold for newsprint. Enough trees there for one Sunday edition of the *New York Times*, he said. Many others around had already been "pulped"—no longer lush with spruce and the undergrowth natural to the forest. He couldn't bear to see this one go, too.

He hadn't money to buy the island himself but he corralled relatives and friends, organized a non-profit society for the preservation of such rare lone spots and did buy the island right out from under the axe. That is the kind of person who is publishing this book, he and his wife and two small sons beginning a new business out of the blue with courage and imagination. (He hasn't given me permission to write this but I hope he will let it stay here.)

POSTSCRIPT

Whenever we meet someone who read this book long ago we are asked about our boys. Were they in the war, did they return safely, what are they doing and, especially, did they accept our "philosophy " of living?

Those questions point up what Dad Chevalier once said to us somewhere back in this book: "Well, here you are again with two boys and two suitcases to show for the years you have been gone." For, sure enough, there is only that one immortal achievement to show for any life: offspring, as healthy and happy and courageous as possible. Poems, songs, stories, new knowledge, great inventions are less ephemeral than objects but generations alive to enjoy them are the without-which-not!

Both boys were in the war, Bob in the Navy, North in the Army. Both returned well and as whole as a war can leave any human soul. Bob's girl with whom he had grown up in the summertimes here on Waldron Island met him at the San Francisco dock. They were quietly married down there, now have two girls and two boys from nine to two years old, each of them more beautiful than the others and all so unbelievably good and sweet.

North met his Baltimore girl in graduate school, had three years of knowing her and they, too, were married without families or to-do in their college chapel. They have a girl, seven, and a boy, five, also radiantly lovely and showing quite special talents.

Bob took his degree in Meteorology at the University of Washington but soon came down out of the skies for a life as summertime captain of a fishing boat in Alaska so that they could live on Waldron Island which he and his wife so much loved.

Before he went off to war, North had taken his degree in Political Science at the University of Washington. He went out to Fletcher School of Law and Diplomacy for his graduate degrees in Foreign Service. The girl who became his wife got her degrees in the same subject at the same time and now lectures on International Law at the Foreign Service Institute in Washington D.C. where they live at the moment between foreign posts. (They live very near the 100 acres where Farrar and I met. The Cabin in the Woods is gone and a golf course spreads its manicured way over those sweet hills, across Minnehaha, up the laurel slope and on.)

Sydney, Australia was North's first assignment, Manila the second. He got polio there, is now paralyzed almost exactly in the degree Roosevelt was, but has altered his life in no way nor has his wife. Woodworking is still his hobby. He even puts up shelves, builds furniture for their new home, sails, rows, drives with hand controls and works full time at the State Department. Life goes on as usual for that family, for they are very brave and intelligent people.

If by accepting our philosophy of life you mean trying to live fully on almost no money at all, then neither boy is going our way. They try to live fully on as much as they can possibly make (a much harder thing to do!). North used to call himself the white sheep of our family, announced early that he wanted the best possible American "standard of living" with all the appurtenances. Bob has finally turned to his wood-working hobby, which all my menfolk have, as his way of making a living. He built their house here on Waldron so well it might have been carved from a single log, so integrated it is, so stout and tight. He is very skilled and incredibly fast. Now he is carpentering in Seattle with contracting jobs as he can get them, all set to be a "big-time" contractor. More power to them both!

If our sons' children give their parents as much satisfaction and pride as ours do us, that will be a mighty big hunk of joy to add to the "gayety of nations"! And what more can any one actually do for the world than to be himself busily and fruitfully happy?

People ask continually about life on Waldron Island. Well, we have managed to live here only occasionally in the summertimes and only this one entire year since 1934. But we have seen two big changes since this book was written. First, seven charming, well-educated, idealistic and beautiful young couples came swarming here in search of "the good life" for the families they meant to have. All of them wanted to work creatively while somehow earning their livings in the time margins. One taught the school, one went to the mainland a week of every month to work in a chemical laboratory, another fished on the reef nets in the summertimes, another did labor on the island, the trained nurse took cases in Seattle as seldom as possible, our son went in the summers to Alaska with the fishing fleet, another sold plastics on the mainland at intervals, one ran a small resort here. Most of them had their children here, one six boys, another four girls and so on. Soon the island rang and swarmed with children!

But nobody did any creative work. They had too much time. Waldron became a sort of delightful suburb of the mainland. Dances in the handsome log post office, children rolled in blankets around the walls, homemade cakes and coffee at midnight, home in the early mornings in rackety old cars kept up at all because we have one bachelor here who is a magic mechanic and also a philosopher and never seems to need the money we haven't got to pay him. Beach parties with vast home-grown suppers, folksongs and talk, the children rolled in their blankets at ten o'clock sundown behind the logs above high tide level. Visiting endlessly, going to the dock three times a week for mail and freight. Old-fashioned cider bees, roof-putting-on bees, fireplace or road-building bees, talk fests whenever anybody comes to visit which is nearly all the time. Reading endless books whether good or bad. But writing, painting, composing or studying not at all.

Second, they all swarmed away again. With children ready for high school, the need for money increasing, inevitable tragedies (but not one death or serious illness among all that tribe these many years), the young people went off, leaving only one of them here for seed, so to speak, or to keep the school going. All of them have splendid jobs with good salaries, all find it hard to make ends meet, live less well as for joy and companionship but better in other ways, all come home for the smallest vacation. Now that they are so busy they can hardly call their souls their own, perhaps they will begin to do the creative work they used to dream of.

From now on Waldron will be a place of retirement for old people, for a good many of these have come here in the last two decades. What with this beauty, the fishing, the spirit of friendliness the young people left behind them, the old are rejuvenated. There is a twice daily airplane service to the mainland, groceries from Friday Harbor or Orcas by the mail boat which, however, now refuses passengers. There are low tides for clams, all tides for fishing, tall straight trees for building, water from below for the digging or from above for the catching in cisterns.

Meanwhile Farrar and I have not retired. Farrar is getting "social security" and I soon will be, so that we are richer than ever in our lives. We are free in every way to work at what is our hobby of hobbies, whereby hangs the tale of our best adventure so far.

In 1947 I went to Honolulu where I came to know Dr. V. G. Clark, an osteopath, who taught me the importance of good food for health, introduced me to that shocking book, *Tomorrow's Food*, by Dr. Vincent Norman and journalist James Rorty. I was so shocked that I came home to Bellingham and sold a radio program to our faithful Bornstein Fish Company on which I studied nutrition out loud over the air. It was a great success. I had wonderful help from many friends, dentists, doctors and accumulated a research library free. The study of nutrition led quite inevitably right back into conservation with which "Puget Soundings" and *The Puget Sounder* had been so much concerned, this time especially conservation of the soil through better farming and of human health through better (and especially non-poison-sprayed) food from that soil.

Farrar had been lecturing, building in adobe, carpentering, entertaining at schools, writing songs as always, but all the time getting more and more interested in what I was doing. Together we began to go all out for nutrition and agriculture as the America needs we most wanted to help supply. We agreed that I should go back to school and take a master's degree either in nutrition or in agriculture. (I took it in both—Agricultural Extension.)

We had by now heard of the world-famed soils authority, Dr. W. A. Albrecht of the University of Missouri. We decided I should go there. We actually went by way of a covered wagon drawn by a wonderful team of mules along the side roads of Oklahoma, Arkansas, Missouri. This was to get material for a still unpublished book, *Side Roads*, and to study eating habits, signs of erosion, farming methods and so on along the way.

In Columbia we lived in our wagon parked in the pasture of Mrs. Marie Nash on "The Fulton Gravel" a mile or so from the University. We grew so close to that family that the daughter, now married, named us godparents to her children and thus gave us two more loved grandchildren free.

Farrar worked on the University maintenance crew that year, "Grandpa working Grandma's way through college, " he said.

It is no easy thing getting a master's degree in scientific subjects some 37 years after a B.S. It took me 12 full months of 1950-51 to do it but I couldn't have done it at all if I hadn't had those long months of hard study for the radio program. Dr. Albrecht's lectures on the soil were so

POSTSCRIPT

On their way to the University of Missouri, 1950.

SEVENTEEN YEARS LATER

Driving the donkeys.

They lived in the wagon while June earned her master's degree in Agricultural Extension. The photograph on the shelf is Skye Burn, their first grandchild.

interesting and, I thought, so terrifically important, that I took them down on a wire recorder and with his help and encouragement made them into a fat outline which we called OUR SOILS AND OURSELVES. The matter is all Dr. Albrecht's of course but the "popular" phrasing of his outline is mine, he a big enough man not to mind in the least.

June and Farrar in their health food store at 43 Bedford St., NYC.

Since 1951 we have been teaching nutrition, experimenting with seaweed gardening, studying "Organic farming," even running a natural-foods store in New York—a wonderful experience. Last year I went to England to see the immense profitable organic farms there, some of them a thousand acres big, and especially the world's only scientifically-controlled experiment in comparative farming methods at Haughley, in Suffolk.

This year we have applied for a Guggenheim Fellowship grant to go over America to study the entire organic—or "natural" or "non-chemical"—farm movement together with community conservation and waste-disposal programs. We will write a handbook of methods and progress. If we get it that will absorb us for two years.

If we do not get it, and in any case when that is done, we may take one more walking-and-bus trip all over America to see again the lovely places we remember and to find out a thousand more. Oh, peach orchards in bloom! Niagara roaring. Bluets across an Oklahoma meadow. A shore of Lake Erie. Maybe the whole thousand-mile trail down the Appalachain and Blue Ridge mountains. Miles of house-deep snow in western mountains. Yellow pastures in haycocks in New England. Sweet side roads still leading off into pine woods, every fallen needle a letter from home...

And at the last, our homestead island, Sentinel, where we began forty years ago with its farmable few acres, the seaweed fertilizer only 100 feet down the bluff away! From the top of that parklike island we can look out over blue channels, snowcapped mountains and islands all around. Ferries pass and small boats. Our hearts are always honing for Sentinel. We live for the day when we can feel it is time to retire there once more with a little milk goat, a few chickens, the fish right around us, a world of beauty at our feet.

We've had our gravy!

And together is home.

Goodbye again.

      J.B.

      Waldron, Washington, 1958

EPILOGUE

Inez "June" Chandler Harris, 1917.

EIGHTY-ONE YEARS LATER
By granddaughter Skye Burn

Inez "June" Chandler Harris was born June 19, 1893, in Anniston, Alabama. In explaining her adventurous spirit, June wrote, *"My father was a child of Esau, the wanderer. Not even a Methodist circuit-riding life moved fast enough for him. My shy, gentle-eyed fireball of a mother protested every move—and loved them all. When I was sixteen, we moved to Oklahoma where I finished college at Oklahoma A & M. In 1917, I came to New York with a friend to cast about finding what we most wanted to do in life."*

June and her friend made a pact to take turns supporting one another so each had an opportunity to explore what she wanted to do in life. June worked as a staff writer for *McCall's Magazine* for fifteen dollars a week.

When it was her turn to be supported, June rented a cabin in the woods near Washington D.C. where she could write uninterrupted. Writing ran in June's family. I have been told, but have not confirmed, that June was related to Joel Chandler Harris, the journalist and folklorist who collected stories from the African American tradition, published as *The Complete Tales of Uncle Remus* in 1881.

Farrar Burn was born September 22, 1888, in Fort Smith, Arkansas, and grew up in Van Buren. In their teenage years, Farrar and his brother Robin fabricated a flatulent sounding "musical" instrument in a neighborhood garage, which they called a Bazooka. Robin later gained fame as Bob Burns, a musical comedian who performed in movies and on radio from 1930 to 1947. Bob's show was so popular with the troops during World War II, the U.S. military named a weapon the Bazooka in his honor.

EPILOGUE

Although June did not receive the Guggenheim grant mentioned in Seventeen Years Later, her interest in the correlation between soil fertility and the nutritive value of food became a lifetime commitment. In 1951, when June was studying and working with Dr. Albrecht at the University of Missouri, she wrote, *"This concept of soil fertility as earth's great gift to man, as man's responsibility to maintain, as a source of man's nutrition in the most literal sense and, also, therefore, as a source of his behavior should be given to every farmer. It would give him dignity."* (June lived in a time when people still called the whole of Humanity man and mankind.)

In 1954, after closing their health food store in New York City, June and Farrar returned to the island and set up camp in the cove at Sundown Farm. They lived in the camp while Farrar and Bob built their cabin. The cabin construction took four months, for a total cost of $500.

After June and Farrar moved into the cabin, I watched her turn sand into fertile soil and a bountiful garden which produced the most flavorful vegetables that I have ever tasted. They raised goats and chickens and grew wheat on the bluff, which they ground to make cereal and bread.

June and Farrar grew the wheat and ground the flour to make the bread.

June and Farrar's camp.

Farrar and Bob during a break from construction.

EPILOGUE

Skye, age 5, June's mother, June, and Doris Burn, Bob's wife.

June's writing area and Farrar's piano. The hob where I sat and listened to him play.

Looking through the cabin to the kitchen. The sleeping area was in the loft, with a ladder from the kitchen.

June and Farrar left the island in 1962 when Farrar developed skin cancer. June wrote a friend, *"He is thinner than when you saw him and is merely walking bones."* Farrar's mother and brother both died of cancer after they had surgery. Farrar had several minor operations to remove cancerous lesions but faced with major surgery they instead chose the Gerson Therapy. To produce the quantity of organic food the Gerson diet required, June and Farrar needed a longer growing season. When they left the island, Farrar wrote, *"It is going to pull my heart out to leave, but change is the thing we seem to need most. Even for the worse. Nature is everywhere changing. Every change exercises a new faculty in us which will die if not used and leave us somewhat unbalanced."*

EPILOGUE

June on their farm in Marianna, Florida.

They purchased a small one-level factory building in Marianna, Florida, which had been used to make sausages and came with enough acreage to grow produce and pasture cows. After scrubbing and painting the floors and walls, Farrar built shelves for their books, June pinned a print of Van Gogh's Sunflowers on the wall, and they called it home. They had a dog named Pat and cat named Mandy. Farrar recovered from the cancer. In 1964, when I was fifteen, I travelled across the country by bus to visit them in Marianna.

June grew disturbed in her later years. World War II damaged her trust and faith in life. She stopped singing while she went about her daily chores. June wrote, *"It is far, far easier to comprehend deep within ourself the birth and death and resurrection of Jesus than in the possibility that humans could and did murder five million of their neighbors in cold blood."* She was distraught to see how the war changed Bob and it broke her heart when North contracted polio. When North was in the hospital, and they didn't know the prognosis, Farrar recorded an LP, which was sent to the Philippines by diplomatic pouch. The record begins with Farrar's calm voice, "Hello North, I'm going to sing you some songs." It ends with "So long Northy." The love expressed in those softly spoken words has always moved our family to tears.

Farrar cared for June with profound devotion. When she became too frail, he sold the place in Florida and they moved to Van Buren, where he felt comfortable in familiar surroundings. June died there in 1969. Farrar died in 1974.

I visited Farrar in Van Buren in 1970. He met me at the bus depot with a box of chocolates. He missed June dreadfully. We had chicken boiled with collard greens for dinner. After dinner, Farrar picked up his guitar and sang a few songs in his old slightly quavering voice. I am grateful beyond words for the legacy of life given to me by June and Farrar and by my maternal grandparents.

Skye Burn
Bellingham
2022

June and Farrar in Van Buren, Arkansas, shortly before her death.

*To be yourself, to live true to your own nature,
to fruit in your own way—that's heaven.*
Farrar Burn

Farrar, singing with his guitar.

PHOTO AND OTHER CREDITS

Except as noted below, all the images are from the June and Farrar Burn Papers and used with permission from Western Libraries Archives & Special Collections and the Center for Pacific Northwest Studies (CPNWS) at Western Washington University.

Some of the images from the June and Farrar Burn Papers have been subject to quality enhancement and cropping by the editors prior to publication.

p. 49 *San Juan II* at Patos Light Station, Washington, 1915. Louis Borchers, photographer. Patos Island Lighthouse Collection, Orcas Island Historical Society. Used with permission. https://www.washingtonruralheritage.org/digital/collection/patos/id/607/rec/1

p. 60 The cliff dwellers of the north. Eskimo settlement, King Island, Bering Sea, Alaska. LOT 10557, Prints & Photographs Division, Library of Congress, LC-USZ62-62721. Photo copyrighted by Lomen Bros., Nome, c. 1913. https://loc.gov/pictures/resource/cph.3b10360/

p. 116 Rooster and Crate, original drawing, © 2022 Skye Burn.

p. 214 Looking up the Rogue River from Agness, Oregon. National Archives at College Park, Public domain, via Wikimedia Commons. Sands, photographer, c. 1938. NARA record: 518371 https://commons.wikimedia.org/wiki/File:ROGUE_RIVER,_OREGON_-_NARA_-_520152.jpg

p. 230 New York City, Seventh Avenue looking south from 35th Street, 1935. Berenice Abbott, photographer. New York City Public Library Digital Collections, Public Domain Picks. The Miriam and Ira D. Wallach Division of Art, Prints and Photographs: Photography Collection Changing New York. https://digitalcollections.nypl.org/items/2077b2b0-878c-013a-d84a-0242ac110004

www.ingramcontent.com/pod-product-compliance
Lightning Source LLC
LaVergne TN
LVHW070525070526
838199LV00073B/6705